New Technology
and Industrial Change

NEW TECHNOLOGY and INDUSTRIAL CHANGE

The Impact of the Scientific-Technical Revolution
on Labour and Industry

Ian Benson and John Lloyd

Kogan Page

First published 1983
by Kogan Page Limited
120 Pentonville Road, London N1 9JN

British Library Cataloguing in Publication Data
Benson, Ian
    New technology and industrial change.
    1. Labour supply — Great Britain
    2. Technological innovations — Great Britain ¹
    I. Title. II. Lloyd, John
    331.12'5'0941   HD5765.A6

    IBSN 0-85038-284 X
    ISBN 0-85038-698 5 Pbk

Printed in Great Britain by
The Anchor Press Ltd and bound by
Wm Brendon & Son Ltd,
both of Tiptree, Essex

Contents

Part 2: A New Framework for Agreement 153

Acknowledgements

The authors are grateful for the stimulation, support and encouragement of Mikuláš Teich, Kristan Nygaard and John Forrester. We benefited greatly from their critical comments and suggestions, and those of many other colleagues. We owe a particular debt to Christopher Freeman and Kurt Hoffman of the Science Policy Research Unit at the University of Sussex, Robin Williams of the Technology Policy Unit at the University of Aston, Jostein Fjaelestad of the Norwegian Computing Centre, Roy Laslett of the Engineering Industry Training Board, Tør Haug, Harry Smith, Russell Moseley, John Evans, Dr Ian Mackintosh, Max Wilkinson, Alan Cave and Roy Green. Our thanks are also due to the librarian and staffs of the Marx Memorial Library, and the libraries of the TUC and Cambridge University.

We are grateful to Jean Williamson, Gladys Ashdown, Anne Smerdon and Claire Harrap on whom fell the considerable burden of typing and retyping the various drafts of the manuscript, and to Loulou Brown our editor, and Fiona Barr who compiled the index.

The authors and the publisher wish to thank the following who have kindly given their consent to the use of copyright material: Pergamon Infotech for a figure they first published in the Pergamon Infotech State of the Art Report *Microcomputer Systems*, 1978; the National Computing Centre for a figure from their *Computer Technology and Employment*, 1979; the Controller of HMSO for illustrations and text from official publications; Dr Alex Reid, and the Royal Society for illustrations from the *Philosophical Transactions of the Royal Society*; Dr Roy Rothwell for tables from *Industrial Innovation and Public Policy*, 1981; and the Trades Union Congress for *Technological Change*, 1980.

We are grateful to Glenwyn, Naomi and David Benson for their forbearance during the innumerable weekends and evenings in which the book was put together.

Foreword

Since 1978, an ever-growing stream of books, articles and television programmes has been flowing on the subjects of microelectronics and related new technologies and their impact on industry and society. This book is not just one more to add to the flood, it is one of the few which goes further and tries to place new technology firmly within the context of political change. This is very important. Far too many writers attempt to predict seemingly inevitable consequences, either good or evil, stemming from new technology. Ian Benson and John Lloyd share my own view that we can, through conscious political and institutional action, shape and determine its effects.

At the present time the great wave of microelectronic technology is breaking upon industrialized countries when they are undergoing a severe recession. That recession places labour at a disadvantage: unemployment has sapped its strength and exposed division and weakness in the trade union movement. Labour is thus at a critical point in its development, with no guarantee that its influence on society can continue to grow as it has done since the war.

Two alternatives face the unions and the Labour Party: to decline numerically, or to put themselves at the head of a powerful coalition of forces.

The search for a strategy appropriate to the UK must begin by recognizing the importance of social control of technological development. This is one of the central political questions of our time.

Why is the question so central? Let me set out what I believe to be the main reasons.

Firstly, we are beginning to see a shift in employment patterns on all fronts at once — a quite unprecedented series of movements. Manufacturing will need fewer and fewer workers as more and more plants introduce automated equipment. The motor vehicles industry is an obvious example. Certain categories of office work will decline, while others, for example data processing, will expand greatly. Service industries can generally be expected to grow.

Second, labour must be aware of those momentous changes, be able to adapt to them and bend them to its interests. Luddism has never been the position of the organized workers movement, and it is not now. After all, organized labour is, to a very considerable degree, the *creation* of technological change. But it cannot allow its position to be weakened and eroded by it. Trade union organization must adapt more rapidly than in the past, and must use the new media of communications and information processing for its own ends.

Third, labour must be able to bargain effectively with the growing power of transnational capital, a power greatly strengthened by technological developments which are often created by it. Information technology provides a nervous system to enable direct management control of global organizations, underpinned by a global financial system; while new technology increases the capital intensity of production and thus adds to the concentration of ownership. The only power which labour can harness to effectively counterbalance transnational power is state power. That is why the state must be built up, especially in the areas of research and development and national economic planning.

For these reasons labour's policies on technology must, I believe, be revised to meet changing circumstances. We have too often been content to see technology as peripheral to economic planning. The first decisive break with that tradition was a bold experiment: the National Enterprise Board, of which I was a member. The NEB involved intervention by the state and by labour at strategic levels to initiate and control technological change. The creation of new bodies, such as Inmos, against many misgivings and City cries of 'foul', gave labour its first experience and responsibility in the field of strategic planning.

I believe that the policy then developed should go much further. Technology and planning must in future be linked at a number of levels and in different ways. State-supported research and development must be brought closer to both industrial and social uses. It must be opened up and made to serve in the creation of new employment.

We must complement state intervention by strengthening the unions and streamlining their internal communication with their members. The process of decentralization, which is a feature of union organization, must continue, and can be greatly aided by the use of new information technology; negotiation over a range of issues can become much more local when planning becomes so too.

There are many questions raised by the advent of new technology. These include the following.

☐ How do we develop an appropriate strategy towards the transnational companies?

☐ What is an appropriate division of labour in new technology-based industry?

☐ How can the democratization of state research and development be carried forward?

☐ What new information and education systems need to be developed to support social negotiation of economic and technical plans at local, national and international level?

☐ How can trends in technological development and their short-term social and economic impact best be monitored?

☐ What forms of interdisciplinary research might be required to survey the long-term social and economic consequences of rapid technological change?

These questions form the subject matter of this book. Ian Benson and John Lloyd are active participants in the attempts to widen the area of choice for our society: the choice of technology and planning.

It is this which makes this book a refreshing change from the seemingly endless succession of commentaries by academics, all too often betraying a lack of understanding of the real world beyond the 'chip' and the gadgetry. I hope the authors' call for a response to the scientific-technical revolution, based on Harold Wilson's: 'conscious, planned, purposive use of scientific progress to provide undreamed of living standards and the possibility of leisure, ultimately, on an unbelievable scale', will be heard and taken up not only by those who are already politically conscious, but by all who are concerned about the social impact of changing technology.

Both authors are to be congratulated on the content and timing of their book.

Lord Scanlon
October 1982

Introduction

'Let us remember that the automatic machine . . . is the precise economic equivalent of slave labor. Any labor which competes with slave labor must accept the economic conditions of slave labor. It is perfectly clear that this will produce an unemployment situation, in comparison with which . . . the depression of the thirties will seem a pleasant joke.' *Norbert Wiener*[1]

'There is plenty that still needs doing. The first and hardest step is to use our present knowledge to remove known evils. The second is to use research to find new means for removing evils that we cannot at present avoid, to cure diseases and to maintain life and happiness for all. But beyond that there lie still further tasks, those of continuing and extending research to discover the unrecognized evils that we must in turn fight and destroy. Conversely, in a more positive way, we need to discover new good things, new processes, and most of all, new and effective bases for social action. What this means, in effect, is that the task of human thought only begins in knowledge. Knowledge must result in constructive change before it can renew itself.' *J D Bernal*[2]

We, the citizens of the advanced countries, are consumers of the fruits of the *scientific-technical revolution* (STR). Our houses, food, clothing, means of transportation, recreation and methods of earning a living are all creations of that revolution.

We not only consume the products of this revolution; our lives and relationships are shaped by it. Our visions of the future are dominated by two broad economic and political models which reflect the impact of the STR, and form opposing foci in debate and organization.

AN OPTIMISTIC MODEL

The first model considers that the creation of very high levels of consumption will be made possible by the immense productivity gains attendant on the widespread adoption of automated equipment. These high levels of consumption in the advanced countries will be paralleled by more rapid growth in the lesser developed countries as more capital is exported to them to create plants for labour-intensive industries, and as new breakthroughs in agricultural chemicals and equipment boost food production.

In the course of this development many industries at present providing employment in the advanced countries will decline very rapidly. Large employers, ie steel, shipbuilding, motor vehicles, will (or have already) shed labour fast, and bureaucracies which are adopting automated office equipment will follow suit. In some cases, (for example, in the steel industry) the advanced countries will lose their market share to the developing countries because of the latter's relatively low labour costs.

However, productivity growth will release more spending power for an increased range of services and products which will create new kinds of jobs. There will be widespread job restructuring, which sometimes will be a painful and prolonged process in the more conservative and rundown of the advanced economies, such as the UK. Yet this process must be undergone if real gains are to be made, and short-term misery will be compensated for as capital is moved out of old sectors into new ones, or as old sectors are modernized in order to make them competitive and profitable.

This first model has, in the past decade, greatly appealed to political and academic circles as well as popular movements in Western Europe (particularly in the UK) and in the USA. These themes, stressed by Margaret Thatcher in the UK in 1979 and Ronald Reagan in the US in 1980, helped win commanding majorities for the present UK and US governments.

Behind these conservative movements lay a list of individuals, and institutions who had underpinned them and provided intellectual backing for their campaigns. The two most distinguished individuals were Milton Friedman and Friedrich Hayek, both of whom had many followers who preached monetarist principles (a central concern by governments to ensure that inflation is not fuelled by increasing the money supply) and who stressed the connection between capitalism and liberal democracy.

In the UK and the USA, think tanks were founded devoted to the promulgation of neo-Conservatism. The Institute of Economic Affairs, the Adam Smith Institute and the Centre for Policy Studies (set up by senior Conservatives while in opposition) were the best known and most influential theoretical bodies in the UK; while major academic centres, such as the London and Manchester Business Schools, were developing monetarist economics in a more practical way.

The monetarist economists took a series of insights from Friedman and Hayek (and, standing tall behind them both, Adam Smith). The most practically important insight for the UK government was the perception that the public good was best served by the pursuit of private greed. Professor Israel Kirzner, approving Hayek's view that the free market is a 'discovery procedure'[3] says that:

'It can be stated with confidence *that human beings tend to notice that which it is in their interest to notice.* Human beings notice "opportunities" rather than "situations". They notice, that is, the concatenation of events, realized or prospective, which offer *pure gain.* It is not the abstract *concatenation* of these events which evokes notice; it is the circumstance that these events offer the promise of pure *gain* — broadly understood to include fame, power, prestige, even the opportunity to serve a cause or help other individuals . . . a concatenation of possible events may not be noticed at all unless the potential discoverer stands to gain from the price differential. *In order to "switch on" the alertness of a potential discoverer to socially significant opportunities, they must offer gain to the potential discoverer himself* . . . what is important about the market economy is that unexploited opportunities for re-allocating resources from one (low-market-valued) use to another of higher value offer the opportunity for pure entrepreneurial gain . . . *the most impressive aspect of the market system is the tendency for such opportunities to be discovered.'*[4] (Italics in original)

The incoming UK Conservative government in 1979 was an enthusiastic convert to these views, and sought to increase the area of freedom of market forces by cutting back on state ownership and decreasing the monopoly powers of public enterprises. State subsidies were to be withdrawn from manufacturing industries, such as steel and vehicles, and concentrated in promoting the 'sunrise' sectors of information technology or robotics. The scope for productivity improvements in the state and private sectors was large, and began to be realized from 1981 onwards — though much of this was simply an effect of redundancies outstripping falls in production. Productivity improvements, especially when associated with the introduction of new technologies, almost always meant large-scale redundancies. By 1982, unemployment had almost doubled from 1979 to three-and-a-quarter million, and a growing proportion of the total were long-term unemployed, whose prospects of finding work diminished steadily the longer they remained on the unemployed register.

It became clear that the labour movement had lost the political initiative in the late 1970s, and was prevented, by unemployment and internal struggle, from recapturing it. The loss in 1978-79 of general acceptance by union leadership of Labour's anti-inflation strategy, based on an incomes policy, and the enormous publicity given to the strikes in the National Health Service and elsewhere in the public sector set the labour movement back on its heels. *Post mortems* have been conducted largely by the left, and much of the analysis in these *post mortems* explicitly blames the working of incomes policy for Labour's failure and hence proscribes it for the future. Thus, the joint plans drawn up by the TUC and the Labour party, embodied in a report 'Economic Planning and Industrial Democracy', issued in 1982,[5] fudges the incomes policy issue because no political agreement can be gained for its operation.

Labour thus has no credible counter-inflation strategy to set up against the Conservatives' use of unemployment to force down wages. While its present strategy incorporates more explicitly radical elements than its previous policy, it is a strategy with a hole in the middle.

The SDP-Liberal alliance is, at the time of writing, still formulating its main policy, though it is clear that it favours a mixed economy, coupled with an incomes policy of some kind. In other words, what seems likely to result from the plethora of study groups and conferences mounted by the SDP is an overt diplomatic commitment to the kind of policies most past Labour administrations followed.

So long as Labour and the Alliance cannot convincingly represent the unemployed and the low-paid, and draw their needs into a coalition with skilled and professional workers, the government's policy remains secure. Free market principles and policies, though often mixed with substantial interventionism, could and did accomplish some of the necessary modernization of the UK economy. The much heralded economic recovery, however, kept receding into the future as it became apparent that there were some sectors of the economy which had permanently contracted.

A PESSIMISTIC MODEL

The precipitous economic decline of recent years has reinforced the views of those who adhere to a different model of the impact of the STR. In this scheme, automated equipment in clerical, mass production and service sectors will be adopted unevenly in the advanced economies, raggedly in the advancing economies, and scarcely at all in the less developed countries.

The more technologically dynamic advanced countries, such as Japan and West Germany, will be able to sustain high rates of growth while worldwide markets expand — though they may be very much constrained by the high price of imported energy. In the more techno- logically conservative countries, such as the UK, the displacement of labour by automated equipment will not be compensated for by growth in demand for other products and services, because that growth will not be rapid enough, investment will not be large enough, foreign competition in products and services will be too strong and because the potential labour force is growing.

The result could be any or all of the following: the polarization of society into the 'technologically advantaged' and the 'technologically disadvantaged', increasing crime and delinquency rates, and a growth of totalitarian political formations.

These two models are rarely as sharply and as mutually exclusive as they are represented here. Yet they tend to throw up broad approaches to the impact of new technology, which conflict. For those who see that the microelectronic 'revolution' means largely better and better gadgets and increasingly intelligent machines doing increasing amounts of work, then the problem becomes one of how to fill ever increasing periods of leisure time.

However, those who do not believe that full employment can be achieved naturally (given time and movement of capital) will be concerned to stress what they consider to be massive problems in the fields of capital restructuring, job creation, training and retraining, educational provision, import penetration, export potential and research and development programmes.

Once we distance ourselves from the absolutes of party political rhetoric, there is little question that the demanning which took place in a number of corporations was essential for their efficient working. In so far as it feather-bedded inefficiencies, because it did not wish to, or could not, take on union conservatism, Labour has suffered by being identified with loss-making and protected public sector industries. The 'free market' was and is of value in identifying the unnecessary if inflated production costs which society pays, and which ultimately bear most on its poorest members.

However, the authors of this book do not identify with the first model. Rather, they align themselves with the second model, for one reason above all others which has become clearer in the course of the Conservative government's term of office. That reason is that rapid technical change, ushered in under 'free market' conditions, imposes an enormously high economic, social and personal cost upon a part of the population least able to support it: the cost of unemployment.

The authors do not believe that a society, which rightly sets out to raise productivity, output and the general technical level of its productive forces, needs to exact this cost from its workers. We also believe that those who hold this to be true have much to do to convince others that there *is* a better way to operate, and even more to do to ensure that it *is* better. The purpose of the book is to provide an argument for a better way by attempting to understand the nature of rapid technical change, and to develop policies to deal with it.

THE SCIENTIFIC-TECHNICAL REVOLUTION

In developing their approach to the impact of technical change, the authors have found it useful to re-examine the attempt by J D Bernal and his colleagues in the 1930s to draw together a whole range of material, economic and political consequences in their all-embracing concept of the 'scientific-technical revolution'.

They argue that the STR is a genuine revolution as there is: 'a change in the course of which the succeeding state of affairs acquires qualitatively new features which were not present in the preceding situation, and since it has aspects which clearly mark it off from the scientific and industrial revolutions.[6]

The first, scientific, revolution of the fifteenth to seventeenth centuries, was the gradual discovery of objective natural laws made by men who usually worked in isolation and often in secret. Further development of their discrete discoveries was only made possible as scientific journals and societies were founded, and as objective science gradually became less heretical.

The second, or industrial revolution of the eighteenth to nineteenth centuries, was largely an 'applications revolution'. The makers of the early steam-driven machines had little interest in pure science — though the most eminent of them, James Watt, conducted systematic experiments and participated in the work of the Birmingham scientific society.

According to Bernal, in the early twentieth century the STR completes this process by incorporating science into production — making both scientific advance and its application routine in much the same way as other aspects of production. In this way, the once sharp division between discovery and application, the scientific and the technical, has been blurred. Bernal wrote:

'The first revolution actually discovered the method of science, the second only applied it. The new revolutionary character of the twentieth century cannot be confined to science; it resides even more in the fact that only in our time has science come to dominate industry and agriculture. The revolution might perhaps more justly be called the first scientific-technical revolution.'[7]

Bernal differed from many contemporary commentators in his belief that the material changes which followed from the 'ever-accelerating stream of new techniques and improvements of old techniques' were less important than their indirect effects.[8] In part, this was a result of the economic weakness which flowed from the close association of science-based production with monopoly, an unproductive relationship which forced the state to intervene increasingly in the running of the economy. He argued that:

'the well advertised successes of monopoly-directed science, such as nylon and television, are apt to blind us to the things that are not done. For the possibilities of applications of science are known only to a few. But these see well enough how little of the immense resources of actual knowledge is used, owing to the misdirection and restriction of everything that does not promise immediate profit. In one way or another science has been kept from the service of mankind.'[9]

17

In this way although:

> 'the first growth of science itself was a product of economic and political factors, once science was established as a means of securing economic and political power its very progress became a factor in political and social life. No modern industrial state can exist at all without science, it cannot continue for long without making the fullest use of its resources of intelligence to advance science and its utilization. The political patterns of our time are therefore in part a result of the material effects of science.'[10]

Mikuláš Teich has added precision to this concept of the STR by placing its origin in the theoretical developments which led up to the splitting of the atom at Cambridge University in 1932, and identifying its revolutionary characteristic in the subsequent development of the twin disciplines of nuclear energy and electronics.[11] In both cases, it is impossible to separate the technical from the scientific.

Both technologies accelerated the emergence of transnational corporations as the dominant form of industrial organization. Both owe their existence and continuing development and exploitation to new forms of state economic activity.

A HIERARCHY OF SOCIAL CONSEQUENCES

Bernal identified three broad levels of social effects as flowing from the STR: changes in the production or labour process; changes in the structure of the economy and international division of labour; and changes in the role of the state.

These levels are, of course, interdependent. Changes at every level have an impact on, and are acted upon, changes at every other level. Any schematic presentation such as that set out below must of necessity be simplistic. We have represented the processes taking place at each level as if they were largely autonomous. However, it must be understood that the processes are, in fact, interlinked.

These processes are not merely 'products' of the STR. Government and company structures were affected very considerably by changes in the production process during the industrial revolution, and the state apparatus has always been directly influenced by, and has intervened heavily in, the economy over which it holds sway. Our point, following Bernal, is that the STR greatly accelerated state intervention and forced it to become more conscious and more apparent.

The most conspicuous technical result of the STR to date has been the developments in electronics, including computers. The new technology has emerged since the war as the basis of the most important manufacturing sector of the world economy, producing commodities which are increasingly in demand, and increasingly replacing mechanical or electrical-mechanical *products*. Of greater importance in our context, however, is that the electronics industry provides the material basis for revolutionizing *means of production* through automated or computerized equipment. Where earlier technologies replaced muscle power with mechanical energy or human rule of thumb with mechanical precision, automation replaces human brain power with electronic intelligence and memory.

This already has, and will continue to have, the most profound effects. The first of these, in the field of employment, relates to direct labour displacement by new technology and the need to re-order the labour process to adapt to that technology. Further effects arise from the relationship of these changes to the business cycle, leading to a greater concentration of ownership into transnational companies, and, as a consequence, to the increased mobility of capital. These effects, in turn, raise questions concerning the appropriate role of states in education, research and application of new technology, and the nature of their relationship with the transnational companies.

The Changing Production Process

The potential changes generated by automation have been grasped since at least the early 1950s, when the first great automation debates were stimulated by engineers, managers and mathematicians associated with the development of computer technology, such as Diebold and Wiener. They felt that automation would lead to significant labour displacement, although some (including Wiener) underestimated the time which would be taken for the technology to be adopted.

The displacement only emerged as a serious political issue when American trade unions began to blame automation for the unemployment of the late 1950s. The US government responded by establishing a National Commission, whose six-volume report, produced in 1966, endorsed the traditional view that unemployment stemmed from demand deficiency rather than automation. This view was strengthened when the US unemployment rate subsequently declined as a result of the economic activity surrounding the Vietnam War.

The automation debate of the late 1970s concentrated on the employment implications of the microprocessor, or silicon chip. It was held that five million people in the UK might become unemployed during the 1980s as a direct result of adoption of the new technology. In West Germany alone, it has been calculated that two million clerical jobs will disappear.[12] Here it is worth noting that Professor Tom Stonier predicts that 10 per cent alone of the working population will provide all our required commodities — food, shelter, clothing, means of transport and sources of energy — by the end of this century.[13]

Such speculative forecasts can gain currency (and may indeed be correct) because of a lack of hard data about employment effects. During the latter half of the 1970s unemployment rates rose in most advanced countries, more because of a worldwide slump in demand than as the result of a widespread introduction of automated systems. It seems likely, however, that many employers will take advantage of high levels of unemployment, and the related decline in trade union power and militancy, to introduce (where they can afford to) labour-saving systems. Certainly, job shakeouts in many industries — steel, shipbuilding, chemicals, electronics and motor vehicles — are unlikely to be reversed significantly when there is an upturn. As we shall see later, where employers have concluded new technology agreements with their workforces, these are often also productivity agreements requiring less labour over time for the same or increased output.

The early part of the automation process, however, has been more a question of job restructuring than job destruction. Many commentators have remarked on the expansion in clerical and supervisory functions, which Daniel Bell has called the 'information occupations'.[14] It is anticipated that these occupations will continue to grow, as traditional economic activity in the primary (production of raw materials) and secondary (manufacturing) sectors declines.

The expansion of the information occupations has to be related to the progress of automation. Fully automatic systems of data collection and control are only now becoming technically and commercially feasible. The process of integration with material handling systems is scheduled to extend until the end of the century. Much of the expansion of clerical and supervisory functions in the recent past has been related, not to the creation of permanent jobs but, to the temporary reorganization of work at the interface between manual and maturing automatic data processing information systems. These restructured jobs have often been degraded versions of the jobs performed in the older, less mechanized, systems.

A report on the training implications of new office technology, prepared by the Royal Society of Arts, anticipates that up to eight million workers will be affected by automation. The examples of those occupations which will be abolished, or radically changed, include: 'post room workers, typists, secretaries, invoice, filing, shipping, stores, insurance, sales and stock clerks, draughts people, accountants, supervisors and junior and middle managers'. The report continues: 'If care is not taken the result could be to degrade the job content and reduce job satisfaction. Employees might become disenchanted and bored with their work, leading to social isolation and psychological stress'.[15]

A critical constraint on the rate of progress towards this new pattern of employment lies in the ability of employers and employees to assimilate the new knowledge being generated and to incorporate it in product and process design. Under free market conditions a permanent imbalance between skill supply and demand tends to develop. The further the process of technical change advances, the greater this imbalance becomes.

The Changing Economy and the Widening Technology Gap

We are witnessing not only very great underlying technical changes in the domestic economy, but also steadily growing internationalization of production. These factors have an interconnected effect on national employment patterns and policies.

Where new technology is introduced in a competitive sector of industry, a technology gap opens up between the leading firm and its rivals. During a boom period of the business cycle, markets are expanding and the leading company often chooses to maintain prices at a level appropriate to the old production technology in order to maximize its return. In this way, a price umbrella is provided under which other companies may shelter. An expanding economy will also generate opportunities for redeployment of workers displaced by automation and unemployment, and any negative economic consequences may be contained.

However, a recession in the business cycle will bring the technology gap into the open. When markets contract, price competition will become more fierce, as the technologically advanced capital intensive producers seek to maintain production volumes. Over a series of cycles of booms and slumps this can have the effect of driving weaker competitors out of markets altogether, leaving the remaining companies in a more dominant position.

Since this process takes place throughout the economies of the Western world, it has the effect of bringing about a new international division of labour. It is apparent for example that certain high-level skills, associated with the head office operations of transnational corporations, are not present in the UK labour market. Similar deficiencies exist in research and development areas, where the absolute gap between countries widens as the rate of technological progress increases. As the MIT Centre for Policy Alternatives noted in a recent report for the UK Department of Industry:

> 'Firms late in entering the race (for the exploitation of microelectronics) may be seriously disadvantaged when compared with those that are today beginning to develop skills and understanding of this new technology . . . Entry today can be achieved with more standardized parts, and with more powerful tools and assistance in their use than was true earlier. *How long this strategic window for entry will be open to all-comers remains to be seen.*'[16]

Another American commentator, Victor Basuik, has anticipated the probable reappearance of the wider 'technology gap' between the US and Western Europe which caused much concern in the 1960s. The 'brain drain' disappeared after the 1960s because the US government appropriation for science and technology declined in the late 1960s and early 1970s, giving rise to a surplus of American PhDs in almost all sciences. In addition, European-based companies, like their Japanese

21

counterparts, began to challenge America in certain non-military products such as consumer electronics, plastics and automobiles.

However, the gap has not been closed in advanced technology proper: space technology, satellite communications, weather modification, lasers, fusion, MHD power, solar energy, etc. As Basuik has noted: 'The real test of the technology gap will come in the future when these technologies become economically important.'[17]

The developing technology gap manifests itself as an increasing integration of production facilities themselves. The most technically advanced corporations *must* also be international in marketing scope (and usually transnational in manufacturing) to recoup the investment required to become and remain technically advanced. The design of advanced capital-intensive manufacturing units reaches its greatest efficiency when the world is considered as a whole. Their location, whether producing car engines or semiconductors, then becomes an increasingly political question whose outcome depends on the result of an auction by national governments competing with grants for plant construction, tax exemptions, etc. Viewed from the UK, according to a recent government report: 'it is clear that the quickening pace of technological change', introduced in such circumstances, will mean that: 'The optimal scale and location of industrial plant may also change. A further consequence may be an acceleration in the rate at which enterprises enter and leave particular markets.'[18]

The Role of the State

This increasingly mobile nature of capital, together with the changes in the pattern of employment, has, as Bernal noted, forced Western governments, of all political persuasions, to become involved in the detailed running of the economy. A wide variety of forms of state intervention has developed, ranging from the *laissez-faire* biased policies of the UK to the 'state capitalism' of the French and the Japanese. In the countries that were late to industrialize, governments have played a far more direct role in industrialization, and have stimulated the emergence of science-based transnational companies. As early as 1887, when science-based industry was in its infancy, T H Huxley remarked:

'We are entering, indeed we have already entered, into the most serious struggle for existence to which this country was ever committed. The later years of the century promise to see us in an industrial war of far more serious impact than the military war of its opening year.'[19]

It was a warning to England which is now heard throughout the Western world, from America to Germany. Today, Huxley's 'industrial war', in the form of a growing contest between transnational companies with control of technological development, and nation states with increasing responsibility for economic welfare and the application of technology, has become a key feature of world politics.

FORGING THE LINKS

Bernal's particular contribution to the analysis of the social impact of technology came in the way that he saw the three processes — of changing production methods, the changing economy, and the increasing role of the state — being linked. In his model, links were forged, not only by the flows of capital, as envisaged by Adam Smith and his latter day disciples, but also by social forces of which by far the most important were organized science and organized labour.

To Bernal, organized science not only created the potential for technological change, but also heavily influenced the social choices which were made regarding the direction in which the application of science to production would take.

This interaction of scientists and society was, to Bernal, central to the transition from capitalism to socialism. He paid special attention to the role of scientists organized in trade unions alongside other workers. Such scientists, he believed, had responsibilities to open up new options for scientific and technological development in the social interest by research, education and political action. Indeed, Bernal himself was active before the war in attempting to assess with the TUC the consequences for labour of emerging industries, materials and processes.

Bernal's view that technical change can be heavily influenced by social forces is somewhat contentious, even in left wing circles. For example, David Noble, a modern historian, has noted that we:

'confront a world in which everything changes yet nothing moves. The perpetual rush to novelty that characterizes the modern market place, with its escalating promise of technological transcendence, is matched by the persistence of pre-formed patterns of life which promise merely more of the same. Each major scientific advance, while appearing to presage an entirely new society, attests rather to the vigour and resilience of the old order that produced it. Every new, seemingly bold, departure ends by following an already familiar path.'[20]

Others on the left have denounced 'Bernalism' as little different from state capitalism.

Yet Bernal and his colleagues had a clear idea that the STR was associated with the most profound changes in the old order. Unaided, the private sector was unable to take into account the external effects and the costs of technological change. Only the state could mobilize resources on the required scale, adopt broader time horizons, and ensure adequately against risks.

While Bernal regarded the increasing economic importance of the state as a progressive change in the old order, he acknowledged that science and technology were applied in many instances to buttress the traditional structure of managerial authority. He saw this as being management's response to a developing shop floor militancy, which he regarded as a necessary accompaniment to the convergence of political and economic power. Thus, in Bernal's model the STR becomes both a *factor* in the transition from capitalism to socialist forms of industrial organization, by stimulating the growth of the state, and a *product* of this transition, as managements develop and apply new technology to roll back inevitable pressures for industrial democracy.

According to Bernal, transition from capitalism to socialism did not follow automatically from the progress of science and technology, but required the interaction of scientists and society. Science progressed most rapidly when presented with a range of social problems, a steady stream of capable recruits to its workforce, and an economic environment which was capable of 'fixing' the beneficial results of research so that scientific frontiers could be steadily advanced. It was evident to Bernal (though not to us) that these conditions could not exist in the West. He believed that the misuse of science in order to produce weapons of mass destruction would create a situation in which capable people would be repelled by rather than attracted to scientific work. As long as the short-term profit of monopoly concerns remained the major objective of industrial research, conditions for 'fixing' research results would remain poor, while the stream of problems which could stimulate a socially responsive science would be reduced to a trickle.

The salvation of science and scientists required an alliance of both with society to break these unacceptable economic and political patterns. Before the war Bernal and his colleagues helped organize a national and an international scientific trade union, and argued that the TUC should take science policy seriously. They found a ready audience in socialist and labour movement circles, and their analysis had a major influence on the development of Labour politics; from the drive towards the liberalization of Soviet science in the 1950s, Wilson's white-hot technological revolution and (in Czechoslovakia) Dubček's reform movement in the 1960s to the programme of Mitterrand's socialists in the 1980s.

Bernal's ideas have been influential in the social and political events of the post-Second World War period. The development of labour movements has been closely connected with the process of global industrialization. The concept of the STR and the interventionist economic and political programmes which were based on it, promised to reconcile the two conflicting aspects which technical change presents to labour: the threat of change and structural unemployment, and the opportunity of release from scarcity — aspects which are reflected in our two models. Bernal's reconciliation made the control of technological change, through the socialization of the economy, a major part of the most recent, and successful, socialist programmes in, for example, the UK and France.

While Bernal's vision of society has from time to time inspired electoral majorities, the application of his prescriptions has been rather less effective. Labour was slow to build on its early efforts to make scientific and technological policy an area of creative activity. When in power, Labour governments were equally lax in building on their predecessor's interventions in state research and development.

In part, this was because the early post-war decades have presented a mixed picture of the impact of the new technologies for Labour. While it led to a declining number of jobs and industrial strength in many traditional sectors of the economy, the influx of new groups into key white-collar areas (such as computers, telecommunications and air-traffic-control) served to mask the overall threat to Labour's bargaining position. It was only with the stagnation of the 1970s that the question of social control of technological change emerged as a serious subject for debate within the labour movement.

The strategy which emerged was based on extending collective bargaining, and using political influence to construct a patchwork of negotiated agreements concerned with the sharing of power over the new production processes: data agreements, concerned with restructuring the organization of work, and creating computer-based production and management systems which serve a variety of interest groups; technology agreements which extended from bargaining over new technology to economic and manpower planning demands; and planning agreements which sought to bring in the state as a partner in a collective bargaining process at the level of strategic planning.

THE STRUCTURE OF THE BOOK

The structure of the book which follows corresponds to Bernal's model of the social aspects of the STR. The first part describes the three-tier hierarchy of social consequences and the role of the labour movement in linking the semi-independent processes taking place at each of the three levels. We begin by examining the role of engineers and managers in shaping the production process (Chapter 1); and chronicle the development of labour awareness of technology and its attempts to control it (Chapter 2). Then (Chapter 3), we consider transnational companies which are the most advanced form of economic organization resulting from the STR, a development which has pushed towards the internationalization of production. In Chapter 4 we examine Labour's response to this new challenge, and then (in Chapter 5) we show how the nation state has been obliged to develop its role to match the changing production process, and the expansion in trans-national activity. In the final part of Part 1 (Chapter 6), the influence of the unions on the UK government's policies on technology and strategic planning is discussed in relation to the 1974-79 'Social Contract'.

In the second part of the book we attempt to point out some recent developments in legislation and employee bargaining (Chapters 7 and 8) and in Labour policy (Chapter 9) which appear to us to be promising ways of harnessing the benefits of the STR and coping with its effects. We argue that these initiatives contain the nucleus for a democratic socialist strategy in the late twentieth century.

REFERENCES

1 Norbert Wiener (1950) *The Human Use of Human Beings*, p 220. Eyre, USA.

2 J D Bernal (1965) *Science in History* (3rd edition), p 928. C A Watts & Co, London.

3 F A Hayek (1978) 'Competition as a discovery procedure'. In *New Studies in Philosophy, Politics, Economics and the History of Ideas*. University of Chicago and Routledge and Kegan Paul.

4 I M Kirzner (1980) 'The primacy of entrepreneurial discovery'. In (ed) A Sheldon *Prime Mover of Progress*. IEA Readings, 23.

5 Economic planning and industrial democracy (1982) TUC and Labour Party.

6 M Teich (1970) Three revolutions, scientific, industrial and scientific-technical. Unpublished lecture, Cambridge.

7 Bernal, op cit, p 1,014.

8 Bernal, op cit, p 876.

9 Bernal, op cit, p 886.

10 Bernal, op cit, p 876.

11 Teich, op cit.

12 C Hines and C Searle (1979) *Automatic Unemployment*, p 14. Earth Resources.

13 T Stonier (1980) 'The impact of microprocessors on employment'. In T Forrester (ed) *The Microelectronic Revolution*, p 305. Blackwell.

14 D Bell (1979) *The social framework of the information society*. In M L Dertouzos and J Moses (eds) *The Computer Age: a Twenty Year View*, p 163. MIT.

15 *Consultative Report on the Educational and Training Implications of Modern Technological Developments* (1980), p 13. Royal Society of Arts.

16 R T Lund (1979) Microprocessor applications, cases and observations, p 208. MIT Centre for Policy Alternatives (Unpublished).

17 V Basuik (1979) *Technology, World Politics and American Policy*, p 51. Columbia University Press.

18 *Technological Change: Threats and Opportunities for the UK*, p 30. ACARD, HMSO.

19 T H Huxley (1887) Letter to *The Times* (March 21).

20 D Noble (1977) *America by Design: Science, Technology and the Rise of Corporate Capitalism*, p xvii. A A Knopf, New York.

Part 1:
Social Aspects of the
Scientific-Technical Revolution

CHAPTER 1

The Changing Production Process

INTRODUCTION

The perfection of electronic technology and its integration into manufacturing, distribution and exchange has become the major engineering task of the second half of the twentieth century. In developing this technology, engineers have been indirectly transforming the pattern of employment. New occupations, industries and production processes have been created, and conditions of employment and job security have become more uniform across the working population. In designing the new technology a new social structure is being fashioned.

The outcome will not be determined by the designers alone nor by those whose lives they are seeking to fashion. The development of automation at every stage throws up tensions between these groups which fuel political and industrial conflict. This chapter seek to analyse the process of technical change as seen by its designers, and remarks on the tensions thrown up.

TAYLORISM, or SCIENTIFIC MANAGEMENT

Factory labour gradually evolved into the dominant method of production during the nineteenth century, towards the end of which the organization of factory labour by management was first studied as a science by F W Taylor in the USA.

The full development of craft-based industries was a prerequisite for the introduction of the new machinery of the science-based industries. This was achieved by the introduction of what Taylor termed, 'Scientific Management', which was methods developed and applied for the purpose of raising productivity, using existing techniques of managerial control.

Taylor described his system in this way:

'Perhaps the most prominent single element in modern scientific management is the task idea. The work of every workman is fully planned out by the management at least one day in advance, and each man receives in most

29

cases complete written instructions, describing in detail the task which he is to accomplish, as well as the means to be used in doing the work . . . This task specifies, not only what is to be done, but how it is to be done and the exact time allowed for doing it . . . Scientific management consists very largely in preparing for and carrying out these tasks.'[1]

It is important to underline the obvious fact that Taylorism was not the cornerstone of the factory system but its ultimate expression: it was a bold attempt to refine factory labour according to its quantifiable, mechanical essence and a precondition for transcending it which only became possible in our own times. Taylor already had, as his 'raw material', a factory labour force; his rigorous division of labour within production allowed a much more rational and effective exploitation of that labour than previously, and the perfection of new techniques of mass production, such as the assembly line. Taylorism entirely refashioned the pattern of employment by:

☐ greatly increasing the demand for engineering and design specialists;
☐ greatly increasing the specialization of skilled and semi-skilled workers within the new division of labour;
☐ creating a mass demand for semi-skilled labour competent in operating machines but not being required to be trained in a craft.

Taylor's system was far from universally adopted in factories, and, indeed, quickly attracted a good deal of criticism on the grounds that it caused more trouble among workers than it was worth. Nevertheless, the system and its many derivatives, succeeded in establishing, developing and buttressing the central importance of technical expertise and managerial control. In the twentieth century, 'managerialism' has become a largely unquestioned ideology relating to industrial life. Its acceptance is so widespread that an alternative is, for many, unthinkable. The theory is often supported by the observations of trade union officials that it is 'management's right to manage'.

The organization of work groups engaged in complex tasks is an intricate skill which has to be learned and practised as a profession separate from the skills which are being organized. However, this skill should not be confused with the terms under which managers exercise their necessary function. Taylorism revolutionized the production process, but was concerned only with the given social structure prevailing in late nineteenth and early twentieth century industries. Since that structure was dictated by the patterns of private ownership, Taylor's system was adapted to these patterns and was seen by many workers as an attempt to extend the power of capital over those organizations which they had developed for their own representation and defence.

It is important, therefore, to bear in mind the dual nature of Taylorism, for that dual nature appears again and again in trade unions' and workers' responses to automation in our own time. It is *revolutionary* in the attack it made on craft-based working patterns, and thus inevitably on craft union organization; it is *conservative* in its attitude to the given structure of ownership and power.

Taylorism made possible the organization of production in a scientific way. The fundamental importance of the approach was its methodical division of work into major phases. It was these divisions, and the further sub-divisions within them, which have produced the pre-conditions for its transcendence. By treating human labour as machine labour, Taylorism paved the way for real machines to take over — once the necessary level of intelligence had been incorporated into the machines.

Taylor identified five major production phases:

1. Product identification, classification and design.
2. Production scheduling and forward planning.
3. Production standards and control.
4. Material handling.
5. Inspection and quality control.

Of these five processes, the fourth (material handling) most concerns us here as it attracts the largest investment in terms of land and capital, and requires a large and disciplined labour force. Material handling can take three main forms.

Flowline production, which is the manufacture of a product by successive processes, each component proceeding to the next operation as soon as the preceding operation has been completed.

Batch production, which is the manufacture of a product in small or large batches or lots, by a series of operations, each operation being carried out on the whole batch before any subsequent operation is started. This is by far the most common method of working in manufacturing industries and it is estimated that approximately 75 per cent of all parts produced by the metal working industries are produced in batches of less than 50.

Job production, which is the method by which single articles are manufactured. Job production takes place in all engineering concerns, whether in the manufacture of small components required for the maintenance of plant, the production of prototypes or tools, small jobbing contracts for other concerns, or large-scale job production such as shipbuilding.

These broad sub-divisions under the general heading of material handling have been the basis of industrial production. They have shaped the labour forces, and have been influential in determining the form of organization labour adopted in order to gain a measure of control over working conditions. Factory labour, which created industrial armies, was, Marx believed, a necessary pre-condition for Communism. It proved not to be a sufficient one — though it was the creator of trade unionism.

DIEBOLDISM

The transcendence of Taylorist methods of production was postulated by John Diebold, in his *Automation: the advent of the automatic factory.*[2] In this book he described how electronic technology was to revolutionize the production process.

The first major tasks, he believed, were to develop a general purpose material-handling machine which could replace the batch production shops; the development of automatic data processing machinery; and an extension of special purpose automatic production processes to new sectors such as food processing, printing and paper board, and glass and cement manufacture.

The second major task was the integration of information and material handling. As Diebold underlined:

'in manufacturing firms, the function of the office is fundamentally related to the function of the plant. The admission of this fact is of considerable importance to a fruitful analysis of office methods. When this basic relationship is overlooked the introduction of new machinery often perpetuates existing procedures instead of eliminating or replacing them.'[3]

Diebold's scheme thus foresaw and prescribed the process which is now under way — the automation of office and design tasks and the application of computerization to production machines. The concrete development of the process depended upon further innovations in electronics and microelectronics. In the 30 years since he adumbrated this process, these developments have been exceptionally rapid and are now at the core of most of the major innovations in production techniques.

THE DEVELOPMENT OF MICROELECTRONICS

The new electronic devices required the development of a technology for interconnecting many thousands more electronic components than had hitherto been possible. The key to this was the switch from electronic valves to semiconductor components, connected via printed circuits.

The origins of the printed circuit board can be found in a series of pre-War patents; F W Seymour's on the Plated Circuit in 1927, H H Wenmine's System for Stamped Wiring in 1929, H G Arlt's Sprayed

Circuit patent in 1937 and Heinsch's Swiss patent for Cast Connection in 1939.

The development of semiconductor components proceeded steadily, from the fabrication of the single germanium transistor in 1948, to the production of the silicon transistor in 1954. The first integrated transistor circuits (ICs) appeared in 1962, and these were superceded by Medium Scale (MSI) then Large Scale (LSI) and Very Large Scale Integration (VLSI) in the 1970s. A significant milestone in this development was the microprocessor, or computer on a chip, which appeared in 1971.

There is a general consensus in the semiconductor industry that progress towards higher levels of integration will continue to be made over the next 10 years, but at a decreasing rate as optical limits are approached. Noyce anticipates that a million bit memory chip should appear by 1991, at a cost of around $1,000, accompanied by single chip computers with greater power than today's large processors costing $100 or less.[4]

The integrated circuit formed the basis of a range of general purpose circuit elements whose function could be changed by program, without the necessity of rewiring. The ease with which they could be used meant that over the decade 1968-1978 the majority of new products were electronics based (see Figure 1).

It was with the electronic computer that the flexibility offered by these new circuits was most fully exploited. In 1963 computers were the largest single users of transistors, taking an equal share with the whole consumer electronic sector. Over the period from 1955 to 1968 the number of computers in use in America increased from 250 in all, with a growth rate of 150 per annum, to 69,400, and a growth rate of 14,700 per annum. Spectacular growth rates continued into the 1970s, and there are now millions of these machines in use around the world.

Their power, which had been restricted in the 1950s to carrying out complex numerical calculations, was enhanced in the 1960s by the addition of cheap magnetic and semiconductor storage. This made it possible to automate the processing of non numeric data and led to the development of equipment for the construction of computer communication networks in the 1970s, and the assembly of information systems incorporating automatic data collection and control.

A complete hierarchy of computer applications has developed, based on these machines, automating *discrete* aspects of the production process. Figure 2 is a schematic diagram showing the information flow from the design function through to manufacture. Computer-aided design (CAD) and computer-aided manufacture (CAM) are most advanced in the electronics industry. There, circuit design, the layout and manufacture of circuit boards and their testing is carried out automatically. Although these devices are not generally applicable to

33

Commerce
Word processors
Cash and stock control terminals
On-line ordering systems
Visual information systems
Desk-top computers

Communications
Subscriber trunk dialling
Global TV and telephone services
 by satellite
Viewdata
Push-button telephone dialling
Compact radio telephone systems
Solid state TV cameras

Defence
Night viewing equipment
Microwave blind landing systems
Battlefield radar
Advanced weapon-guidance systems
Infra-red surveillance equipment
The cruise missile

*Home entertainment and consumer
 products*
Video games
Teletext — Ceefax and Oracle

Video cassette recorders
Stereo broadcasting
Electronic calculators and
 wristwatches
Electronic musical instruments

Manufacturing industry
Electronically controlled machine
 tools
Advanced instrumentation systems
Electronic measuring equipment
Electronic motor speed and
 temperature control systems
Automated welding

Medicine
Body scanners and other advanced
 diagnostic equipment
Heart pacemakers
Patient monitoring systems
Computer-produced speech for the
 vocally impaired
Kidney dialysis equipment
Electronic aids and sight for the
 blind

Source: Microcomputer Systems
(1978) Infotech.

Figure 1. Electronics-based products 1968-1978

mechanical design, various efforts are being made to extend them in this direction.

In parallel with these developments, discrete administrative functions have also been automated; for example, payroll processing, stock control, production scheduling, accounting and the monitoring of time-keeping and performance.

The development of communications capabilities has enabled data to be transmitted between these discrete functions so that they can be assembled into information systems which automate the flow of information. This development has enabled the second stage of Diebold's plan — the integration of information and material handling — to be realized.

A widening array of products (for example the telephone, computer, television, radio, copier, typewriter, machine tool, and mechanical

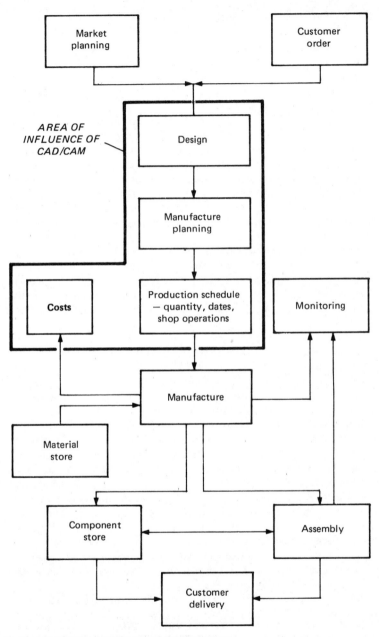

Source: Computers and Employment (1979) NCC

Figure 2. Information flow in manufacturing

handling device) with largely separate technical developments are now being yoked together. This is because of a number of related developments, the most important being the miniaturization of computing and memory power, made possible by the advances in electronics, assisted by the progressive substitution of digital for analogue signals, and the growth in use of satellites and optical fibre cables.

The most heralded convergence has been that between the computer and the telephone exchange: more accurately, the exchange's metamorphosis into a computer. Signals from the subscriber to the exchange may now be processed electronically rather than electro-mechanically: the twin benefits are greater speed and, depending on the programming in the exchanges, the provision of a range of services (such as abbreviated dialling and audio conference calling) previously unavailable. The telephone, now becoming a keypad instrument (eg push button telephone) rather than a dial one, has become more flexible and rapid.

Developments *within* computers have had even more profound effects. The increasing power and very much smaller size and cost of components, and of the central processing and memory units of computers, means that data processing is now available to millions of amateurs rather than to a few professionals. As the transmission of data via phone lines becomes more common (and more simple, as transmission switches from the analogue to the digital mode) a new and vast network of small data users, or thousands of data networks, becomes possible.

The union between the telephone and television is likely to be as fruitful as the union between telephone and computer. It has already produced viewdata, (such as the UK's Prestel system) a system by which computer-stored information is accessed through telephone lines and displayed on the television screen, which is coupled to the telephone. This development is capable of much further refinement, especially in the direction of increased interaction. Already, with Prestel, there is the facility for drawing down computer programs into the television set, then using them as stand-alone microcomputers. As the scope of these viewdata networks grows, it will become increasingly possible to exchange information with sales outlets, work, local and national agencies, and even to use them as voting machines.

The broadcast counterpart of viewdata, CEEFAX and ORACLE, already offer a restricted version of such a data network to over one million subscribers in Europe.

The video disk, which began appearing in commercial quantities in the early 1980s, is a 'merger' between television and records. However, the disks, which contain sound and picture, are digitally encoded. The video disk will become cheaper than video-tape, if less flexible. It is likely to greatly increase the home viewing of pre-recorded material, and will find applications in training and education.

The typewriter, which, when electrified in the 1950s, was merely made easier to use, has recently been given intelligence and a memory and is now close to a computer. The electronic typewriter/word processor has transformed the typewriter from an instrument which made a record on paper only to one which can discriminate between making records on paper and storing data electronically, communicating with its fellow typewriters, receiving messages much as a telex does and 'personalizing' standard letters and other documents. The possession of memory and intelligence enables the typewriter to be active, even when human hands are not at its keyboard. Henceforth, many of its operations will be performed without human intervention, and in response to signals transmitted to it down phone lines, to which it will be coupled.

The copier is now also in the orbit of the telephone, because of developments in the field of the 'intelligent' copier. These are copiers which, when linked to copiers elsewhere, can transmit a copy of a document by sending signals through phone lines.

New technology has also affected the nature of telecommunication networks, increasing their electromagnetic bandwidth so that they can carry a wider range of services, from voice and data to video. Indeed, Dr Alex Reid has pointed out that the ranges of services now available over wireless and wired networks have become almost identical (see Figure 3).

We are beginning to develop means of mass communication which are no longer one-way (such as radio and TV) but are instead genuinely interactive. These forms go under the collective name of 'teleconferencing', and include computer, audio and video modes. Equipment and telecommunications costs for all three forms of teleconferencing have declined by 30 to 50 per cent over the past six years, and they are rapidly becoming cost-effective, compared with the time and money spent on long-distance meetings.

The speed with which these developments will take place will be accelerated by progress in satellite transmission, because of the ease with which satellites can handle vast quantities of data, voice and vision. The effects of these developments are held to be the emergence, in the office, of integrated work stations and of entertainment and information/education centres in the home.

THE AUTOMATION OF THE MATERIAL HANDLING PROCESS

The shape of the factory of the future is slowly emerging: the robotized plants, or sections of plants, in Japan, the US and parts of Europe are signs of this happening. Much of their chemical and steel production, as we have already noted, is largely automated.

Number of Recipients

	1	1–10	$10 - 10^2$	$10^2 - 10^3$	$10^3 - 10^4$	$10^4 - 10^5$	$10^5 - 10^6$	$10^6 - 10^7$
Alpha-numeric and graphic data	Telex data facsimile	Electronic mail and computer conference		Viewdata				
Audio	Tele-phones	Audio conference		Audio information services				
Audio-visual	View phones	Video conference		Cable TV				

Figure 3a Wired electronic communication services

Number of Recipients

	1	1 – 10	$10 - 10^2$	$10^2 - 10^3$	$10^3 - 10^4$	$10^4 - 10^5$	$10^5 - 10^6$	$10^6 - 10^7$
Alpha-numeric and graphic data	Packet radio conference				Broadcast CEEFAX/ORACLE			
Audio	Mobile telephone	Citizens' band radio				Broadcast sound		
Audio-visual	Satellite video conference					Broadcast TV		

Figure 3b Wireless electronic communication services

Based on: A Reid (1978) 'New telecommunications services and their social implications'. *Phil Trans Royal Soc,* **289.**

Figure 3. The convergence of telecommunications services

The 'convergence' is between computer and production equipment of all kinds. Automation was first possible in handling equipment which is required to pick up, carry or place materials with wide margins of error. However, as the tolerances narrow so the equipment must become more sophisticated, and its intelligence increase exponentially.

The first generation of 'blind' robots, now operating in car plants are the most intelligent machines now in general use. They are able to weld, spray and turn nuts and screws. They depend upon the parts on which they are working to be lined up precisely — otherwise they will weld, turn and spray in the wrong places. Their 'intelligence' is rote learning.

The evolution of really intelligent production machines depends on their intelligence being complemented by 'senses': of sight, hearing and touch. Robot technology now being developed by Japanese, US and a few European companies uses TV cameras to feed back information for processing by computers, or audio equipment to respond to commands, or devices known as 'remote centre compliances' which allow the machine to sense when its arm is next to a solid object.[5]

It is not yet certain whether or not such robots can be made: there are, at present, no operational robots which can see, touch or hear so well that they make autonomous decisions about the right and wrong ways of assembling products. However, there is an increasing amount of research being focused on this field. The central problem is not the machines but the enormously complex software required to deal with the vast amount of information fed back from, for example, TV cameras.

In production, as in communication and office work, intelligence is now being injected into operational systems in large doses. The process is slowing somewhat because of the technical (usually software) problems. Yet many innovations in production equipment have already been made at the research and development stage, and now wait for production techniques and marketing opportunities to catch up.

THE INTEGRATION OF MATERIAL AND INFORMATION HANDLING

The advanced companies now researching this area are spurred on by the prospect of replacing workers who currently assemble products by machines, that is, for example, one-third of all employees in an average car plant. The most optimistic believe that a wholly automated factory is a realizable prospect in the medium-term future. General Electric believes that:

'eventually, all the individual parts of a computerized factory could be linked up. Draughtsmen would design objects by computer with keyboard and screens; the workers would feed the production details to computer-controlled machine tools which turn out the parts; and then they would instruct robots to assemble the parts to make the product. Virtually no one would be directly involved. As a final move, the company is developing voice recognition equipment so that people can talk to the machines and tell them what to do. The day of the moving, feeling, seeing and hearing robot will then be at hand.'[6]

Figure 4 shows how such integrated business systems might be constructed. Design programs are used to program computer-controlled machine tools directly. Shop floor data collection systems may be used to input data for production control and other administrative purposes. Point of sale equipment can collect sales information directly for use by inventory programs. Inspection and machining equipment collects statistics on its own performance and transmits the information to remote computers which supervise the overall production process. Taken together, these developments make it possible to envisage the bulk of manufacturing changing from batch towards a much more intensive use of machinery — the second stage in Diebold's programme (see p. 32). This is likely to take place fairly rapidly. Limp materials, such as paper and cloth, will be handled in fully automatic factories in the 1980s.

The automation of metal machining and assembly will be a slower process, but should be largely complete by the last decade of the century. In 1977, The American Society of Manufacturing Engineers (ASME) and the University of Michigan conducted a survey of 124 experts on manufacturing and assembly to obtain forecasts of future developments in technology. They reported that:

by 1982, a practical adaptive-control assembly machine will be available for small component assembly;

by 1985, 75 per cent of all assembly systems will use automatic inspection, and 75 per cent of all automatic inspection will use programmable control;

25 per cent of the direct labour in automobile final assembly will be replaced by programmable automation;

programmable assembly techniques will be used in 25 per cent of automatic assembly operations;

by 1987, 15 per cent of assembly systems will use robotic technology;

by 1988, 50 per cent of the direct labour in small component assembly will be replaced by programmable automation;

by 1990, development of sensory techniques will enable robots to approximate human capability in assembly;

by 1995, 50 per cent of the direct labour in automobile final assembly will be replaced by programmable automation.[7]

The UK Institution of Production Engineers have complemented such US projections with projections for Britain and Japan. They anticipate that:

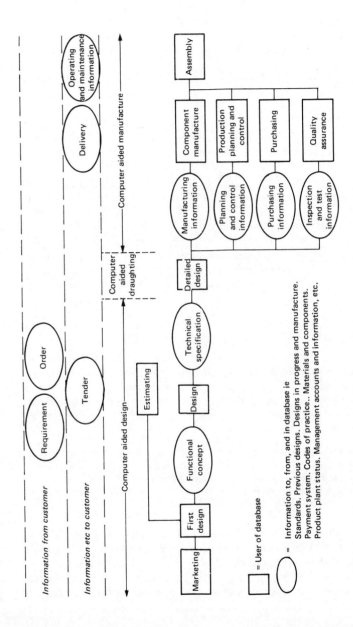

Source: ACARD (1980) *Computer Aided Design and Manufacture* HMSO.

Figure 4. An integrated business system

41

by 1985, 25 per cent of US companies will use computers for component design, a level which will not be reached by the UK and Japan until 1990;

10 per cent of US companies, 7½ per cent of Japanese, and 5 per cent of British firms will use CAD for both component and tool design;

by 1990, 25 per cent of machine tools in US factories will have sensory devices for inspection, a level which will not be reached in the UK and Japan until 1995;

20 per cent of US and UK manufacturing companies will have integrated materials and production planning systems. Japan is expected to reach this level by 1986.[8]

The automation of production has proceeded in fits and starts. Some sectors (eg steel and chemicals) were capable of automation by early generations of computerized equipment in the late 1950s and 1960s. Other sectors, such as cars only saw fundamental changes in their production process when robots began to appear in the mid-late 1970s. And the arrival of automated equipment for the huge and varied office sector, has been delayed until the early 1980s, when microelectronic equipment comes into its own and the market is prepared for it. Now, however, the process is speeding up. The time lags between the automation of discrete sectors are being rapidly cut back; more and more industries and companies are being required to plan a new mode of production to replace, or co-exist with, their present one.

Thus, just as Taylorist techniques required engineers to divide and discipline labour for methodically limited tasks, the requirement now is for more engineering generalists with the necessary knowledge to conceive of the production, distribution and exchange process as a whole, in order to bring about the totally new use of the new machinery. Diebold remarked that:

'one of the impediments to rethinking of products and processes has been that the traditional division of responsibilities has the effect of localizing the areas in which rethinking is done. Almost by definition, however, rethinking must be done on an extremely broad basis — viewing the objectives of the entire organization as a whole.'[9]

In search of these new skills, engineering companies have taken a more intimate part in the construction of university curricula. For example, GEC have been closely associated with the design of Bath University's engineering course, which highlights these system skills. The Finniston Report on the education and training of engineers in the UK has noted that the work of engineers:

'has direct and indirect effects on the tasks of other workers in the enterprise, the jobs and systems of which those tasks form a part and the total organization of work. Engineers must, therefore, be concerned not merely with technically optional solutions and systems but with the human and organizational factors involved in the operation of the system.'[10]

BRINGING DOWN THE COST

Engineers and managers have always been concerned with the maximization of efficiency and profit or surplus. Under Taylorist principles, much of this was achieved by labour discipline. At the present time, new technology removes the need for such measures by cutting down on the requirement for mass workforces or by monitoring electronically.

The battle to reduce costs and increase efficiency is being carried out on four major fronts, as set out below.

Reducing Labour Costs
The new clerical automation and data collection devices may act as a direct replacement for labour. In other areas, such as computer system operation, automation enables less skilled operators to be employed, as the machine takes on maintenance or supervisory functions previously carried out manually.

Raising the Intensity of Labour
Numerous devices have been developed for monitoring attendance and activity at work. They have been particularly associated with the widespread reintroduction of the clock, under the guise of 'flextime' working which may be used as a means of cutting down rest periods and time lost through absence. Other devices supervise the operation of machinery, such as typewriters, telephones or vehicles. Information collected on typewriter key depressions, telephone use, or engine performance and driving times, introduce the possibility of management control into areas of working life where previously a good deal of autonomy existed. Information collected by these new monitoring devices can form the basis for a new, 'automatic' Taylorism, in which work is planned and organized by machine.

Increasing the Rate of Through-flow
Production planning automation, as used in Japanese car manufacture for example, can dramatically replace the requirement for work in progress. There the KANBAN system ensures that authority to manufacture a part is only issued when the next stage of the production process requires it. The buffer stocks held in between stages are progressively reduced in the light of experience.

Increasing the Flexibility of the Production System

New technology offers the possibility of less direct dependence, by the operator and the group, on machines, with work organized on the basis of 'semi-autonomous' groups. There are certain degrees of freedom for work organization associated with any given production technology, and the task of management is seen as optimizing not only the technological system, but also the social organization, that is, the optimization of the overall socio-technical system. An optimum social organization would have certain desirable characteristics related to opportunities for a degree of independence and decision-making, variety, opportunities to learn, meaningful work, etc. These demands have been particularly influential in recent Scandinavian experiments in work place democracy, while in the UK the method has been refined into a strategy for computer system design by Enid Mumford and her colleagues at the Manchester Business School.

INFORMATION SYSTEMS AND CONTROL

It is implicit in much of what we have described above that information systems are not merely concerned with the transmission of neutral data, but also embody lines of social and economic control. Standard texts on information systems design identify a two-dimensional framework for decision-making, based on the level of managerial activity and the nature of the decision-making process.[11]

Operational Level

At this level, decision-making rules are fixed and results are deterministic. Examples are acceptance or rejection of credit, process control, payment transmission, scheduling, receiving, distribution, stock control and the allocation of work. Operational decision-making is a process of ensuring that specific tasks like these are implemented in an efficient manner. In his book on *Information Systems*, Burch notes that 'the primary management function is control, with planning performed on a rather limited scale.'[12]

Tactical Level

Tactical decision-making refers to the allocation of resources to meet objectives. This decision-making relates to areas such as budget formulation, cash flow analysis, plant layout, product improvement, and research and development. Where operational decision-making is largely a control activity, Burch notes that 'tactical decision-making requires a fairly equal mix of planning and controlling activities.'[13] This decision-making has little potential for programmed decision-making, as the decision rules are, for the most part, ill formulated and are not amenable to routine and self-regulation.

Strategic Level

Strategic decisions are oriented towards the future, and characterized by a great deal of uncertainty. Long-range plans are produced which state the goals of the organization and the range of strategies which are to be pursued. Goals and strategies might cover, for example plant contraction, the nature of product lines, mergers, acquisitions, capital expenditures, or the sale of the organization. Burch defines the strategic level as being largely a planning activity concerned with 'establishing objectives, policy making, organizing, and attaining an overall effectiveness for the organization.'[14] Strategic planning support systems would be concerned with economic data bases and models, and 'what if' simulations.

Normative Level

Normative decisions are concerned with the regulation of capital flows between countries and enterprises. Under a system of free trade and free capital movements this is the business of governments and private institutions concerned with the financing of trade and investment. Their instruments of control vary from granting or withholding credit, fixing exchange rates and interest rates for deposits and loans, to outright share ownership and board representation. Normative decision-making, like strategic decision-making, is a planning exercise not amenable to programming. Decision-making may be supported by economic models and various information systems concerned with the production and exchange of financial statistics relating to enterprises, stock and money exchanges and money markets.

THE EVOLUTION OF INFORMATION SYSTEMS

Computer-based information systems have been designed to meet the needs of each level of activity. As they have been developed and implemented, their impact on the workforce has steadily increased.

The system development process helps to shape the working environment. Information systems are developed for management by systems analysts. Since the analyst is concerned with gathering information from the workforce, he or she needs to gain the co-operation of the workforce. The traditional approach seeks to minimize any possible resistance, which is assumed to be an unreasonable fear of change, by various devices. Thus, Burch notes:

'the systems analyst, when acting as a change agent may attempt to move individuals . . . by employing a participative change strategy, a coercive change strategy, or a combination of both . . . Participative change begins when the systems analyst educates the individuals affected by the new system (in the hope) that this . . . will cultivate the development of the appropriate attitude towards the new system . . . Coercive change, on the other hand, is initiated from a position of power (and) is most effective when the target group is composed of dependant people.'[15]

The implementation of computer-based information systems has proceeded over the last 20 years through four generations: discrete systems, database systems, shop floor data entry systems and computer communication networks. All major organizations have by now passed through the first two phases and are entering the third phase. Advanced transnational companies, especially those in the finance and electronics sectors, are at present implementing the fourth phase.

Phase 1: Discrete Systems
During the first phase of computer-based information systems, central data processing departments are introduced, and various administrative routines such as payroll processing are transferred to the machine. Clerical and shop floor procedures of the organization are little changed, although a new job function concerned with encoding data for entry to the machine is created. Printed reports are generated on the machine for posting back to the user.

Phase 2: Database Systems
During the second phase of the development of automatic data processing, tentative electronic links are radiated from the computer room and connected to terminals in the user departments. Some information is now collected at source, by-passing the key punch operators, and a few reports are made available at VDU terminals. Personnel and accounting programs have been joined by production control and inventory management systems. At this stage, the reduced requirement for data preparation staff to encode the input leads to some staffing changes and redundancies, but the major part of the organization remains intact.

During this phase, data used by the enterprise is progressively centralized to ensure its compatibility with the various application programs. Often a new function of Database Administrator is established to control access to it.

Phase 3: Shop Floor Data Entry
By now all programmable operational functions have been transferred to the machine and VDU terminals are deployed throughout the organization. The data preparation section is now redundant, and redundancies also take place in clerical areas.

Phase 4: Computer Communication Networks
In the fourth phase, independent computer centres are linked together into networks to enable each of their terminals to access any database. Specialized terminals, dedicated to document production (such as word

processors) or telecommunications (such as facsimile machines) begin to proliferate.

Having gained instantaneous access to data about the movement of cash and materials, senior management is able to obtain a clearer picture of the day-to-day operation of their enterprises. This data could be used as a basis for the simulation of alternative modes of operation, throwing up options for rationalization at strategic and normative levels.

CONCLUSION

In the early part of this century, Taylor and his associates not only developed a new system of production, but also heavily influenced contemporary industrial relations, as will be shown in Chapter 2. Alongside a new framework for the division of labour in industry, they created the conditions for corporate collective bargaining to regulate relations with their 'collective workers'.

Engineers and managers are now designing a new social structure which radically alters Taylor's division of labour in the following ways:

☐ Production, distribution and exchange are linked together by a computerized 'loop' around which information and commands circulate.

☐ The large workforces in production industries are growing proportionally smaller and smaller as they are replaced with capital.

☐ Service industries of various types are also becoming capital intensive.

☐ Workers with systems skills are at a premium; but skilled and semi-skilled workers with a specialized trade are a glut on the labour market.

☐ Operational discipline is being replaced by machine discipline, or by self-discipline.

REFERENCES

1 F Taylor (1911) *The Principles of Scientific Management*, p 39. Harper and Bros.

2 J Diebold (1952) *Automation: The Advent of the Automatic Factory*. Van Nostrand.

3 ibid, p 91.

4 R Noyce (1979) 'Hardware prospects and limitations'. *The Computer Age: A Twenty-Year View*, p 333. MIT.

5 P Marsh (1981) *New Scientist*, pp 845-47, 25 June.

6 ibid, p 847.

7 'What's to come in assembly' (1978) In *American Machinist*, 22, August.

8 *Current and Future Trends of Manufacturing and Technology in the UK* (1980) Institute of Production Engineering, London.

9 Diebold, op cit, p 2.

10 Report of the Committee of Inquiry into the engineering profession, p 40 (1980) HMSO.

11 G Anthony Gorry and M S Scott Morton (1971) 'A framework for management information systems'. *Sloan Management Review*, pp 55-70, Autumn.

12 J G Burch *et al* (1979) *Information Systems, Theory and Practice*, p 52. Wiley, New York.

13 ibid, p 52.

14 ibid, p 52.

15 ibid, p 461.

CHAPTER 2

Labour's Response to Scientific Management

INTRODUCTION

Scientists and engineers have played an essential part in the evolution of labour movements, which have been an integral feature of industrialization. The 'machine question', that is the recurring struggle over the control of technological change and its consequences, testifies to the very strong links between the history of technology, economic history and labour history. The exact nature of this interaction, between technology and socio-economic change, is a subject of debate.

THE TECHNOLOGICAL PERSPECTIVE

The history of technology appears as one of steady progress from the time of the industrial revolution. The primary industrial revolution, concerned with the development of steam engines, was followed by a series of secondary revolutions — those of the railway, electricity and electronics.

THE ECONOMIC PERSPECTIVE

Classical economists, from Adam Smith to Milton Friedman, have presented history as a continuous process of advance since the primary industrial revolution. They use measures such as energy, or food consumption or life expectancy to show a general pattern of technological change leading to higher standards of living in the advanced world. It is acknowledged that fluctuations occur in this pattern, which are associated with regular short-term cycles in economic activity. These, however, are attributed to the temporary operation of self-regulating market mechanisms, which adjust to changes in the supply and demand for goods and services, mechanisms known as the 'invisible hand'.

This view of economic history has not gone unchallenged by economists who have been as influential in the past as monetarists are at the present time. Marx and the socialist economists, and Thorstien Veblen and the Institutionalists, have argued that uncontrolled market forces threaten to destroy the very prosperity that they have created. Writing at a time when science-based industry was only in its infancy, Marx noted that, with the development of the factory system, a new method of production is introduced which lies in:

> 'an analysis of the process of production into its constituent phases, and in the solution of the problems that then arise by means of the application of mechanics, chemistry, etc — in a word the natural sciences.'[1]

To Marx, the development of labour-saving devices in this way, and their incorporation into production was central to the antagonism between capital and labour, as those who were not required in production formed an evergrowing 'industrial reserve army' while technological improvements gained ground. As the purchasing power of workers provided the major demand for consumer goods, the effect of this unemployment would be to reduce demand substantially, giving rise to periodic crises of over-production leading to depressions. This view of the impact of unregulated technological change is central to socialist, as well as to Marxist, thought.

Thorstien Veblen was an American economist who was to provide much of the economic analysis which underpinned Roosevelt's New Deal. Veblen was concerned with the increasing importance of science and technology to the post-First World War economy, and, like Marx, he came to regard it as a central factor in production. Since it was not thus regarded in classical economic theory, Veblen believed that any economy which actually operated on classical lines was bound to fail. Writing immediately after the First World War he noted:

> '. . . it has been usual, and indeed is still not unusual, to speak of three co-ordinate "factors of production": land, labour and capital. The reason for this three-fold scheme of factors in production is that there have been three recognized classes of income: rent, wages and profits; and it has been assumed that whatever yields an income is a productive factor. This scheme has come down from the eighteenth century . . . (and) seen in the light of later events . . . is notable for what it omits . . . The state of the industrial art . . . is the indispensable foundation of all productive industry, of course, but except for certain minute fragments covered by patent rights of trade secrets, this joint stock is no man's individual property. For this reason it has not been counted in as a factor in production.'[2]

According to Veblen the failure to take into account the impact of technological change on the functioning of the American economy in the 1920s would soon cause a disaster. Its origin lay in the unscientific business practices which Taylor and his colleagues had tried to rationalize within the factory, and similar 'conscious withdrawal of efficiency' outside it arising from an operation of the price system, which placed a capital value on an enterprise according to its earnings record and not its productive capacity. Inefficiency would lead to: distribution costs which would add more than 50 per cent to the price paid by consumers; waste from the unemployment of capital and labour, either deliberate or arising from ignorance; production of 'superfluous goods'; and withholding of information, monopoly of resources, and ignorance on the part of businessmen of industrial requirements. Veblen likened the post-First World War economic system, with its greatly expanded engineering base, to an interlocking mechanical process, interdependent and delicately balanced. What equilibrium was achieved was unstable. He believed that the cumulative effect of the derangement and sabotage arising from business methods of control 'will paralyze the whole outright'.[3] When the crash Veblen had anticipated did occur, some 10 years later, his analysis was to become a commonplace.

Kondratiev's Wave Theory

Around the same time as Veblen was working out his economic theory, a Dutch economist, Van Gelderen, proposed the idea that there might be 'long-waves' in economic activity, lasting over half a century or more. At first, this was not directly related to technological changes. The earliest systematic attempt to collect data to clarify the turning point of these long cycles was undertaken by Kondratiev at the Institute of Applied Economic Research in Moscow in the 1920s. Kondratiev saw these cycles being related to the durability of certain types of investment, such as buildings and transport. His work, cut short by Stalin, was of limited success. Joseph Schumpeter took up Kondratiev's work in the West and introduced the idea of technological revolutions as the basis of the 'Kondratiev cycles'. In particular he identified the role of steam power in what he termed the 'first Kondratiev' (1787-1840), the railroads in the 'second Kondratiev' (1843-1897) and electric power and the automobile in the 'third Kondratiev'.

Schumpeter argued that these cycles arose from bursts of creative activity by entrepreneurs, although it was noted by contemporaries such as Kuznets that he provided no explanation why such innovative activity should be sporadic. Kuznets did, however, accept that innovations and investment activity associated with basic innovations such as steam power and electricity, might be 'bunched' in some way.

Kuznets noted that with major innovations there was evidence of big time lags between their first appearance and general adoption, and suggested that this might have more to do with the functioning of the economic system than with the appearance of the innovations themselves. He argued that Schumpeter and Kondratiev had both failed to substantiate their theories by reference to statistics on production, trade and employment and that references to prices and interest rates which they had made were unsatisfactory because these are dominated by external events such as war. The problem is that, while later statistics are relatively easy to obtain, it is difficult to reconstruct retrospective statistics for production. Because of this, controversy has continued amongst economic historians on the 'myth' of the Great Depression of the late nineteenth century, the reality of the 'boom' which preceded it, and the existence of the industrial revolution itself. Attention has only been focused on undertaking the necessary detailed work at the time of depression, and interest in Kondratiev's theory has only recently revived.

UK Industrial Production	1827-1847	3.2%
	1848-1875	4.6%
	1876-1893	1.2%
	1894-1913	2.2%
	1914-1938	2.0%
	1939-1967	3.0%
	1968-1981	0.8%
Germany (to 1945) FRG (after 1945)	1850-1874	4.5%
Industrial Production	1875-1892	2.5%
	1893-1913	4.3%
	1914-1938	2.2%
	1939-1967	3.9%
	1968-1981	3.0%
USA Industrial Production	1849-1873	5.4%
	1874-1893	4.9%
	1894-1913	5.9%
	1914-1938	2.0%
	1939-1967	5.2%
	1968-1981	2.5%
Variations in the Rate	1820-1840	2.7%
of Growth of World Trade	1840-1870	5.5%
	1870-1890	2.2%
	1891-1913	3.7%
	1913-1937	0.4%
	1938-1967	4.8%
	1968-1981	5.5%

Sources: E Mandel (1967) *Late Capitalism*
OECD (1976) *Main Economic Indicators* (1960-75)
OECD (1982) *Main Economic Indicators* (to 1981 3rd Quarter)
UN (1982) Monthly Bulletin of Statistics

Figure 1. Variations in the rate of growth of industrial production and trade

Those production statistics which can be collected are shown in Figure 1, and would appear to support the case that long waves of economic activity can be seen. Nevertheless, Schumpeter was not able to show why these cycles took the form they did.

Electronics: A Fourth Kondratiev?

Recently, Chris Freeman has argued that an explanation might be provided for the period of these waves if it could be shown that the early prosperity phase of the wave tipped the balance of economic activity in the direction of full employment, and if the recession phase shifted the balance in the opposite direction. The upswing would correspond to a period of parallel operation of old and new industrial methods; the infrastructure of the new industries being built up, products and production techniques becoming standardized and skilled manpower being trained. Here the critical limiting factor would be the training time to establish a corps of teachers, and an associated engineering discipline. This, Freeman argued, is of the order of a generation, ie 25 years. After this time, the labour displacing effects of the new technologies would predominate. Old industrial processes would become obsolete and the effects of the diffusion of new technology could lead from unemployment to demand inflation. This would be a self-reinforcing process, because when there is low profitability, entrepreneurs will be more inclined to adopt labour-saving technologies.

The role of innovation in stimulating long waves of economic activity has been widely discussed in recent years. One of the more influential participants, G Mensch, has proposed a theory of 'bunching' of basic innovations to explain how Kondratiev waves start. He maintains that historically such a pattern can be observed to occur in the depression periods of the 1830s, 1880s and 1930s, and he predicts a new cluster of basic innovations in the 1980s. Mensch argues that the depression creates an 'accelerator mechanism' to shorten the lead time between invention and innovation. During the technological stalemate of the recession phase, these basic or radical innovations are crowded out. As a result, unexploited basic innovations cluster together in the decades of the deepest trough, providing the opportunity for subsequent recovery.

This theory has been challenged by Freeman and his colleagues in their recent book *Unemployment and Technical Innovation*. They argue that, by explicitly denying the link between science and technology, and ignoring the impact of war-induced reflation, Mensch's analysis of the innovative bunching which occurred in the 1930s is superficial.[4]

In the early post-Second World War decades in the West, a series of actions by state and industry succeeded in putting in place a new industrial infrastructure based on electronics. The expansion of further and higher education began to meet some of the need for new vocational skills, while government and privately sponsored research and development led to the emergence of the new technologies. By the 1970s, the majority of new products were based on this new technology, and now it is having a major impact on production processes.

In the 1950s and 1960s, the few workers displaced by this process

53

were absorbed into less technically advanced sectors of the economy. Harry Braverman refers to this as: 'the paradox that the most rapidly growing mass occupations in an era of scientific-technical revolution are those which have least to do with science and technology'.[5] Now, however, this apparent contradiction is rapidly being resolved as the new technology diffuses across the board, replacing the old electro-mechanical processes of production, distribution and exchange with electronic information systems.

Appeals to the argument that falling production costs will ultimately increase the range of potential production and the size of markets are met with the evidence that production in many sectors is coming up against limits of energy costs and market saturation, from cars to washing machines and televisions. On this evidence, Freeman has argued that electronics-based industries may well form the basis of a fourth Kondratiev wave, the upswing or development phase lasting over the 1950s and 1960s, and the downswing or application phase lasting until the end of this century.

THE LABOUR PERSPECTIVE

The progress of the Kondratiev waves has shaped the development of the labour movement, and it is in the history of the labour movement that the discontinuous nature of technological change can be seen most clearly. Its very essence is one of alternating advance and retreat; of gains secured, eroded and restored; of organizations formed, degenerating and reformed. Here we find the periods associated with steam, rail, electricity and electronics notable for the introduction of new words into our vocabulary to articulate novel social events: luddism, unemployment, technological and now structural unemployment.

Each successive period of economic advance presented contradictory faces to labour, undermining the old framework of economic security and, at the same time, creating opportunities for new and enhanced forms of labour power. Machinery increased the economic strength of the more technically advanced employers while undermining the traditional basis of workers' bargaining power. Labour's attempts to compensate for this weakness by experimenting with new forms of organization inevitably led to clashes with employers over the control of new technology.

During the two nineteenth century Kondratiev waves it was the British labour movement, in the country with the most advanced capitalist system in operation, which had to resolve these questions. The first Kondratiev based on steam power, split working people into two groups. While the new textile factories undermined the economic position of the weavers and stockingers, the same process enabled the millwrights to develop craft unions and pioneer local collective bargaining. These were to be absorbed into national unions following the attempts of the textile machinery manufacturers to smash the embryo unions in a lockout over the machine question in 1851.

The second, 'railway', Kondratiev was associated with equally momentous changes in working class life. In response to growing pressures in the middle of the cycle the craft unions came together in 1868 to form the Trades Union Congress (TUC) which campaigned successfully, with middle class support, for the reform of the franchise. By the end of the century, millions had moved to the cities as unskilled workers to man the infrastructure of transport and utilities which underpinned large-scale industrialization. In the factories, the introduction of the mass production of machines led to a further struggle between unions and employers over the machine question and working time, culminating in the lockout of 1897. The unions' defeat paved the way for socialists within the labour movement to argue for the formation of an independent working class political party to compensate for the shift of industrial power to the employers. This led to the establishment of the Labour Representation Committee, forerunner of the Labour party.

The rapid advance of mechanization prompted unions on both sides of the Atlantic to campaign for a reduction in working time, a campaign which was to provide the basis for the establishment of the first international trade union centres. In America, the fight for the eight-hour day required the adoption of the British pattern of trade union organization. In contrast, in Germany, which was industrializing within a feudal state, the trade unions were subordinate to the working class political party, the Social Democratic party, which fought to first establish a framework of democratic rights.

At the turn of the twentieth century the major elements of the modern labour movement were in place: national and international trade centres, central funding and the beginnings of labour parties. With the development of science-based industry in the third Kondratiev, the locus for the evolution of the movement shifted to America. There, scientific management created the 'collective worker'. The new workers ultimately realized their organizational potential by forming industrial trade unions to undertake corporate collective bargaining, involving the science-based combines and the state. US government regulation of collective bargaining was enshrined in two acts which mark the opening and close of this wave of organization, the Wagner Act of 1935 and the Taft-Hartley Act of 1947. Since this time the pattern of state regulated collective bargaining has been imposed throughout the advanced world, with the exception of Britain where aspects of corporate collective bargaining, notably legally binding agreements, have been repeatedly rejected.

Each of these earlier waves has seen the shifting of the centre of industrial bargaining power. Firstly from the home to the factory tool-room, then from the toolroom to the mass production line. Now the shift is from the production line to remote control and administration machines. While the shift benefits many groups of newly organized workers (in air traffic control, computers and telecommunications, for example) it is unwelcome to many traditional areas where labour strength is based on union control of machine manning.

There are two threats to traditional groups: direct labour displacement, and unwelcome opportunities for machines to be used as substitutes for one another during a dispute. According to the TUC, to counter the threat posed by telecommunications and flexible manufacturing systems:

> 'trade unionists need to take a great interest not only in the computer equipment − the hardware − but also in the software − the programs that control the information system. Who will write the programs? What jobs will the programs do? What say will the employees have in the way the programs work?'

Furthermore, union organizations will have to be brought together within and across companies so that:

> 'discussion of union strategy takes place throughout the workforce. And to make sure that unionists working on design and marketing get involved in discussions with members of production workers' unions.'[6]

Concern over the implications of new technology for labour has not been confined to Britain. A recent report by the European Trade Union Institute, research arm of the European TUC remarks:

> 'A central requirement for a satisfactory resolution of the problems associated with new technology is that trade unions should be involved at the earliest opportunity at all levels of policy-making − the enterprise, company or industry level, the national level and the European and international level.'[7]

In America, too, the labour movement has been alerted to the implications of the new technology. The United Auto Workers described the present situation in their Ford newssheet in September 1979 in graphic terms:

> 'If, in 1973 someone had told workers at the *Washington Post* that new technology would rob them of their jobs, eliminate their skills, or destroy the power of their union, the workers, especially the highly skilled printers and pressmen, would have laughed at, or ignored, such a ridiculous idea. Yet, by the end of 1973, management of the *Washington Post* had totally destroyed the union, taken away many benefits, and eliminated a number of jobs − all almost solely through the use of new technology. A similar story can be told of countless newspapers across the country.
>
> 'If someone had told workers in the aerospace industry in 1974 that

new technology would rob them of some of their jobs, eliminate some of their skills, or weaken the bargaining power of their union, the workers would have laughed at, or ignored, such a ridiculous idea. Yet, aerospace management through the use of new technology did just that in 1976.

'Workers at McDonnell Douglas in St Louis had the bitter experience of seeing management through the use of computerized machines run their plant while the workers were on strike.

'Even though the plant was run at a greatly reduced level, enough was run to meet important government contracts and greatly lessened the strike power of the union.'[8]

Union concern over the impact of the new technology has been slow to develop. The post-war economic expansion, associated with the development phase of the fourth Kondratiev wave, eased the problems of adjustment to technological change where they occurred. In addition, the piecemeal way in which discrete functions were automated made it difficult for unions to detect any overall pattern to the changes which were taking place during this time. New thinking was evident, however, in the Automation Debate in the mid 1950s, and this was given concrete form in the struggles that developed round the early mechanization agreements.

In the UK in the early 1960s, Harold Wilson took up some of these earlier themes of new technology and made them a feature in the run-up to the 1964 election. The attempts of the Wilson Governments of 1964-70 to modernize the economy, though far-reaching, fell short of their stated aims. (In the early 1970s, more radical solutions, including a National Enterprise Board with specific responsibility for new technologies, planning agreements and an extension of industrial democracy were proposed.)

By the 1980s, the international labour movement had developed two clear strategies for responding to the implications of technological change. American unions attempted to build outwards from the system of corporate bargaining in North America to establish global collective bargaining with the transnationals. International joint union councils for individual TNCs such as Ford, Massey Ferguson, IBM and Philips, had been established under the auspices of the international trade centres, and efforts were made to synchronize pay settlement dates, and obtain a measure of international recognition from the companies.

The Western European unions, jealous of their sovereignty, were concerned to develop a nationally centered strategy which aimed to use state power as a means of regulating the TNCs together with data and technology agrements to control technological change at the workplace. In Chapter 7, we look at the first component of their strategy which is the experience of bargaining over data agreements in the 1970s, and in Chapter 8 we examine the second component, technology agreements. The third component of this strategy is concerned with using state power to regulate TNC strategic planning, in so far as it affects the domestic economy. In theory, this involves a state presence in each major industrial sector of the domestic economy which equips the government with first-hand knowledge of the industry's economics and and an element of independent bargaining power in its negotiations. Mutually agreed strategic plans, known variously as planning agreements, agreed development plans, or *accords de planification* are to be drawn up between the state and each TNC with the unions as interested third parties to the negotiations. In the UK, it is now intended that these agreements should be compulsory.

These three components of the labour movement's strategy are aimed at extending the principles of collective bargaining to encompass the whole of the decision-making process concerned with technological change. Where the social impact will be felt at the workplace, negotiators will be accountable, through the unions, to those directly affected. Where the impact is more diffuse and affects many social groups, the bargaining agent is the state, accountable through parliament to society as a whole.

STEAM POWER, LUDDITES AND MILLWRIGHTS

The beginnings of the first phase of mechanization, and, as a corollary, the first phase of unionism, were marked by the creation of one class of worker and the destruction of another.

The entrepreneurs and inventors of the late eighteenth century turned to the millwrights, blacksmiths, carpenters and masons working with hand tools to engineer their new machines. The success of their steam-driven machines, particularly in textiles, created a demand for quality and quantity which these handicraft methods were unable to meet. To meet this, a revolution in the basis of machine-making was necessary — the transformation from machine-making by hand to machine-making by machine. Between 1800 and 1840, a series of inventions and improvements were perfected which paved the way for this transformation. The development of new tools led to differentiation in the trades. Division of labour into pattern maker, iron and brass founder, smith, hammerman and fireman, viceman and filer, turner and planer developed in place of carpenter, millwright and blacksmith. The new engineers worked in factories rather than in isolation, while the expansion of the industry drew many thousands more into employment.

At the same time, the rapid spread of these new machines and factory production began to undermine the traditional textile crafts. Weavers and stockingers in the East Midlands were particularly affected. This changing pattern of employment took place in last decades of the wages/prices system of Elizabethan times. Under this system wages were fixed by Justices of the Peace and those groups, whose incomes were being undermined, looked at first to the state to defend their economic livelihood. When this failed, weavers turned to machine breaking and political action to defend their living standards.

Between March 1811 and July 1812, the major phase of Nottinghamshire Luddism took place and a thousand frames were destroyed. Luddism went beyond machine breaking into general revolutionary political activity: its shadowy existence, exhumed by E P Thompson and others, fed the radical culture of the early nineteenth century. Thompson expresses both its limit and potential:

> 'Luddism may be seen as the nearest thing to a "peasant's revolt" of industrial workers; instead of sacking the chateaux, the most immediate object which symbolized their oppression — the gig mill and the power loom mill — was attacked . . . (yet) . . . even while attacking these symbols of exploitation and of the factory system, they became aware of larger objectives, and pockets of "Tom Painers" existed who could direct them to wider aims.'[9]

Political action, for workers such as millwrights, took the form of attempts at collective bargaining to regulate wages. By 1779, their local organizations had become so strong that in London the Masters themselves combined to petition Parliament to enable wages to be fixed in the trade by Justices of the Peace, and to outlaw combination amongst the journeymen millwrights. The Bill proposed by the Masters was withdrawn and replaced by a more comprehensive piece of legislation which included all trades and which, together with more stringent amending acts passed the following year, known as the Combination Acts, outlawed all forms of trade unions.

While the millwrights maintained their organization, the smiths, iron and brassfounders, mechanics and engineers struggled to form societies and clubs which would provide assistance in times of unemployment, sickness, old age and death, and provide a cover for illegal collective bargaining.

The repeal of the Combination Acts in 1824 and 1825 provided a major stimulus to these new organizations whose growth was encouraged by the social consequences of the Industrial Revolution. By 1838, the strongest society, known as the Journeymen Steam Engine and Machine Makers Friendly Society or 'Old Mechanics', had nearly 3,000 members, and by 1850, as a result of amalgamation with most of the other craft unions, a new body, the Amalgamated Society of Engineers (ASE), based on the 'Old Mechanics', had been formed with 10,000 members.

The trade policy of the new union was aimed at eliminating redundancy and unemployment and it had four major planks: the abolition of systematic overtime, and of piecework, an end to the use of men who had not served an apprenticeship or seven years at the trade, and a restriction in the number of new apprentices to one to every four journeymen.

The ASE held firmly to the rule that membership depended on the acquisition of craft status. According to Clegg, Fox and Thompson: 'Craft attitudes and policies were rooted in the doctrine that by serving an apprenticeship a man secured the right to exercise his skill and receive the customary wage.'[10] In their book, the preface from the ASE rules are quoted to the effect that:

> 'if constrained to make restrictions against the admission into our trade of those who have not earned a right by a probationary servitude, we do so knowing that such encroachments are productive of evil, and when persevered in unchecked, result in reducing the condition of the artisan to that of the unskilled labourer, and confers no permanent advantage on these admitted.'

At the same time as taking over and strengthening craft exclusivism, however, the ASE and other societies like it, such as the Boilermakers, marked, as the Webbs noted, a 'new model'[11] in trade unionism. These societies established a central headquarters, usually in London; they carefully built up funds and membership and made routine the necessary bureaucracy of union organization.

The employers responded to the founding of the ASE and its early successes by establishing their own organization, the Central Association of Employers of Operative Engineers, which, from its inception, declared its uncompromising right to manage. A statement issued in January 1852 declared that: 'we must take leave to say that *we* alone are the competent judges of our own business; that we are respectively the masters of our own establishments; and that it is our firm intention to remain so'.[12]

THE FOUNDATIONS OF THE MODERN LABOUR MOVEMENT

When the ASE introduced a national overtime ban in support of their demands for the abolition of systematic overtime and piece-work on 1 January 1852 the employers responded by locking out 3,000 members. The lockout was to end in a victory for the employers. Despite this setback, the union managed to recover and rebuild its organization so that by the end of the century it was in a leading position in the country's trade union movement. Membership reached 91,000 out of the 1,447,000 employed in the industry by 1901.

The steady progress of industrialization saw the creation of an infrastructure of service industries, in particular, gas and transport. In general, these were manned by unskilled workers who suffered from poor living conditions and periodic bouts of unemployment from which little relief was provided by the state. The term 'unemployed' first became commonplace in the later decades of the nineteenth century.

It was at this time, too, that the long period of stability in the stock of tools used in the engineering industry came to an end with the mass production of machines. The manufacture of sewing machines, type-writers, machine guns, etc required the replacement of the old centre lathe by a host of new machine tools.

These changes to the patterns of employment took place under a restricted franchise, with the unions' legal position still in jeopardy. Unions had no protection for their funds; strikers were still liable to be jailed for 'conspiracy' or 'intimidation'; and the Master and Servant Act, which made workers' breach of contract a criminal offence, was still applied. The prospect of stiffer anti-union legislation, following the appointment of a Royal Commission on Trade Unions in 1867, led the craft unions to unite in the first Trades Union Congress (TUC) in 1868. The representations of the trade unions were successful and the Trade Union Act of 1876 recognized the unions as corporate bodies, granted the right to peaceful picketing and repealed the Criminal Law Amend-ment Act, passed in 1871, which had been interpreted by the courts as making any trade union industrial action an illegal conspiracy.

The principal industrial disputes of the 1860s and 1870s were concerned with the reduction of working time from 10 to nine hours per day. The victory of the Nine Hour Campaign contributed towards an upsurge in TUC affiliated membership, which reached nearly 1,200,000 in the early 1870s.

To the socialist minority in the unions the changing structure of employment meant that the craft unions would have to rely on joint action with unskilled workers and make use of parliament for legislation on working conditions. By 1890, the leadership of the labour movement was shared between the conservative ASE, and the socialists, who argued for an independent working class political party, and new unions of unskilled workers.

Tom Mann, perhaps the most perceptive of the union left-wingers, was among the first to notice that technology's advance would erode, if not destroy, the exclusiveness of craft unionism. He wrote in 1890 that: 'Labour-saving machinery is reducing the previously skilled to the level of unskilled labour, and they [the craft unions] must, in their own interests, be less exclusive than hitherto'.[13]

Unions in the USA
In the 1850s, the emergence in America of trade unions in the printing, engineering and iron moulding crafts was stimulated by the attempts of employers to introduce division of labour into the production process and distribute the de-skilled jobs among apprentices. Since most skilled workers believed that wages were fixed in relation to supply and demand for labour, they feared that the increasing supply of apprentices would lead to a fall in wages, and the new unions therefore intended to limit their number. New machinery was viewed favourably

by the craft unions during this period. Mechanization was principally the substitution of mechanical for hand energy; tools were left to be steered by the craftsmen.

The American Federation of Labour (AFL) became the first permanent national trade union centre in America. It drew together the old craft unions, the newer engineering unions, and the units of unskilled workers organized by the Knights of Labor. At first, engineering workers gained from the expanding markets for their output, while savings from mass production lowered the cost of manufactured goods and led to increased real living standards for those in work. However, by the mid 1870s, because of the rapid spread of machinery (made easier by the new division of labour) and the depression, the general optimism about the individual unions' ability to control technological change disappeared, and pressure began to mount for a substantial reduction in working hours.

It was during these depression years that the Knights of Labor developed, organizing unskilled workers and those whose national trade unions had been disrupted. In 1886, at the height of their strength, their membership reached 700,000. The Knights' leaders stressed the need for political rather than industrial action to secure labour's goals: the solution lay in the establishment of co-operative control of machinery. Both the craft unions and the Knights were responsive to Samuel Gompers' call in 1881 to the founding congress of the AFL. The founders noted that in Great Britain annual Trades' Union Congresses were held, and the work done by their assemblies revealed that 'only in such a body can proper action be taken to promote the general welfare of the industrial classes.' A call for a national eight-hour law figured prominently in the list of resolutions adopted at the founding conference.

This campaign for shorter working hours, arising from the depression and the spread of machinery, provided a link between the old and new unions on both sides of the Atlantic and the developing socialist movement. One of the earliest acts of the AFL was to call for strike action to be taken on and after 1 May 1886, to secure an eight-hour working day. In many trades, a 14- or 16-hour day was reduced to 12. In many places the Saturday half-day was adopted, and Sunday working ceased in most industries. Although the employers subsequently clawed back a longer weekday, by 1889 it was apparent that their efforts had not fully restored the earlier position. The AFL's campaign for an eight-hour day continued into the 1890s, linked explicitly to the need to counter the social consequences of new machinery.

It was the AFL, carrying its concern for the consequences of rapid mechanization into the international trade union movement, which gave rise to the May Day traditions. The idea of organizing a great international demonstration on a fixed date to give workers the opportunity to simultaneously demand the reduction of the working day to eight hours emerged at the Paris International Trades Union Congress in 1889. The result was the first May Day demonstration which took place in England on the first Sunday in May, 1890. Described by a *Times* reporter as the 'greatest [rally] in modern times', it was estimated that half a million people took part in the event which united both old and new unionists.

It was not only the unions in Britain who were influenced by developments in America. British employers also looked to America for guidance in new managerial techniques. It was an American, Colonel Dyer, who organized the Engineering Employers Federation (EEF) in order to mobilize the British employers' resistance to their unions' claim for a 48-hour week. The EEF threatened a national lockout in July 1897, after the unions had begun to make some progress in local bargaining. The lockout took place when the unions refused to recognize the EEF, and tens of thousands were left without work.

To British employers, influenced by Colonel Dyer, the dispute was about far more than the length of the working week. The Board of Trade's report noted that:

'Though the immediate cause of the general dispute was the demand for the eight-hour day in London, the real questions at issue between the parties had become a more far-reaching kind and now involved questions of workshop control and the limits of trade union interference.'[14]

The lockout lasted for 30 weeks and ended with defeat for the unions. The terms of settlement established a procedure for national collective bargaining, and involved concessions on union policy in major areas. There was a commitment to working with non-union men, acceptance of overtime up to 40 hours a week where the union had opposed systematic overtime and recognition of the management's 'right to manage and select, train and pay according to ability' which was to lead to many conflicts over the machine question.[15]

Science-based Industry and Collective Bargaining

At the beginning of the twentieth century throughout the world, the unions represented a very small proportion of the workforce. At the heart of labour movements were the craft-based unions in the engineering industry.

Since 1900, the critical factor in favour of the trades union movement, in the UK as elsewhere, has been the development of science-based industry, which has made it impossible for the modern state to survive a war without enlisting the co-operation of the organized working class. The growth of the electrical power and vehicle sectors rapidly changed the structure and location of the UK engineering industry. In 1907, 25 per cent of engineering workers were employed in the shipbuilding industry and only 12 per cent in electrical engineering and vehicles. By 1935 the figures were 7 per cent and 50 per cent

63

respectively, with the newer sectors concentrated in the Midlands and South of the country.

New tools and scientific management led to a radical change in the pattern of employment. New methods of planning required the introduction of new men into the workshop, alongside the managers and the draughtsmen: works engineers, rate fixers and progress chasers. In the workshops the new methods meant job-cards, drawings in place of sketches, gauges, 'work-hustlers', 'speed-and-feedmen' and increased supervision.

However, growth in these 'white-collar' occupations was over-shadowed by major changes in the composition of the manual work-force. In 1914, the division between skilled, semi-skilled and unskilled workers in engineering was 60 : 20 : 20, but by 1933 the equivalent figures were 32 : 57 : 11. A further consequence of the move to capital-intensive production was the concentration of employment in large factories. Overall, 1.6 per cent of factories employed 48 per cent of the engineering workers. In vehicles, 53 per cent were employed in factories of more than 1,000 employees; in electrical engineering 60 per cent and in aircraft 75 per cent.

These radical changes threw up problems of organization and tactics for the unions. Although they had established the principle of collective bargaining over wages, employers still insisted on control over all other aspects of employment, including machine manning, apprentice conditions and overtime.

At the same time, union recruitment was inhibited by the craft sectarianism of the existing membership who feared the dilution of their bargaining power and the difficulties of organizing first-generation workers, who were often immigrants in America and newcomers to city life in Britain. Faced with these obstacles, the growth of the unions was not straightforward.

Taylor versus Workers Control: the US

It was Taylorism, that is, scientific management, which enabled management to reassert their control over the workplace. The discipline of Taylorism was developed in the US against a background of the depression and labour unrest at the turn of the twentieth century. Its progress was slow, and by 1917 only 20 companies had adopted Taylor's system in full. Taylorism was aimed at precisely those areas of the labour process which the nineteenth century craft unions had controlled through their regulation of the work rate and craft rules. Its implementation was part of the attempt to weaken union power in these areas, and it met with fierce resistance.

At the turn of the century, the American engineering unions were led by the International Association of Machinists (IAM) who organized 10 per cent of the 280,000 engineers. It was known as the 'wardog' of the AFL. Carefully noting the failure of the ASE in the 1897 lockout they waited until 1900 to mount a campaign to win a nine-hour day, a closed shop, seniority rule for lay-off, recognition of shop stewards and a minimum wage. The campaign was launched by a strike in Chicago, and was then extended to Cleveland, Detroit, Pittsburg and Philadelphia. The union was assisted by labour shortages associated with the birth of science-based industry and employers were forced to partially concede the claim in the Murray Hill Agreement. They resisted the recognition of the closed shop and shop stewards and instead agreed to national collective bargaining and a system of arbitration. In exchange, the union pledged to place no restrictions on production.

The Recession of 1903-4 enabled employers to refuse to renew the Chicago Wage Agreement and they mounted a national 'open shop' drive to rid themselves of the craft unions. Their association provided employers with strategic advice, financial assistance, private detectives, legal advice and a black list. In addition, they organized a strike breaking association entitled 'The Independent Labor League of America', infiltrated the unions with spies, and began a policy of harassing trade union activity through the courts. The open shop campaign was to reverse almost all the gains the union had made outside Chicago, and, around 1910, most American factories had incorporated some elements of Taylorism.

The craft unions resumed their attack on Taylorism during the First World War, despite the AFL official no-strike agreement with the government. Innumerable strikes took place against dilution and for a simplified wage classification system in place of the individual incentive pay schemes of Taylorism. By 1918, strikes for an end to the premium system, standard rates, the eight-hour day, and recognition of shop committees were common. By the end of the second decade, 48 per cent of American workers had gained a 48-hour week, compared with eight per cent 10 years earlier, and membership of the IAM had grown from 54,000 to 331,000.

Gains for the union and management after the First World War were won, with the help of a significant level of economic growth. Rationalization and new technology helped output per man-hour to rise by 5.6 per cent between 1919 and 1929, compared with a 1.7 per cent increase in the following two decades. With their monopoly power in the market the science-based industries were able to control prices, and, through the American Plan, establish a measure of stability for their workforces. The Plan contained both a carrot and a stick. The carrot was corporate welfare, job security, seniority-based privileges and employee representation through company unions. Skilled workers were encouraged to purchase their own homes, and join patriotic societies. The stick was state repression of industrial action. The net effect was to reduce the membership of the AFL from a high of 4,078,740 in 1920 to a figure of 2,933,545 in 1929.

On the surface it appeared that Taylor had been right in his belief that the interests of capital and labour could be harmonized. It was the Great Depression in 1929 which undermined the optimism of scientific managers, and re-opened the pre-war debate on the social implications of their work which had lain dormant during the 1920s.

In 1932, Howard Scott, an engineer and a member of the International Workers of the World (IWW), and Walter Rautenstrauch, the Chairman of the Columbia University Department of Industrial Engineering, established the 'Committee on Technocracy'. After carrying out an analysis of the economic trends in 300 industries they put forward the concept of *technological unemployment* to explain the basis of the crisis. Employment in manufacturing, transport, mining, construction and agriculture had reached its highest level ever in 1918 and had then declined by five per cent, while output had gone on rising until 1929. The committee argued that the destruction of jobs during the 1920s had led to a fall in demand which had precipitated the 1929 crisis.

When the Committee published its findings in the middle of 1932 there was an immediate public response. Whereas in the 1920s the health of the economy belied the predictions of instability, businessmen were now less confident in operating capitalism, and were prepared to admit the possibility of technological unemployment.

As organized labour became acclimatized to Taylorism, and the system itself was modified, labour's hostility to the principles of scientific management receded. In 1919, the AFL Convention called on the Federal Government to subsidize research in science and industry in order to raise productivity, and in a 1920 policy statement called for 'co-operation between the scientists in industry and the representatives of the organized workers'. One of the earliest examples of practical co-operation between unions and Taylorism was seen in the policy of Sidney Hillman of the Amalgamated Clothing Workers, who turned to an associate of Taylor, Morris Cooke, for advice after the War, when the garment unions were successfully exerting pressure on employers to replace piece work with day work. After 1924, the staff of the union were available to union plants that sought help in cutting costs.

Scientific managers were to provide much of the ideology behind American politics in the 1930s. Hoover had attempted limited reforms of the economy but was frustrated by his conservative backers. To break this log jam, Roosevelt saw the need to construct a counter-vailing political force and adopted the prescription of scientific managers such as Cooke for a campaign for the extention of trade union rights. In 1933, the National Recovery Act granted the 'right of labor to representatives of its own choosing' and signalled a temporary reversal in the traditional hostility of the state towards the labour movement. Under the slogan 'Roosevelt wants you to join the union' the Committee for Industrial Organization (CIO) organized mass production industries. However, the labour movement which emerged, split between the old AFL and the new CIO, was much weaker in influence than the united movement in Britain. Unable to found an independent labour party, the unions had failed to win organizational demands during the Second World War, and when peace was declared they found themselves on the defensive in Congress.

Employers were able to use Congress to take back the gains of the industrial unions, and restrict them to a legal framework regulating corporate collective bargaining which remains in place today. Overall it was the 'military-industrial' complex which was the main beneficiary of Roosevelt's wartime administration.

Shop Stewards, Industrial Democracy and Demarcation: the UK

The introduction of Taylorism to British industry was made slightly easier by the employers' victory in the 1897 lockout. Attempts to introduce incentive pay schemes or the use of semi-skilled men to man the new machines were often met with refusal or hostility by skilled workers, even when the ASE had approved of these schemes. Three developments during the period between the wars deserve to be picked out.

Shop Stewards

The Clydeside revolts over 'dilution', which was the introduction of unskilled labour into factories, highlighted the emergence of shop stewards in British industrial life. They emerged in the ASE in the last decade of the nineteenth century, and grew in numbers as the national executives of the union found it difficult or impossible to resolve the increasingly complex problems referred to them. The historians of this period note that:

> 'The failure of the national negotiators to settle so many issues, either by revision of the agreement or by dealing with individual disputes, gave encouragement to local action, particularly over payment by results . . . changes in products, tools and machines and in workshop practice and organization.'[16]

The shop stewards' period of influence was brief: by the 1920s, they were broken by heavy unemployment, by selective dismissals of stewards, and by the defeat of the ASE (by then the Amalgamated Engineering Union — the AEU) in yet another lockout by the EEF in 1922. A 1919 shop stewards' agreement, signed by a local union and an employer, stipulated that: 'shop stewards shall be subject to the control of the trade unions, and shall act in accordance with the rules and regulations of the trade union and agreements with the employers'; many stewards accepted these provisions and their organizations survived, albeit with diminished influence. The more militant, many of whom were members of or were influenced by the fledgling Communist Party, formed the backbone of the National Unemployed Workers

Committees Movement. The power of the stewards grew again in the 1930s, but it took the Second World War to increase their numbers, authority and influence to the point where it could not be reversed.

Interestingly, it was not their revolutionary ambitions which attracted mass support: rather it was their activities as co-ordinators of increased war production through Joint Production Committees (JPCs), roles which the left-wingers among them adopted with special enthusiasm after the Soviet Union entered the war. Len Powell, secretary of the Engineering and Allied Trades Shop Stewards National Committee, describing his own and others' role, wrote:

> 'Shop stewards, representing the point of view of their members, together with charge hands and foremen meeting regularly with the management, can bring forward the quickest methods for doing jobs, which means that where managements are capable and responsive, much more production results.'[17]

Industrial Democracy

A substantial section of the trade union movement, active at all levels, attempted to spread ideas on industrial democracy, or workers control. These ideas, derived from syndicalist thought, were based on the logic of the industrial process and the desire of workers to control machinery.

The idea of industrial democracy, though a minority one, at times attracted wide support and could be used to organize opposition to the imposition of scientific management techniques. It came to the fore particularly in the early 1930s, in a debate at the Labour Party Conference on workers' representation on the boards of nationalized industries. These boards — according to Herbert Morrison, who, as Minister of Transport in 1929 had laid out a blueprint for the takeover of London Transport — were to be under the supervision of a government minister but were to be run by technical experts.

The attempt in 1932, and again at the 1933 Labour Party Conference, to get the principle of workers' representatives on public boards accepted was only partly successful. Concessions were made in 1933 to a compromise Party/TUC document which conceded the right to trade union representatives at board level only. Reluctance was felt by both the Party and many union leaders, including Ernest Bevin, who were ambivalent about the independent position of unions whose representatives sat among the employers.

This problem within the labour movement has continued to the present time, when debate has been particularly sharp. Many of the issues are at root ideological: Are unions to co-operate with capital? Is industrial democracy only possible under public ownership? However, the labour movement was then and is now also concerned with technology and how labour is to be organized for it. The more sophisticated machinery becomes, the more it sets, or appears to set, the work method and pace. Therefore, the more it demands, or appears to demand, a highly disciplined response from labour, and the more labour will seek direct control over it to mitigate the effects of automation. The forms this search for control take are by no means pre-determined; but the form is less important, in this context, than the imperative of industrial democracy which, in an age where capital is replacing labour at ever-faster rates, now appears too strong to halt.

Demarcation

The final development of note concerned an attempt by the unions to regulate their internal conflicts over spheres of influence at the workplace. The Bridlington Agreement of 1939 was an attempt to set down guidelines for orderly inter-union conduct, on the grounds that only one union should organize any given class of workers in any given plant.

The Bridlington Agreement has stood the test of time well enough, though it is frequently tested before TUC disputes committees. Its establishment grew out of a need to mark off certain industrial processes as certain unions' preserves. These industrial processes change under the impact of new technologies, and at present are changing rapidly. Unions and the TUC are having to cope with a variety of disputes as the old lines wobble and are erased.

LABOUR AND THE SCIENTIFIC-TECHNICAL REVOLUTION

The period since the Second World War has been marked by the increasing power and influence of the trade union movement in the UK. From a membership of 7.8 million in 1944, the TUC reached a peak of 12 million members in affiliated unions by 1980. Although, by 1982, membership had fallen back to 11 million, because of recession, the *degree* of unionization remains unchanged (see Figure 2). The influence of the TUC was at its height in the 1974-79 period of Labour government, when it was brought into a central position in the governance of the country.

It was during this period, when the first effects of the microelectronic revolution began to be generally felt, that the then Labour government initiated a widespread 'awareness programme', paralleled among the unions by various documents on the effects of technical change for workers in particular sectors, and on how union officials could incorporate new technology issues into bargaining at every level.

These 'official' responses were the most visible signs of a debate within the labour movement, a debate which ranges from rejection to near-total acceptance of automated systems on any terms. The major area of debate, however, centres on how labour can use its organization and strength to obtain greater leverage over the new production processes.

Year	Male	Female	Total	Year	Male	Female	Total
1901	16.2	3.2	12.4	1951	55.6	24.6	44.9
1911	21.7	6.2	17.1	1952	55.8	24.9	45.0
1921	41.2	17.6	34.3	1953	55.1	23.9	44.3
1923	40.5	16.4	32.9	1954	54.7	23.8	43.9
1924	41.1	15.9	33.1	1955	55.0	23.6	44.2
1925	40.1	16.0	32.4	1956	54.5	24.4	43.9
1926	37.4	15.4	30.4	1957	54.7	24.2	44.1
1927	34.8	14.9	28.4	1958	53.6	23.7	43.1
1928	33.5	14.6	27.5	1959	53.0	23.4	42.6
1929	33.3	14.3	27.2	1960	53.3	23.9	42.8
1930	32.6	13.7	26.5	1961	52.8	24.0	42.5
1931	30.5	13.2	25.0	1962	52.0	24.2	42.1
1932	29.0	13.0	23.9	1963	51.9	24.5	42.0
1933	28.5	12.7	23.5	1964	52.2	24.9	42.3
1934	29.8	12.7	24.4	1965	52.3	25.2	42.4
1935	31.3	13.0	25.0	1966	52.1	25.2	42.2
1936	33.6	13.4	27.2	1967	51.6	25.6	42.0
1937	36.2	14.4	29.3	1968	52.8	26.8	43.1
1938	37.0	14.5	29.8	1969	54.3	28.3	44.5
1939	40.0	15.0	31.6	1970	58.3	31.6	48.3
1940	44.6	15.2	33.9	1971	58.6	32.1	48.6
1941	48.5	17.5	36.3	1972	59.9	33.0	49.1
1942	54.3	20.2	39.3	1973	60.2	33.0	49.2
1943	57.5	22.8	43.1	1974	60.5	34.2	50.1
1944	59.0	23.0	44.2	1975	(separate male/		50
1945	53.3	21.9	41.5	1976	female figures		51
1946	54.4	22.9	43.5	1977	not available)		52
1947	54.9	23.9	44.4	1978			53
1948	55.6	24.2	45.1	1979			53
1949	55.1	23.8	44.5	1980			53
1950	54.6	23.4	44.0	1981			53

Sources: Historical Abstract of British Labour Statistics 1886-1968
HMSO 1971; B Burkitt and D Bowers (1979) *Trade Unions and the Economy.*
TUC.

Figure 2. Degree of unionization in the UK

As we noted at the beginning of this chapter, labour displacement during the fourth Kondratiev (associated with automation) has been, in its early period, difficult to detect because of its piecemeal and discontinuous nature. However, these first effects of automation were obvious enough in the mid 1950s to stimulate a wide-ranging debate, which cut across older debates over public ownership, and was in many ways a rehearsal of the more urgent, contemporary debates.

The TUC and Science
The labour movement emerged from the Second World War in its strongest position ever. The wartime co-operation between the government and the unions was extended to involve the TUC in the corridors

of power: unions, for the first time, glimpsed what a 'social contract' might look like. The building blocks for this co-operation were to be found in the network of Joint Production Committees (JPCs) which brought together unions and management within the plants; these remained very largely intact after the war.

In October 1941, in order to direct the attention of members to production problems, which had contributed to the military defeats of 1940-41, and analyse what had gone wrong, the AEU undertook an inquiry into the state of munitions production throughout Britain. The main recommendation, accepted by government and industry, was that the employers, as a step towards improving production and ending frustration and cynicism, should establish JPCs of management and workers in every factory. By 1944, over 4,000 of these Committees had been established.

They did not survive long after the extraordinary conditions of wartime. Employers fought as hard against them as they were to fight 30 years later (successfully) against the Labour government's plans for industrial democracy. Then, as in the mid 1970s, the unions showed a distinct schizophrenia about exercising control. A motion to the 1946 Congress calling on the TUC to: 'survey new methods, materials, machinery and power tools and prepare reports which will help workers' representatives to play a full part in the activities of joint production machinery' was lost, and replaced with a more anodyne motion which noted the General Council's: 'intention to consult affiliated organizations within the various industries in regard to the practical application of proposals to be made after the discussions taking place with the government' on the Economic Survey for 1947.[18]

The growing differences between the government and the unions during the late 1940s reflect not so much a conscious attempt to damp down moves for greater participation, as reliance on traditional, bureaucratic methods on the part of the government, and a reluctance on the part of the unions to form a closer relationship to management at plant and national level.

Thus, the JPCs and other joint bodies tended to become mere extensions of the government's efficiency drives. What might have been structures for exercising influence over new production processes were regarded as instruments to convince workers that more output was required in the national interest.

The issue of new production technologies was dealt with simply as one of job displacement. Here, the TUC took a measured view, noting, after a fact-finding mission to the US in 1949, that:

'it was expected that some displacement of workpeople would take place . . . Readjustment may, however, create personal difficulties for individual workpeople and certain unions had found it necessary to negotiate agreements providing compensation for members becoming redundant owing to technological advance in such circumstances.'[19]

The possibility of increasing industrial democracy was largely closed off for the unions in the 1945-50 period. This did not inhibit the TUC unions in their organization, as they continued to grow steadily up until the late 1970s. While that growth was not reflected in a growth of influence at government level in the 1950s, once the governments of the early 1960s took up economic planning in a serious way, the TUC was back in the corridors of power, in a position strengthened in the 1970s. What they lost by not taking up the battle for industrial democracy was a place in decision-making in plants and offices, where such decisions most directly affected their members. However, they gained freedom from this responsibility, a growing ability to block unwelcome managerial initiatives and, in time, large corporate power.

Although the unions turned away from industrial democracy, collectively they took a close interest in the advance of technology. The chief instrument for this interest in the post-war period was the TUC's Science Advisory Committee.

The Science Advisory Committee

Ernest Bevin, President of the TUC in 1937, first put forward the idea of a committee of eminent scientists and General Council members who would advise the Council on scientific matters. He said, in his Presidential Address:

> 'Science has made amazing progress, but society has not kept pace with it in making the fundamental readjustments, and assimilating the results of research, discovery and invention. There is not only a "time lag", but the inertia and rigidity of our social and economic structure to be overcome. The General Council believe that men of science can make a great contribution to progress by assisting such a movement as ours with their counsel and knowledge. The General Council have decided to establish a Scientific Advisory Council, whose purpose will be to enable this Congress and its constituent unions to secure the help and advice of leading scientists in some systematic and regular way. We are convinced that their pre-vision and foreknowledge of the significance of scientific discovery in all fields of research will be of incalculable value not only to our movement but to the community.'[20]

A committee of 12 scientists, drawn from the ranks of the British Association for the Advancement of Science, together with 10 TUC nominees, was constituted as the Science Advisory Committee (SAC). It was given the general brief of informing and advising the Council on new research, processes and related technical matters, and of assisting the Council in formulating a policy on planning and industrial reorganization. The outbreak of war suspended its work; its re-establishment was called for at the 1945 TUC conference.

However, the Committee, which met in March 1947, never lived up to Bevin's ambitious brief. When it was reformed, no specific functions for it were outlined, although several subjects for consideration were suggested, including technical developments in particular industries, such as plastics in engineering and prefabrication in building, and scientific or technical information relating to nationalization proposals. The panel of specialists, available for consultation but not on the committee, was not used, and the agenda centred on the special interests of the scientific members of the committee – notably atomic energy policy.

The meetings of the SAC became less and less frequent. In 1954 it was passed from the Research to the Production Department of the TUC. The TUC reviewed the functions proposed for the 1938 committee and considered that it would be impossible to embark on projects with the detail apparently envisaged at that time, given the available resources. Nevertheless, the TUC concluded that: 'although the implications for the trade union movement of scientific developments are not always obvious, there are both fundamental and immediate questions of science and technology on which the General Council needs informed advice from some quarter'.[21]

Here, as with the JPCs, the central problem was felt to be the existence of a parallel piece of government machinery – in this case, the Advisory Committee on Scientific Policy (ACSP), established in 1947. Thus, motions from the strongly left-wing Association of Scientific Workers on extending the planning of scientific research were opposed on the grounds that the ACSP was the body competent to deal with it. Yet the ACSP, though very largely concerned with the ways in which scientific research could improve productivity, did not at first consult the SAC. Only after it established a study committee on industrial efficiency was trade union involvement sought 'on appropriate committees and panels'.

The First Automation Debate

It was against this background that the first automation debates in the labour movement took place. These debates effectively laid down TUC policy for the next 25 years.

Although public concern about the social implications of the new computer technology had been aroused in the early 1950s, much of that concern was speculative. Automation had only been in existence for some time in the chemical process industries, and elsewhere it was in its infancy. Nevertheless, in response to general public concern, the General Council commissioned their reconstituted SAC to conduct an inquiry in early 1955 amongst the affiliated unions on the social and human implications of automation. On the basis of this preliminary inquiry, a report was put before the 1955 TUC Congress. The report identified four major problems for the unions. First, the scale of application of the new techniques would sharpen problems of labour displacement, causing the craft and technical unions to grow and other

73

unions to decline. Second, if the number of direct production operators became very small and scattered, the unions anticipated problems of communication and organization. This would be especially true if the smaller work groups were integrated by management into vertical work teams. Third, there would be a need to put productivity gains from automation into general improvements in conditions of employment. Finally, the Council stated that:

> 'The major job of the trade unions will be to keep automation within the field of industrial relations. Automation can make a substantial contribution to social wellbeing, but there is no automatic transfer scheme to ensure this. The trade unions will see as one of their main duties the performing of this function.'[22]

The debate on the General Council report was concerned with the question of whether public ownership was a necessary prerequisite for the solution of the complex human, social and political problems thrown up by automation. The left wing, who held that it was, were defeated when they put this proposition to the vote, by 4.4 million to 3.3 million. The debate continued in 1956 when the General Council presented its considered view in a paper entitled 'Trade Unions and Automation'.[23] The document reflected the relaxed attitude of the previous year. Its spokesman, J Crawford, in his closing remarks successfully argued that it was too early to make any judgement on the need for more radical measures than those already proposed by the General Council. He stated that continued monitoring of the implications of automation was necessary, and drew attention to the steps being taken to carry this out. 'If we with our close association with this problem come to the conclusion that our attempts are not enough, surely you can trust us to come back to you and suggest that our present methods are out-of-date and some new methods must be adopted.'[24] On that note the First Automation Debate concluded.

The policy adopted in 1956 formed the basis of the TUC's guidelines on new technology until the end of the 1970s. The General Council's proposed monitoring of the effects of technology proved to be fitful. Pressure for a review emerged in 1962 from the TUC's Womens' Conference, with the call for a close study of the problems connected with the widespread use of electronic machinery. Concern was expressed that employment opportunities should not be diminished and that adequate training facilities should be made available for women to fill the posts requiring high-skilled work. A study, organized by the Non-manual Committee of the TUC, was published in February 1964. It uncovered widespread anxiety about the impact of computers in offices: 'fear of the sack; fear of being unable to keep pace or of absorbing new skills, even if training is available; fear of promotion prospects being eliminated; and even fear of loss of status.'

The 1956 TUC statement was revised in 1965 and 1970, taking into account a second survey on the impact of computers carried out by the Non-Manual Workers' Committee in 1968. The 1970 document noted the accelerated rate of technical change which had occurred since 1956, although it was still prepared within the framework of that earlier debate. The TUC acknowledged that some of the factors which had previously held back the rate of application of automation, such as cost and the shortage of skilled manpower, no longer existed. Concern was expressed that this meant that automation was no longer related only to capital-intensive industries but could also take effect in labour-intensive sectors. Non-manual workers were also now affected. Computer technology was touching such diverse groups as draughtsmen, aeroplane crew, hospital staff, civil servants and local government officers. Nevertheless the TUC felt there was no intrinsic reason why technical change should cause large-scale unemployment. Contrasting the position in 1970 with that in 1870, it noted:

> 'Any trade unionist of that time with the ability to foresee the technological changes that have taken place in the past century might well have feared that all the goods and services produced a hundred years ago could have been supplied with modern techniques, by a fraction of the 1870 labour force. In fact scientific and technological change has made many new products possible and our requirements have increased at least as fast as our industries' ability to meet them.'[25]

Factory and office automation in the 1950s and 1960s prompted a significant expansion in the range of issues covered by collective bargaining, and greatly helped the growth of white collar unionism. Agreements covering the planning of the introduction of new technology, job security and protection of income for those transferred to a lower grade were new features of bargaining during this period, with US unions often providing the lead. The AFL/CIO, for example, began in 1964 to promote joint union-combine negotiations as a replacement for single union-plant agreements.

CONCLUSION

In summary, the official position of the unions in the 1970s was, broadly, one of cautious optimism related to the effects of technological change. There was also a lack of interest in involvement in its control. However, both in the Labour Party and in the unions, new initiatives were being taken — particularly in the field of industrial democracy — which were to imbue the second round of automation debates at the end of the 1970s and early 1980s with a new sense of urgency. These will be examined in Chapter 8.

REFERENCES

1 K Marx (1933) *Capital*, 1, p 496. Dent, London.

2 T Veblen (1963) *The Engineers and the Price System*, p 56. Harcourt Brace.

3 ibid, p 57.

4 C Freeman, J Clark and L Soete (1982) *Unemployment and Technical Innovation: A Study of Long Waves and Economic Development*. F Pinter.

5 H Braverman (1974) *Labour and Monopoly Capital*, p 348. Monthly Review Press.

6 TUC (1981) *New Technology and Collective Bargaining*, p 23 and p 94.

7 European Trade Union Institute (1979) *The Impact of Microelectronics in Western Europe in the 1980s*, p 111.

8 United Auto Workers (1979) *Ford Facts*, 39, September.

9 E P Thompson (1970) *The Making of the English Working Class*, p 603. Penguin.

10 H Clegg, P Fox and A F Thompson (1964) *A History of British Trade Unions Since 1889*, 1, p 4. Oxford.

11 B Webb and S Webb (1894) *A History of Trade Unionism*. Also, *Industrial Democracy* (1897). Longman, Green and Company.

12 J B Jefferys (1945) *Story of the Engineers*. Lawrence and Wishart.

13 H Pelling (1973) *A History of British Trade Unions*, p 104. Penguin.

14 E Wigham (1973) *The Power to Manage: A History of the Engineering Employers' Federation*, p 55. Macmillan.

15 J B Jeffreys, op cit.

16 H Clegg *et al*, op cit, p 431.

17 K Coates and A Topham (1975) *Shop Stewards and Workers' Control*, pp 77-78. Spokesman.

18 Minutes of the National Production Advisory Council on Industry (1947) 10 April.

19 Minutes of the National Production Advisory Council on Industry (1949) 6 October.

20 TUC (1937) *Congress Report*, p 72.

21 TUC (1954) Minutes of the Science Advisory Committee. 3 February.

22 TUC (1955) *Congress Report*.

23 TUC (1956) *Congress Report*, Appendix B.

24 ibid, p 368.

25 TUC (1970) *Automation and Technological Change*, p 10.

CHAPTER 3

Transnational Companies

INTRODUCTION

Transnational companies (TNCs) now form the basis of the contemporary international economy. Of the 100 largest economic units in the world today, half are nation states and the other half TNCs. The science-based company is the prototype of the modern TNC.

From their foundation at the turn of this century, science-based companies operated co-ordinated production facilities in more than one country. These companies now control the main technologically advanced sectors of the global economy: vehicles, chemicals, mechanical and electrical engineering. TNC-dominated products include tyres, oil, pharmaceuticals, electronics and motor vehicles. In the most advanced OECD countries, eight of these companies account for 35 per cent of industrial research and development. Only government action, motivated by strategic considerations, has prevented this pattern of ownership from taking hold in other advanced sectors such as steel and aerospace.

Under post-Second World War economic regimes the pattern of world trade and capital flows has been restructured to accord with the needs of these companies. It has been estimated that the output of overseas subsidiaries of transnational companies in 1966 was approximately twice the volume of exports of the major trading nations, while these exports themselves have increasingly taken the form of transfers within the same company.

The real growth in power of the TNCs has occurred since the war, and was not much talked about until the 1960s. At the end of that decade of dynamic growth, the US journal *Fortune* stated that:

'the real point is that business everywhere is outgrowing national boundaries and, in doing so, is creating new tensions between the way the world is organized politically and the way in which it will increasingly be organized economically.'[1]

Stuart Holland makes the same point when he notes that:

> 'a system in which most trade is conducted between different firms in different companies is giving way to a system in which trade is increasingly conducted between the *same* firms in different countries.'[2]

THE GENESIS OF THE TNC

Transnational companies are not new. Transnational trading companies date from mercantile capitalism, while companies such as Singer, Siemens and Philips have been established for more than a century. Many of the early TNCs were mining or mineral companies, and the great oil companies date from the end of the nineteenth century. However, the most significant TNC sector is science-based, and this now includes the oil, or 'energy' companies, that emerged in the period 1880-1920.

Two indispensable partners to scientific breakthroughs and the development of the TNCs were government intervention, and the operation of the patent system. The latter enabled the new industries to mark out their territories in the field of the development and application of the new technologies, and to enforce their property rights worldwide.

Direct government intervention gave rise to the US chemical and radio industries. The US government intervened to seize German patents in the chemical industry during the First World War and distributed rights to indigenous American companies. Similarly, through General Electric (GE), Woodrow Wilson created the Radio Corporation of America to counter the threat posed by the British Marconi Company to US superiority in radio technology.

THE AMERICAN ELECTRICAL INDUSTRY

Three US companies dominated the early electrical scene. Thomson-Houston Electric and Edison General Electric were two of them. Both controlled a wide range of patents (Thomson in arc lighting and other areas; Edison in lamps, dynamos, electric traction and railways). The range was so wide that neither company could develop far without fear of patent suits, and they therefore merged, to form GE.

The third company, Westinghouse, had also grown (from its beginnings in air brakes) to control a variety of electrical patents. By 1896, GE and Westinghouse faced each other across 300 patent infringement suits. Commercial interests prevailed: they pooled their patents under joint control and kept most other entrants to the market out.

A similar patent monopoly strategy to that adopted by the electrical companies lay behind the rise to prominence of central companies in the new telecommunications industry.

The electromagnetic telegraph, pioneered by Morse in 1837, had become commonplace by 1878 when Bell obtained his two patents for the telephone. In its early years, the Bell organization was involved in over 600 patent infringement suits against competing telephone manufacturing and service companies. To protect its position following the expiry of the patents, a corporate research and development facility was established. Its purpose, according to the General Electric executive, F P Fish, was clear:

> 'The businessmen of the organization knew that . . . every added invention would strengthen their position not only during the 17 years of the main patent but during the 17 years' term of each and every one of the patents taken out on subsidiary methods and devices invented during the progress of commercial development. (Therefore) one of the first steps taken was to organize a corps of inventive engineers to perfect and improve the telephone system in all directions . . . that by securing accessory inventions, possession of the field might be retained as far as possible and for as long a time as possible.'[3]

The manufacture of telephone equipment in Europe was largely controlled by Bell until the 1920s. The Belgium Bell Telephone Company was established in 1882, followed by Standard Telephone and Cables in Britain in 1883, and the two French companies LMT (1889) and CGCT (1892). Following the sale of Bell's European interests to ITT in 1924, a succession of cartel agreements carved up Europe and Latin America — between ITT, Siemens, Ericsson of Sweden and GE.

This systematic application of patents, organized research and development, and technical training was the hallmark of the emerging science-based industry. During the 1920s, the electrification and chemicalization of the old industries led to the creation of further science-based combines; in particular those linked with the development of the automobile, petrol refining, rubber and the automotive industry. However, the fragmentation of the world into various markets and the consequent lack of a world market for most products, together with the lack of transportation or communication technology held back the growth of the science-based TNCs.

After the end of the Second World War, conditions were right for free trade with the establishment of the General Agreement on Tariffs and Trade in 1948. The growth of international capital (especially the Eurodollar) markets and the development of air travel and efficient telecommunications established the pre-conditions for 'true' TNCs, that is, corporations whose home base may be in New York, Tokyo or London but whose production and research and development facilities are worldwide.

THE UK ELECTRICAL INDUSTRY

The UK ignored the development of the electric lamp — the product on which the electrical industry was based — almost until the beginning of the First World War. The three main electrical companies in the UK at that time were the US General Electric, Westinghouse, and the German Siemens. They electrified Britain's tramways, pioneered electric railways and brought electric power to factories. Of these pre-twentieth century originals, only the General Electric Company (GEC) was British owned. The President of the Institute of Civil Engineers remarked in 1898 that: 'electricity has remained in the background in this country because capitalists have given it the cold shoulder', — an observation which contained more than a grain of truth in it until the 1930s.[4]

The post 1914-18 period saw both a strengthening of the large companies in the burgeoning electrical sector, and considerable activity in ownership patterns. English Electric, the British electrical company, was founded in 1919, but was to fall under the effective control of US Westinghouse in the 1920s. British Westinghouse, in turn, merged with a division of the British engineering company Vickers to form Metropolitan Vickers in 1918 with majority British ownership; 10 years later, the US General Electric took control and merged it with its subsidiary, British Thomson Houston, to form Associated Electrical Industries (AEI).[5]

GEC, English Electric and AEI straddled the commanding heights of the electrical industry, producing lamps, heavy electric plant, telecommunications equipment and components. Because of their early tendencies to form cartels, and because much of their heavy electrical production was for public bodies in the US or the colonies, the marketing side of these companies was regarded as relatively unimportant. Also, as their early control had been in US hands, their expansion in the US or into Europe, where GEC and Westinghouse had other large subsidiaries, was blocked. Besides, two powerful companies, (Philips of Holland and Siemens of Germany) held sway in continental Europe, having survived two world wars.

The post-Second World War period saw two contending movements in the electrical sector. The older companies tended to falter while other companies, many of them recent creations, expanded at home and abroad, often at the older companies' expense.

Some companies, such as Ferranti and Elliott, had greatly benefited from expanded electronics production and Research and Development (R and D) expenditure during the war; others, such as Plessey and STC, took advantage of the growing demand for telecommunication equipment and components; others again, such as Pye, Rank, Thorn and EMI successfully inserted themselves into the consumer electronics business. For most of these companies, the 1950s proved to be profitable, as the

UK, parts of Europe and much of the old colonial spread provided markets largely free from European competition.

The new companies were self-confident and resisted government attempts to plan their development. One of the first jobs of Labour's National Research and Development Corporation had been to take over the Manchester University computer patents in 1949. This made the NRDC acutely aware of the sales prospects for computers in America, as American licencees were heavy exploiters of UK technology. Its attempts to alert British industry, however, proved to be abortive. The NRDC set up an advisory panel on electronic computers which met once only in that year. It was attended by all the major electronics and punch card machine companies at the time. The NRDC recorded that:

> 'The outcome of the Advisory Panel meeting was that both the electronic manufacturers and the punch card machine manufacturers respectively represented that they were individually in positions to tackle the problems of an electronic computer development project as well as, for example, the International Business Machines Corporation in the United States . . . It was apparent also that the manufacturers were not willing that the Corporation should take the initiative in launching a development project but agreed that the Corporation could usefully co-ordinate activities.'[6]

As late as 1963, the companies' collective assessment seemed to be adequate. The value of computing equipment installed in the United Kingdom was estimated to be distributed among them in the following proportions:[7]

Ferranti Ltd	25%
ICT	25%
English Electric Co	13%
Elliott Bros	12%
National Cash Register Co (NCR)	11%
Leo Computers Ltd	7%
Others	7%

By the mid 1960s, however, it was becoming obvious to the more clear-sighted people in the industry that 'easy pickings' were over and that substantial efforts would have to be made to preserve the success of the electronics sector. Few, however, appeared to have a clear notion of what to do, while the debilitating effects engendered by the formation of cartels, government contracts and effectively protected markets were hard to expunge.

An exception to the general muddle was Arnold (now Lord) Weinstock. His company, Radio and Allied Industries, was taken over by GEC in 1961, and his business ability and self-confidence, his somewhat un-British concern for efficiency and market growth, and his large share in GEC's equity combined to propel him to the top.

81

He realized that mergers, especially in the heavy electrical sector, were necessary if international competitiveness and domestic efficiency were to be found. This was the driving force behind the consolidation of Marconi, English Electric (which had already taken over Elliott Automation) and AEI into a greatly expanded GEC in the late 1960s, thus creating the third largest electrical group in Europe after Philips and Siemens, and being somewhere around the twelfth largest in the world. GEC in the 1970s took first place in the UK electronics sector. It is the only 'everything electrical' company in the UK (though weak in consumer electronics) and the only one to stand on the two legs of energy and information. The company which made a profit in mid-1981 of £476 million on sales of nearly £3.5 billion, is among the top 100 of world companies, and is a major transnational in its own right. Its major strengths are in the defence electronics divisions and — oddly — power engineering. In other divisions it has been forced to rely on transnational co-operation: its TV production is now shared with Hitachi and it made an abortive sally into mass semiconductor production with Fairchild of the US.

Rationalization was not confined to GEC. The 1960s and 1970s saw the continuing growth of Thorn. Its growth was helped greatly by its ownership of the largest TV rental chains and by the PAL licence system which has had the effect of protecting the country's largest colour TV production. In 1979, the company was strong enough to take over the faltering record and electronics company EMI to give a combined turnover for Thorn-EMI of over £2 billion.

Thorn-EMI is very differently structured from GEC, deriving a large part of its revenue from its dominant place in the UK television rental sector. Its takeover of EMI gave it a small but profitable stake in defence electronics and a large stake in the US record business (through Capitol). However, in order to secure its future as a major force in the European consumer electronics sector it has linked up with the West German AEG Telefunken, France's Thomson-Brandt and the Japanese Victor Company to produce video equipment in plants in Germany, France and Britain. The three European companies will use JVC's VHS system technology. Thorn also has plans to step up its small telecommunications division by relying on injections of technology from Ericsson.

The pattern of technological reliance on foreign companies in the UK electronics industry is a pervasive one, evident in medium-sized companies such as Plessey. New products, particularly in consumer electronics, are often based on US or Japanese designs, while Japanese production technology and methods are widely copied. Investment patterns, too, tend to be abroad, especially in the US. GEC, Thorn-EMI and the fast-growing defence electronics company Racal have all concentrated on the US in their search for companies to acquire.

The companies do not follow these courses for idle reasons. UK technology is frequently in the forefront of world developments, but finds a cut-throat market when it is employed in production. The case of ICL, the UK's largest computer manufacturer, is an exemplary one. Formed from English Electric's computer division and International Computers & Tabulators, with the assistance of the then Anthony Wedgwood Benn, Minister of Technology, in 1968, ICL was, until 1980, Europe's most profitable and aggressive computer manufacturer and ran co-equal with France's CII Honeywell Bull in sales. Since its creation, ICL has taken on IBM, a company 20 times larger, across its product range. It prospered while IBM was under little pressure, but once IBM came under pressure from manufacturers of 'plug compatible' machines, and the Japanese companies began to eat into IBM's market share, IBM responded by price cutting in the late 1970s. The resultant squeeze left ICL, together with other medium-sized companies, gasping for finance and in search of a market share. A senior civil servant, quoted in the *Sunday Times* early in 1981, said:

> 'while the dinosaurs fought for domination of the earth, many little organizations survived by finding the right crevice in which to hide and develop. The question is whether ICL can succeed in finding itself a crevice in the computer business in the future and, if it does find it, whether it is humble enough to stick there.'[8]

By 1981, first quarter losses of £20 million, the soaring costs of research and development, and the need to construct a small business machine presence, forced the UK government to choose between two options: either to find a foreign purchaser/partner for ICL, or to pump in cash. A number of foreign companies were thoroughly canvassed. None were deemed suitable or were willing to take ICL on. Then, on 14 March 1981, the government reluctantly promised a £200 million guarantee on bank loans. Foreign merger talks were ended and a plan for more than 5,000 redundancies pushed through.

ICL's rapid fall from strength and profitability demonstrates the inexorable logic of the world electronics market. That is, that national funding has become the only counterweight to transnational mergers or takeovers — and even this may not, in the long term, be possible.

It is the burgeoning growth of the semiconductor companies in the 1960s and 1970s which revolutionized computer production techniques and the rate of technical innovation within computer companies. The UK's efforts to carve out a stake in semiconductor production depend heavily on the state-formed company Inmos (see Chapter 6). A number of UK electronics companies — GEC, Plessey and Ferranti — began limited chip production in the late 1960s, and 1970s but only Ferranti has so far achieved even modest success in marketing the finished product.

Mass production had been left (until the creation of Inmos) to the transnationals: ITT, Texas Instruments, National Semiconductor,

Motorola and General Instruments. For the most part, these companies used their UK subsidiaries as satellite operators, to churn out chips whose design and development were wholly accomplished in the US. The American transnationals together with the UK electronics companies, fought hard against the creation of Inmos, and succeeded in delaying its funding until after the Conservative government took over its responsibility from Labour in 1979. The habit of acquiescing to the prevailing wisdom that TNC production must always be more efficient is a pervasive one in UK business and government circles.

JAPANESE CAPITAL

The first really serious challenge to the American electronics TNCs is being mounted from Japan. Japanese TNCs will be major investors in advanced and Third World countries in the 1980s. They will be active in engineering of all kinds, especially in electronics, including computers and telecommunications. Western states and Western companies see two Japanese faces. The first is that of the commercial enemy, which destroys or damages native industries by its efficient exporting of superior products. The second is that of the partner, which offers investment or joint production deals. Both faces will continue to be presented but the latter will dominate more frequently in the future.

The success of Japanese companies in the past two decades has been achieved in part because the country: 'represents an extreme in the case of business access to government'.[9] Also in part because it represents an extreme in the case of a national will to achieve growth. Mr Toshio Takai, executive vice president of the Japanese Electronic Association, put it this way:

'the formation of a national consensus is absolutely necessary for the development of electronic industries in any country . . . competitive electronic industries will hardly develop in such countries where textiles or steel industries carry as much weight as electronics industries do.'[10]

US and European companies are now busily adopting such Japanese working practices as 'quality circles', while their executives are buying (and may even read) Ouchi's *Theory Z* and Pascale and Athos' *The Art of Japanese Management*.[12] Meanwhile, at the shop floor, Ford's work-force at Liverpool (Halewood) and East London (Dagenham) have thrown out quality circles, and the attempt implicit in them to 'inculcate shared values' in preference for the older tradition of ensuring the maintenance of separate values.

Though Western management and unions credit the Japanese with all but superhuman business prowess, a great deal of their success stems from a determined application, by government and business working in partnership, of protectionism allied to government support for chosen sectors. The result is a market where IBM takes the lowest share of any of the developed countries (29 per cent, compared with 55-60 per cent worldwide), and where the Japanese companies, especially Hitachi and Toshiba, have now become an international force to be reckoned with. Toshiba has had, in the past three years, a deal with West German Siemens to use German technology for its small machines in exchange for the use by Siemens of its large machine technology. In 1979, Italian Olivetti entered into a similar deal with Hitachi; Japanese semiconductor companies have established several plants in the Republic of Ireland; and Hitachi opened a sizeable semiconductor plant in West Germany in 1980.

In 1980, Japanese companies exported some $600 million of equipment. Their products incorporate more and more Japanese-developed (rather than copied) technology, and with the recently-announced growth in national R and D spending from 1.7 per cent of GNP to 3 per cent, this will increase. They are weak on software but acquisitions and home-grown companies are expected to make up much of the leeway in the near future.

All the major Japanese companies have now established, or will soon establish, bases in the US en route to becoming fully-fledged TNCs. Fujitsu, the largest, owns 28 per cent of the IBM-spinoff company Amdahl, 80 per cent of American Telecom and 100 per cent of Fujitsu America, its distribution company. Hitachi so far plans only direct sales through National Semiconductor, while NEC and Matsushita have established distribution and service centres.

The Japanese have not only acquired the necessary skills, but have grasped the crucial importance of the convergence between data processing and telecommunications technology. NEC has already adopted the slogan 'C and C' (computers and communication) to place in the centre of its strategy. According to Mr Norman Weizer of A D Little, Japanese companies: 'will really take hold when the electronic office takes hold. I see the convergence of computers and communications happening by 1985, and by then the Japanese will have their act together'.[13]

It is important to note that the Japanese companies have taken on IBM by closely imitating the US company. All Japanese machines are compatible with IBM, and have followed IBM's technical advances. This is in stark contrast to the UK lead company, ICL, which has achieved some success in going it alone technically, but is constantly vulnerable to IBM's moves. Japanese strategy has been clear-sighted and realistic; it has been based on acceptance of IBM's technical dominance as *the* fact of data processing life and has adapted to it accordingly. Japan is the one competitor (it usually is the only competitor) which IBM takes seriously.

The Japanese example demonstrates the lengths to which an advanced state must go if it is to carve out an independent niche in the most advanced technologies. When confronted with the massive power of IBM in data processing, the only recourse open is for a state to use its own capital, probably coupled with preferential purchasing and tariff barriers, if a native industry is to be developed — or preserved.

However, the export of Japanese capital in the 1980s will be a different affair from the great periods of US (or UK) overseas investment. The Japanese companies will, when they invest in a substantial way in advanced economies, be obliged to make increasing joint production arrangements of the Honda/BL type because nation states have been strengthening themselves *vis à vis* TNCs at the same time as TNCs have been extending their scope (see Chapter 5).

The great Japanese investment is partly due to pressure from advanced economies on Japanese government and business. A recent Japanese white paper suggested that:

> 'trade frictions between Japan and its chief trading partners would best be resolved by increasing Japanese direct investment in advanced industrial countries and stepping up industrial and technological co-operation.'[14]

The Japanese need to export capital in order to retain and expand their markets. The ability of host governments to set terms and conditions on the nature of that investment suggests the possibility of new deals.

CONVERGENCE

We have seen how TNCs have, as their foundations, the science-based industries of the late nineteenth and early twentieth centuries. A great spurt to their development since the second war has been the developments in production and office technology. They will inevitably become stronger as a result of contemporary technical developments which have been lumped under the title of 'convergence'.

Convergence is generally applied to the growing technical similarity between the telecommunications, computer and entertainment industries. However, it also applies to the non-electronic industries which are having to adopt computerized production technology and/or enhance their products with microcomputers. Thus the car industry is adopting robotized production methods at the same time as the electronic components in a car are rising from a negligible proportion to 10 or 15 per cent of a car's value.

Convergence in both the broad and narrow sense is not limited to TNCs. Quite small companies are being required to adapt their production and marketing practices dramatically to cope with new conditions. But it will be the transnational electronic companies, and those linked with them, which will command the process, set the new standards, determine the new products and shape the new markets. The others will follow.

This process, now well under way, increases the power of TNCs both when they bargain with governments and when they bargain with labour. Ever-larger amounts of advanced technological expertise are concentrated in their hands, and they have increasing scope to determine where and how production is carried out.

All major electronic companies must come to terms with convergence if they are to protect their markets and see them expand. All are, in differing ways and at different rates, doing so. Many are acquiring, or acquiring interests in, semiconductor companies. Others are moving into automated office products ('the office of the future'); still others are building up their software capability – often, again, by acquisition. Crucially, all are attempting to hook into a communications network.

However gradual the metamorphosis in plants, offices and in the home, substantial changes will occur in the nature and structure of the corporations which dominate the market. These technical convergences are forcing business mergers. Convergence of technologies, and the necessity for companies to restructure to cope with these changes, requires much larger R and D and capital outlays; while mergers and bankruptcies are commonplace. Since the process often requires drawing a number of previously independent companies into the net of one corporation, the tendency to monopoly or oligopoly is much accelerated within given sectors.

Convergence and IBM

The structure of IBM, and its strategy relating to its operations, is an example of what convergence means. The French government study on 'informatics', Simon Nora's the *Computerization of Society*[15] attaches exceptional importance to IBM's role in the world:

'The world's foremost user of [electronic] components, IBM has also sought to be the foremost manufacturer. It has succeeded in this with impressive speed and efficiency. Henceforth the company will attach exceptional importance to telecommunications. This was shown by its determination to obtain from the US government the right to launch a satellite . . . once it has committed itself to transmitting voices, images and data it will be led to compete with the telecommunications organizations in their traditional spheres of activity . . . Manufacturing and selling machines, IBM had customers and few rivals. As a controller of networks, the company would take on a dimension extending beyong the strictly industrial sphere: it would participate, whether it wanted to or not, in the government of the planet . . . the extent of its success will sooner or later oblige IBM to take a new view of its environment; this will offer national governments the opportunity to open up a renewed dialogue with the company.'

IBM's present power resides in the computers it has installed in 60 per cent of the world's mainframe users' plants and offices. Its much greater potential power lies in its ability to link these installations and thus become a telecommunications agency for the commanding heights of the world economy. This is what Nora means by the 'government of the planet'.

IBM has kept as low and as grey a profile as the world's largest information company possibly can. It employs nationals in senior positions in the countries in which it operates. It is discretely active in sponsoring cultural and other events. It does not like trade unions but recognizes them when it has to (though not in the UK). Its public relations style is highly informed and cool — in deliberate contrast to the bonhommie and often ignorant hard sell of other corporations.

As Nora and others have identified, the most important element in IBM's strategy of extending its communications effort is its partnership with the Communications Satellite Corporation (Comsat) and Aetna Life Insurance in the project known as Satellite Business Systems. SBS will, in a few years, be in a position to transmit voices, images and data nationally and transnationally, wholly by-passing national networks. It will (or could) be the communication medium for the 'office of the future'. Though the system is currently only licensed for domestic (US) use it logically should expand to overseas markets where IBM makes half of its sales and more than half of its profits. In any future attempts to expand, it will have the backing of the US government, which argues, in various international forums, for the position of unrestricted access, by satellite transmission, to foreign markets.

Launched in 1981 with a rather low-key start, SBS plans to provide point-to-point transmission of voice, data and facsimile. It uses a powerful satellite located in the 'Ku Band' (12-14 GHz) which so far no other carrier or state has laid claims to. Most importantly, SBS provides communications services at lower costs, by-passing potential regulation. It is an obviously attractive alternative to the PTTs' services for large corporations, especially those (like IBM itself) which are multinationals. R E Jacobson summarized the effects thus:

> 'The SBS system will reduce the high costs of information transmission and eliminate reliance on "undependable" local communication networks for users who can generate enough data to satisfy the system's huge appetite for data. Thus SBS could absorb a large portion of the business of terrestrial communications carriers and, by making data transmission "cheap" and dependable encourage SBS customers to once again rely on centralized, compatible IBM computer installations. The consequences for terrestrial carriers (eg AT&T) and "non-compatible" mainframe manufacturers (eg the plug compatibles and European-Japanese firms) are obvious. The removal of cost and efficiency restraints on the communication of digital data would also deal a crippling blow to the minicomputer industry: given the ability to easily access very efficient large mainframe computers from

remote locations, SBS customers could eliminate their dependence on small, inefficient on-site minicomputers.'[16]

As Jacobsen recognizes, the main disadvantages from the increasing reliance upon transnational corporations for information generation and carriage is a loss of domestic employment and expertise to foreign centres, with a corresponding loosening of the safeguards provided by states (or groupings of states, such as the European Community) over the rights of individuals, institutions and companies. Jacobson quotes Mr John Eger, a spokesman for the US information industries, to the effect that national barriers to information flow are, or should be, things of the past because of the interweaving of: 'the activities, the life, the destiny of any nation in the world today with global tele-communications'.[17] The question is: Is that interleaving to be effected by IBM and other enormous corporations? Or is it to be effected by institutions capable of control by the people whose interests it is weaving? It is a question to which IBM ceaselessly strives to provide its own answers. It has already (September 1982) finalized plans to run a joint SBS-British Telecom business communications service, offering computer-to-computer communication and teleconferencing facilities. The service is the first of its kind internationally, and may presage further joint ventures.[18]

IBM's plans are an example of the company's outstanding versatility in being able to make a bid for a ground floor entrance to a reception wholly dominated by state-owned corporations.

Early in 1982, the US government anti-trust lawyers announced they were dropping a long-pending suit against IBM. The world's largest computer company now faces no effective barrier to expansion of its activities in the domestic market. There, it will meet a competitor which fared less well in January 1982 at the hands of the trust-busters — the world's largest private company: AT&T.

TELECOMMUNICATIONS: STATES AS TRADERS AND TRADERS AS STATES

Telecommunications, and information-related activities, are the critical technologies of our times. They will, as Dr Alex Reid has written:

'play an increasingly dominant role as an agent of change in society . . . One social effect of telecommunications is therefore that of pressing forwards, in partnership with computers, a pace of change which is largely indifferent to physical resource and environmental constraints. It is in partnership with transportation that telecommunications has its other main social effect: as a force for increasing cohesion and interdependence at both national and global level. For the movement of material and information, accompanied by the economic specialization which this implies, cannot but make each individual, and each country, the more dependent upon another.'[19]

As Reid makes clear, telecommunications now act on a world stage. Because of this, new configurations are being forced on the states which control, and the companies which manufacture and market, telecommunications equipment. Telecommunications marketing has always been an international business, played according to the rule that international marketing was *from* those countries which possessed a telecommunications industry *to* those countries which did not, and not between members of the first category, with rare exceptions. This rule still holds (though barely) but the stakes have become much higher and the international telecommunications market much more competitive.

While major UK companies which once dominated the scene have seen their share of world trade dwindle to about five per cent, nearly every other advanced country has increased its trade, at least in volume terms. The traditional international telecommunications companies of Philips, ITT, Ericsson and Siemens have been joined by the French CIT Alcatel and Thomson CSF; the Italian Sit Siemens; the Japanese NEC; the Canadian Northern Telecom; the US GTE and, most massive of all, Western Electric, AT&T's manufacturing arm. Britain, having at length developed a computerized exchange − System X − is making a late counter-attack through BTS, a marketing subsidiary for the System X sales abroad.

The conversion of telecommunications production from electro-mechanical to electronic switching, and concomitant changes in production technology, mean that great pressure has been put on manufacturers to keep employment levels steady (or to avoid cutting them back too far) by expanding production further. For most, this means venturing into the export market.

Export markets, especially in oil-rich developing countries, can be enormous. For example, the contract in Saudi Arabia won in 1978 by the Dutch/Swedish consortium of Philips and Ericsson netted these companies over $4 billion.

The cost of developing computerized exchanges is very great. The companies' major customer, typically its 'own' telecommunications administration (PTT), has a large and direct interest in encouraging the manufacturer to offset costs which would be wholly passed on to it, if it were the only customer, by exporting the system.

The fierceness of the battle for the telecommunications market is only partly fought with the weapons of technical excellence. More useful is the weapon of finance. For example, the loan which the Franco-German consortium managed to syndicate to the Egyptian PTT Areto was at five per cent interest, and for the first 30 years of the payback period no interest was charged. It was government backed.

The need to attract trade, preserve jobs and act as a bank has brought the state into the closest involvement with the international telecommunications market. Governments are now becoming trading partners with communications companies; their deals involve the highest level of diplomacy. Trade does not now follow the flag; it is embroidered upon it.

With regard to US companies, the support is in the form of extensive custom put their way by the space and defence programmes, and by the funding of the companies' research and development by these programmes' budgets. US semiconductor companies, like Texas Instruments and Motorola, were partly creations of the US military and the National Space Agency. In the case of European companies, such as the French CII Honeywell Bull and the British ICL, state support has been necessary over short or long periods to avoid bankruptcy.

The computer and telecommunications industries, then, are essentially *state capitalist industries*; state capitalist industries, moreover, which are aggressive on an international scale. The Japanese, French, British, German and Italian governments subsidize information companies at home to make money abroad and the US government does so indirectly.

This involvement paints a different picture to the conventional one seen in some quarters that TNCs now dominate nation states. In the crucial electronics sector, TNCs are more often the partners of nation states competing with other state-company partnerships for markets. These partnerships have mutual dependences, as heavy on the side of the companies as on that of the states.

The state holds legal rights, public funds and popular mandate or acquiescence. The TNC has markets, trained personnel and control of technology. It is this last card which is of the greatest importance in the telecommunications sector in the last two decades of the century, for it is fundamentally advances in telecommunications technology which are pushing along the trend which appears to be of greatest benefit to the TNCs: the trend towards the liberalization of markets.

Technological convergence has played the major role in this trend. As companies break down the barriers previously in place between the various technological sectors, the legislative framework within which they have been contained is being severely strained. This is especially so in the US, where the convergence process has resulted in the cornerstone of US communications legislation, the 1934 Communications Act (and subsequent amendments and consent decrees) becoming restrictive to developments in telecommunications. A 1956 consent decree had limited telephone companies to providing a telephone service, thus shutting them out from data communications and processing. IBM, and other computer companies, have not been so limited. Competition, indeed, is derived more from technological and commercial convergence than (as it is conveniently presented) from the US predisposition to the free market. Monopolies made sense (and were legally sanctioned) when phone lines were the *only* communications channel for two-way speech (since competing lines would clearly increase rather than reduce costs, and thus prices). But microwave and satellite transmission present real competition, while data communications provides extra traffic and new revenue. Competition in the US telecommunications market is now in vogue, because powerful corporations *can* compete (and want to), where previously they could not do so.[20] The presumed result (whatever the rationale) is to better the lot of the consumer by competitive services and pricing.

The Metamorphosis of AT&T

AT&T is at the centre of developments in the US telecommunications market. On 8 January 1982, the day on which IBM learned it would not be broken up, AT&T learned that it would. The decision to strip the company of its 22 operating companies was 'likely to have great international consequences', according to *The Economist.*[21]

However the ownership patterns turn out, it is certain that the cross subsidy, which existed between the lucrative long distance calls for business (which AT&T keeps) and the local service, will end: local calls will get more expensive. It is also likely that significant differences in the standard of telephone service will emerge between areas.

However, more profound effects will flow from AT&T's future activities in the communications market. For although the company was divested of part of its activities — it was, as a *quid pro quo*, allowed to compete in the cable and data transmission markets with all the other companies (like IBM) which had been carving up the new communications traffic between them, secure in the knowledge that the massive presence of AT&T was penned up within the confines of the 'plain old telephone service'.

AT&T has ceased to be a utility and must become, (if it is to survive) a high technology company, selling both equipment and services. In its developing battle with IBM and with other electronic companies, it will develop products and sharpen skills which it is increasingly better placed to market worldwide.

The first rounds in the battle were fired in October 1982, when SBS announced its intention of launching a service called 'Skyline' in January 1983. The service will offer long distance phone services to small business and residential customers, at rates claimed to undercut AT&T by between 14 and 30 per cent. Skyline supplements SBS' Message Service One, designed to service big business users. Others moving into the field include GTE and MCI.

THE IMPORTANCE OF TNC NETWORKS

IBM's moves, and the legislative changes now under consideration in the US and elsewhere, emphasize the absolute importance for advanced electronics companies of acquiring their own networks, or, at the very least, access to the public networks on terms at least as favourable as their competitors enjoy. Xerox, for example, the company which occupies a similar position in the copier market as IBM does in the computer world is busily creating the X-Ten network to link its intelligent machines with other automated office equipment, so that it does not find its position whittled away by interconnected facsimile and word processing terminals. Without national and global networks at their command, the smaller electronic companies will find the balance of power moving further towards the giant corporations, some of which will be able to take on the role of international telecommunications authorities.

TRANSNATIONAL COMPANIES, THE THIRD WORLD AND EASTERN EUROPE

Rules and regulations restrict the operations of TNCs in all countries. However, they have the huge advantage over other companies in that their presence in developing countries often leaves them free to establish cartels and institute discriminatory pricing, patent and labour practices which are prohibited in the home countries and in the other advanced countries in which they are based.

Developing countries have argued that the unequal relationship which they have with TNCs should be redressed in their favour. They have claimed that the activities of TNCs since the war, when their establishment in developing countries often coincided with their countries achieving independence, have tended to discriminate against the development of indigenous industries, and have done little to promote the development of employment.

The United Nations Conference on Trade and Development (UNCTAD), in a number of studies on TNC investment, has concluded that:

☐ The foreign exchange cost of technology represents a considerable burden on the balance of payments of developing countries. TNCs impose formal and informal restrictions on exports, and over- or under-price the exports of their subsidiaries to suit the world market.
☐ The product ranges of many TNCs are aimed at middle and upper income consumer markets. The basic needs of the mass of the population in developing countries are largely ignored because of their low purchasing power.

☐ The transfer of technological expertise and R and D resources is minimal. TNCs are reluctant to commit R and D resources to overseas subsidiaries because of the risk of separate development and loss of control.

☐ Licensing agreements with local companies, and imports, tend to prolong technological dependence; the superiority of TNC production continues the trend, since its production technology remains several steps ahead of any domestic challenge.

☐ Indigenous research and educational activities are often divorced from production: not only are there many fewer universities and other further and higher education centres in developing countries than in advanced countries, but within developing countries there is often a bias against engineering and science skills.

Developing countries' response to these factors has largely been channelled through their development of proposals for the New International Economic Order, begun at the summit of non-aligned countries in 1970. Early efforts at establishing the basis of that Order focused on the reshaping of the legal basis of technology transfer, particularly in two areas: the patent convention and the production of a technology transfer code.

Patents, regulated by the Paris Convention 1883, often restrict local production and protect oligopolistic production; the overwhelming majority of patents registered in developing countries are controlled by foreigners. The current review of the Convention is expected to suggest some changes in favour of the developing countries.

Attempts to draft a code for the regulation of technology transfer have been made since the mid-1970s. There is agreement on the broad aims — to eliminate restrictions and reduce the negative effects of technology imports for developing countries — but the complexities of legal problems have so far been a barrier to success.

At the same time, a number of developing countries have begun to explore the concept of 'technology transfer agreements' — a concept whose practice varies but whose principle is to maximize technology gains by using the lever of the developing country's market against the required technological know-how. A number of these agreements, especially in the field of telecommunications, have been signed between Middle Eastern countries and European states or the US; they are also a feature of East-West commercial relations. In general, the scope of such agreements has increased in recent years as developing countries have become aware of how great is the need of advanced countries and their corporations for new markets.

The Third World's potential bargaining power should not be underestimated. As Sir Edward Fennessy of British Telecom has calculated, existing growth patterns for telephone usage indicate that, by the end of the century, Asia and Africa could well dominate the world market.

There are already signs that developing countries rich in resources (such as Venezuela or Algeria), and countries with a relatively advanced industrial base (such as Brazil), can achieve considerable leverage in bargaining with the TNCs. Algeria, for example, was able to conclude an agreement in 1974 with the US General Telephone Company (GTE) to build an integrated consumer electronics plant which would be staffed with Algerian technicians and managers, trained by GTE in America.

East-West technology transfer agreements have stimulated the emergence of East European-based TNCs. In the case of France and the Soviet Union, for example, a permanent joint government commission oversees the exchange of information, licenses and patents and the development of technical standards in, for example, colour television and space technology. Based on such transfers, three-way co-operation agreements have been established, linking Eastern and Western suppliers to jointly meet developing countries' needs; Western countries supplying the technology with some sub-contracting to the East. In the 1970s, these agreements were mostly in the manufacturing sector, notably iron and steel, chemicals, vehicles and crude oil; some 10 per cent of the agreements were for power plant equipment. The East Europeans gained both business and experience in transnational production methods. The developing countries gained by saving on foreign exchange which was not required by Eastern European countries. It was even possible for no foreign exchange to change hands at all, since Eastern European countries could compensate their Western partners in goods. In this way, for example, the Austrian firm, Simmering-Graz-Panker, and Hungarian enterprises, built two power stations in India. While the collapse of detente has forced a temporary slowing down of this process, once the international climate improves, a tripartite pattern of development will probably redevelop in the telecommunications world.

CONCLUSION

Throughout our survey of the TNCs, we have been concerned to show the two-fold nature of their existence: their immense and growing power through the use of technology, and their immense and growing dependence on the state to finance and legitimize their activities.

On both the domestic and world scenes, a new 'mix' is being created. It cannot be adequately characterized as the growth of transnational power, overshadowing that of nation states; a better shorthand description might be 'the growth of inter-state capitalism'.

Insofar as states and TNCs are in conflict — and they often are — there can be no pre-determined 'victor' on either side. In Chapter 9 we suggest that if positive social benefits are to flow from the deals struck between states and TNCs, it will be necessary for these deals to take another form in the future.

REFERENCES

1 *Fortune Magazine* (1969) 15 August.

2 Stuart Holland (1975) 'The socialist challenge'. *Quartet*, p 75.

3 F P Fish (1909) 'The patent system'. *Transactions of the American Institute of Electrical Engineers*, p 335.

4 Quoted in R Jones and O Marriott (1970) *Anatomy of a Merger*, p 31. Cape.

5 ibid.

6 H J Crawley (1957) The National Research Development Corporation Computer Project, NRDC Computer sub-committee, Paper 132. February.

7 S Lavington (1980) *Early British Computers*, p 84. Manchester University Press.

8 P Stothard (1981) 'Is there a place in the market for ICL?'. *Sunday Times*, 8 February.

9 C E Lindblom (1977) *Politics and Markets*, p 197. Basic Books, New York.

10 T Takai (1980) 'Challenge to US domination: the Japanese electronics industry'. World Electronics Conference, Monte Carlo.

11 W G Ouchi (1980) *Theory Z*. Addison Wesley.

12 R T Pascale and A G Athos (1981) *The Art of Japanese Management*. Simon and Schuster.

13 N Weizer (1980) *Electronics Magazine*, p 116. 27 March.

14 *Financial Times* (1981) 15 June, p 5.

15 S Nora and A Minc (1980) *The Computerization of Society*, pp 71-2. MIT Press, Cambridge, Mass.

16 R E Jacobson (1979) 'Satellite business systems'. *Media Culture and Society*, 1, pp 235-53.

17 ibid, p 250.

18 *Financial Times* (1982) 25 September.

19 A Reid (1978) 'New telecommunications services and their social implications'. *Phil Trans Royal Society*, 289, p 178.

20 *Telecommunications Journal* (1980) June, pp 314-15.

21 *The Economist* (1982) 16-22 January, p 11.

22 Sir E Fennessy (1978) 'The global picture'. Phil Trans Royal Society, 208, p 8.

CHAPTER 4

Labour's Response to the Transnational Companies

INTRODUCTION

Organized labour does not like transnational companies. Unions believe TNCs export jobs, shift plants into low wage countries to escape them, hand down industrial relations systems from foreign headquarters, try to keep unions out of their plants, and subvert socialist governments. There is more than a little truth in most of these beliefs.

THE MENACING MULTINATIONALS

In 1971, the AFL-CIO estimated that some half a million jobs had been 'lost' in the US because US-based TNCs have 'exported' them overseas.[1] A Tarrif Commission Report in 1973 estimated that 1.3 million net jobs had been lost up to 1970, because of overseas production by TNCs.[2] A key passage in the Commission Report argued that:

> 'not all low wage countries are primitive in the sense that they are unable to absorb and profit from techniques and disciplines of modern production. Furthermore, modern technology in some industries is such that relatively unskilled labour can be combined with fairly sophisticated equipment. This contradicts the stereotyped notion of "high technology" as a process in which highly skilled labour always must be available to operate advanced, complex kinds of capital equipment. Usually this is so, but in some industries the stereotype never has described reality. The possibilities for using unskilled labour abroad open up for some firms the opportunity to migrate to low wage countries which have reached a level of development at which they are ready to accept them, without significant divergence from productivity experience in the United States.'[3]

The TNCs' drive to move into low labour cost countries, and the ability to do so, is taken largely for granted by labour and left wingers. It is a major argument, for example, in Charles Levinson's book, *International Trade Unionism*,[4] and is frequently alluded to in trade union and activist literature.

A Labour Research Department report, significantly called 'The Menace of the Multinationals' mentions threats by Ford to expand engine production in Brazil, rather than the UK, because of Ford-UK labour relations, and concludes:

> 'in the last resort, capital is more mobile than the workers it employs in any given place. Multinational companies have greatly facilitated this mobility, and thus have strengthened the bargaining power of management against the workers. By the same token the job security of workers employed by multinationals is lessened.'[5]

Stuart Holland, in his influential book *The Socialist Challenge*, argues that TNCs side-step market conditions internationally by trading with their own subsidiaries, and domestically by exercising joint or shared monopolies. He argues, too, that, while the UK ranks first in the top 500 league of European TNCs, with 140 firms, the reasons for its deteriorating economic performance: 'lie substantially in the extent to which such leading multinationals have written Britain off as the main location for their expansion, and are shunting investment and jobs in modern industry abroad.'[6]

Levinson points to: 'sufficient concrete experience . . . to confirm the fact that global enterprises are centralizing their industrial relations policies',[7] and mentions IBM, Dupont and the major oil companies as showing hostility to unions and keeping them out of their plants when they can. Paul Jennings, President of the US Electrical Workers, told an International Metalworkers Federation Conference in 1972 that 'the concentration of management control and decision-making in multi-national companies is a challenge to free democratic trade unions'.[8] A number of authors argue that centralization of all TNC functions is an increasing trend and that this creates a new 'international class structure', with an international managerial class, a highly skilled, relatively secure labour class and a socially marginal class of unskilled labourers.[9]

The hostility of TNCs to left wing parties and governments is well documented and scarcely surprising. The most obvious, and most often quoted, case is that of ITT's involvement in Chile. ITT, as Anthony Sampson relates, intervened in Chilean politics in a direct and brutal way to protect its telephone company.[10] The company's attempts to manipulate the outcome of the 1970 elections (when the Marxist President, Salvador Allende, was elected) and its subsequent involvement with the CIA in plans to destabilize the country, while negotiating in apparent good faith with the government on the nationalization of the company, earned it muted rebuke from a senatorial sub-committee in the US:

> 'if ITT's actions in seeking to enlist the CIA for its purposes with respect to Chile were to be sanctioned as normal and acceptable, no country would welcome the presence of multinational corporations.'[11]

Shaky Foundations

Many on the left hold views about the TNCs which add up to a conclusive catalogue of evil. However, some of these views are based on shaky foundations and the policies so far adopted by labour in response to the undoubted economic potential of TNCs have tended to be static and ineffective.

The ease with which the TNCs can export jobs and shift production rapidly has probably been over-emphasized. Most TNC investment remains in developed countries. Unions which complain of the export of British jobs with TNC investment overseas at the same time often welcome foreign TNC investment in the UK. Witness, for example, the enthusiasm with which the UK unions in the car industry have courted Nissan in 1982, when the Japanese company announced its intention (subsequently indefinitely delayed) to set up a British plant.

Studies of the gains and losses of jobs in the US due to activity of TNCs differ greatly.[12] The bibliographer of the literature on TNCs and labour notes the subject remains 'a vexed and controversial one.'[13]

TNCs often threaten to move plants — but seldom do so. The case of Ford threatening to switch engine production to Brazil rather than the UK was followed a few years later by a large investment by Ford in a new engine plant in South Wales. New investment is a different matter: many new electronic plants, especially in semiconductor and TV production have been set up in the Far East, and this trend seems likely to continue.

The complaint that foreign production loses domestic jobs is generally based on the assumption of perfect substitute ability, that is, that overseas production fully replaces equivalent domestic production. Yet most evidence points to foreign investment being protected.

> 'Some job loss occurs as foreign production displaces exports or domestic production, but the substitution is far from complete. Overseas production is in response to pressure to protect market shares, both domestically and internationally, (and) cost considerations are an important influence.'[14]

Some TNCs are very hostile to trade unions and keep them out. IBM is perhaps the best example. In the UK, it has successfully resisted unionization, largely by paying relatively high wages. However, the Chairman of IBM UK made clear in a speech to London businessmen that, while: 'our preference is to avoid negotiations with third parties and encourage individuals to participate in the Company . . . in some countries the law requires that we recognize trade unions and in others the unions actually elect some of the members of the Board of Directors'.[15] In the same speech, the IBM Chairman made it clear that IBM industrial relations policies were largely de-centralized: a policy which is followed very largely by most TNCs. Industrial relations vary according to the culture, laws, and labour traditions of each country; salary levels similarly differ widely. Centralization of industrial relations is probably impossible beyond a statement of general principles.

The TNCs dislike governments which seek to hamper or nationalize them; the case of ITT in Chile, however, is unlikely to be duplicated in advanced economies. TNCs are firm supporters of capitalism, and are so openly; they have, however, been prepared to make bargains with the Soviet Union and other Soviet Block states in the past, and have also bargained with democratic socialist states.

Socialist governments dislike TNCs because they believe that they narrow their policy options. This is the burden of Holland's complaint, and of others. Against this, it has been argued from the left that because of increased economic interdependence between states, and of their declining ability for individual manoeuvre, the situation has brought: 'an ever closer relationship between the state and the large firms (both domestic enterprises operating abroad and foreign enterprises operating domestically) and on the whole a strengthening of the nation capitalist state in relation to the constituent firms of the economies concerned.'[16]

COLLECTIVE BARGAINING AND THE TNCs

A possible reason for the tendency of the labour movement to over-estimate the power of the TNCs, and to react very unfavourably towards them, is the fact that unions have had little success in bargaining with them as international entities (though, of course, they do bargain with them in their guise as national companies). Union negotiators have two main frustrations when negotiating with TNCs — first, that a threat of industrial action can often be circumvented by increased production at foreign plants (though there are limits to this, and industrial action in one country can often stop production and supply within its borders) and second, that the negotiators are rarely allowed to sit down with the top management of the company.

International collective bargaining has long been a dream of union negotiators, and especially of those union officials who staff international union secretariats. Charles Levinson, the American head of the International Chemical Workers Federation, believes it will come, and cites with pride the case of St Gobain, where a strike in the company's subsidiaries in West Germany, the US and Italy, co-ordinated by the ICF forced union recognition in some plants, as well as wage increases and workload cuts. Levinson comments that: 'the action was undoubtedly a major step towards the ultimate objective of truly global co-ordination and the progressive integration of collective bargaining'.[17]

The ICF is not the only international union which can claim real success. The International Metalworkers Ferderation has worked hard at setting up world industrial councils, most successful among which have been its world car councils. The International Transport Workers have taken some effective action on 'flags of convenience' vessels, where low pay and bad conditions are frequent, while the International Union of Food and Allied Workers has exerted pressure to some effect on TNCs such as Nestle, Nabisco and Unilever.

Entertainment and Transnational Bargaining

However, so far the only really effective union bargaining with TNCs has been with one industry, which has rarely been thought of as being effectively or militantly unionized. That is entertainment. There, a number of international federations — particularly the International Federation of Musicians and the International Federation of Actors, grouped together in the International Federations of Performers, have struck deals with employers' organizations which guarantee payment to performers on recordings, broadcasts and performances internationally. Agreements between the federations and the producers have successfully covered radio, recordings and television. In the 1970s, cable and satellite transmissions came into the bargaining arena, though agreements have still to be concluded. The international unions have at times shown their muscle: in 1956, a boycott by the performers' unions of European Broadcasting Union Transmissions produced a Eurovision agreement in 1957 which stipulated that European broadcast organizations would make supplementary payments to performers who participated in Eurovision relays.

Philip Miscimarra, who has chronicled these agreements, concludes that two major factors help the trend to transnational bargaining and will probably maintain it, in this area. First, the demand for entertainment, 'traditionally cosmopolitan', is increasing. Second, and more central to our main theme, entertainment technology reduces demand for local performers and technicians in favour of 'international' performers and technicians.

'The introduction of ever more advanced developments (direct television and radio reception from intercontinental satellites, for example) threatens further to extend this type of displacement on the international level. The impact of technological change on local, national and international employment in the entertainment industry is highly visible and seems to ignore national ideological differences and geographic boundaries. This was the force behind the founding of the International Federation of Musicians and the International Federation of Actors, and it remains their predominant ongoing concern.'[18]

By far the biggest job done by unions on the international scene is the passing of information among affiliates — information which is immediately, or ultimately, of use to national collective bargainers. This function will become more, rather than less, important as the scope of TNCs widen and their operations become more complex.

101

Unfortunately, it is often the case that only top union officials are aware of the international dimension to their bargaining. Thus, it is not necessarily simply *more* information that is needed, but much more of the existing information needs to be disseminated to different levels.

The information also needs to be improved. Unions are often antipathetic, or at least indifferent, to government attempts to exert leverage on TNCs at state and international level. These attempts would directly benefit labour, albeit at the price of changes in union practice and views. We do not suggest that better, or better spread, information would guarantee a more realistic appraisal of the international dimension, but it would help.

LEVERS AGAINST THE TNCs

The state, as Bill Warren points out, remains the most powerful counterweight to the TNCs, and one which tends to grow in power *vis à vis* these corporations, though the Thatcher government, at least at times, is a notable exception to this rule. By privatizing nationalized industries, and 'liberalizing' domestic markets, Thatcher is effectively handing over control of these areas of economic activity to the TNCs, thereby reducing the British government's freedom of action. A state concerned with a national economic plan (for example, the UK in 1964-66 and 1974-79, and France virtually all the time) will usually seek to limit TNCs. It may also, for employment reasons, wish to attract them.

TNCs are clearly limited by a country's company law: regulations concerning the export of capital, factory and health and safety acts. However, these are rarely of great concern. More serious for the TNCs was the series of acts passed by the 1974-79 Labour governments, which had the intention of limiting TNC activities, strengthening the state against them, and granting trade unions more power. These acts were:

☐ The Employment Protection Act 1975, which stipulated disclosure of certain information for collective bargaining purposes.
☐ The Industry Act 1975, which brought into its scope all foreign-owned subsidiaries and which called for planning agreements between government and companies.
☐ The Trade Union and Labour Relations (Amendment) Act 1976, which allowed unions greater scope in organizing action in sympathy with an overseas trade dispute, whilst remaining immune from legal action.

All these measures were quickly scrapped by the 1979 Conservative government. Within their brief lifetime, they had limited success.

Unions used the disclosure of information provisions, and took limited advantage of the freedom to organize sympathetic action; however they were constrained, not so much by the law, but by the need for wage restraint under the social contract (see Chapter 6), a restraint which also spread to industrial action.

National Limitations

The Industry Act's provision for planning agreements was used only once — with Chrysler. However, the agreement with an ailing TNC, which was being forced out of much of its world production, could not stop the company from pulling out of the UK in 1979, after receiving large-scale government aid and selling off its plants to Peugeot Citroen, later renamed Talbot.

The Chrysler case has been taken to demonstrate the futility of planning agreements. Certainly it showed up a crucial limitation. That is, that negotiations with a TNC which cannot maintain its investment on even highly-subsidized terms, cannot possibly succeed. However, many people believe that this (limited) lesson proves that all government agreements with TNCs are of no value.

A second limitation is the disparity of geographical scope between unions and companies. Ultimately, a fundamental labour criticism of TNCs holds. Just as TNCs can only rarely be controlled, though they may be damaged, by national action on the part of the state, so they can rarely be influenced by the unions of the host country of their subsidiaries.

International trade unionism has so far met with tight constraints on its actions — constraints which are unlikely to be lifted. Yet at a world level, labour has little on which to base an effective response to TNCs.

Good Practice

The OECD Code of Conduct for TNCs[19] lays down good practice in a variety of areas in which labour is interested. It calls for the divulging of information on collective bargaining, forewarning of redundancies, recognition of trade unions, the observation of local labour standards, and adequate training provisions. It is, however, a voluntary code, providing only an exhortatory effect which is liable to be disregarded by TNCs when they feel it is expedient to do so.

The United Nations Code of Conduct has been in preparation since 1974, when the Commission on Transnational Corporations was established. At the moment it seems likely that the Code will soon be issued dealing with much of the same area as that covered in the OECD Code. It will, however, also be voluntary, and will inevitably be weakened by the need to get agreements between countries which are hosts to TNCs and countries which are the source of TNCs.[20]

The most serious attempt to legislate for control over TNCs at super-national level, is being provided by the European Economic

Community. Two initiatives, closely interlinked, and likely to pass into Community and then member state law in 1983-84 are at the core of this attempt. The first of these, known as the Fifth Directive, proposes employee involvement in the running of companies of more than 100 people. It puts up a number of options for two-tier and unitary boards from which each member state could select which option it preferred. There is a provision, common to all options, that workers' representatives occupy between one-third and one-half of the seats on a board, whether unitary or supervisory. It also calls for three-monthly progress reports for all employee representatives; access to all management reports and consultation on closures, transfers, expansion or contraction; and large-scale organizational changes.

The second initiative, known as the 'Vredeling Proposals' put flesh on the Fifth Directive's bones, outlining the information which must be divulged and the consultation process which must be undertaken. The information, which must be provided to all employee representatives: 'should give a clear picture of the dominant undertaking and its subsidiaries taken as a whole', and should cover the TNCs financial situation, development of the business, employment situation, products, investment programmes and introduction of new working methods. Consultation must be initiated on any decision which has a substantial effect on employees, and must be pursued with 'a view to reaching agreement'.[21]

Employers Against the EEC

These proposals will have the status of national legislation once they are agreed. For that reason, they have attracted increasingly ferocious hostility from European and US employers and governments.

In West Germany, the Federation of German Employers Association, though long used to a co-determination system, criticized the Vredeling Proposals as creating legal uncertainty, which would lead to many compulsory changes in German labour law.

The European Employers Federation, UNICE, has said that the proposals would affect some 40,000 small- and medium-sized companies, as well as TNCs, and it would 'threaten disruption to industrial relations and damage to competitiveness'.

The US State Department has (in a letter to a congressman leaked to the press in early 1982) characterized the proposals as: 'ill-advised as a matter of policy, contains troublesome aspects and would, if adopted in its present form, adversely affect US firms doing business in Europe'.

US congressmen have introduced two Bills on Protection of Business Information, and on Trade reciprocity designed to ensure 'fairness of treatment' for US corporations abroad in the face of EEC legislation. The House of Representatives sub-committee on Oversight and Investments is at the moment monitoring legislation with a view to preparing a legislative response in congress.

The UK CBI has said that the Bills are 'gravely mistaken'; the Institute of Directors has (characteristically) been more militant, loudly claiming that the measures will destroy capitalism and demanding that the UK government veto them.

Right wing members of the European Parliament, led by UK MEPs, have condemmed the two EEC initiatives, and have been leading attempts to block or at least dilute them. Much of this hostility has hinged on the clause in the Vredeling Proposals which calls for consultation on major decisions to be undertaken 'with a view to reaching agreement'. Employers have interpreted this to mean that workforces will be given a veto over, for example, plant closure, mergers or redundancies.

Most trade union centres have warmly welcomed the legislation. The German trade union centre, the DGB, has said that: 'making the economy more democratic is the only way in which the European Community can be brought closer to Europe's workers'. Hermann Rebhan, the General Secretary of the International Metal Workers, has called on all affiliates to support it.

'Multinational companies have been able to operate free of any kind of control or sense of responsibility to their workforce for far too long. This directive will help, albeit in a modest way, to make multinational employees feel less vulnerable and isolated'.[22]

However, the British unions have had little or nothing to say on the proposals — since they have voted to press for an end to UK membership of the EEC.

CONCLUSION

Labour's response to TNCs, as Peter Enderwick has noted,[23] has been slow, ineffective and often based on outmoded views. Much of this ineffectiveness derives from the inevitable national rather than international focus of labour unions and labour and socialist parties (stemming from their own structures and organizations), and the formidable difficulties of bargaining with the TNCs.

REFERENCES

1 AFL-CIO (1971) *Needed: a constructive Foreign Trade Policy*. Washington.

2 US Tarriff Commission (1973) *Implications of Multinational Firms for Western Trade and for US Trade and Labor*. Washington.

3 Hugo Radice (1975) *International Firms and Modern Imperialism*, p 91. Penguin, Harmondsworth.

4 C Levinson (1972) *International Trade Unionism*. Allen and Unwin, London.

5 Labour Research Department (1974).

6 S Holland (1975) *The Socialist Challenge*, p 77. Quartet, London.

7 Levinson, op cit, p 96.

8 IMF (1972) Conference on multinationals, 13-15 December. London.

9 R W Cox (1976) 'Labor and the multinationals'. *Foreign Affairs*, **54**, 2. January; S Hymer (1972) 'The multinational corporation and the laws of uneven development'. In J Bhagwath (ed) *Economics and the World Order*. Macmillan.

10 A Sampson (1975) *The Sovereign State*. Coronet, London.

11 ibid, p 242.

12 R H Frank and R T Freeman (1975) *Distributional Consequences of Direct Foreign Investment*. Academic Press, London.

13 P Enderwick (1979) 'Multinationals and labour'. In *Management Bibliographies and Reviews*, **15**, 3.

14 P Enderwick (1982) 'Labour and the theory of the multinational corporation. *Industrial Relations Journal*. Summer.

15 E Nixon (1982) Speech to Institute of Directors. 6 May.

16 B Warren (1975) 'How international is capital?' In H Radice (ed) *International Firms and Modern Imperialism*. Penguin, Harmondsworth.

17 C Levinson, op cit, p 20.

18 P Miscimarra (1981) 'The entertainment industry: inroads in multinational collective bargaining'. In *British Journal of Industrial Relations*, **XIX**. 1 March.

19 OECD (1976) Declaration on international investment and multinational enterprises and guidelines for multinational enterprises. 21 June.

20 UN (1982) Draft Code of Conduct on transnationals. Economic and Social Council. 5 June.

21 See summary of EEC legislation on consultation (1982) *Personnel Management*, **14**, 5, p 34.

22 H Rebhan (1981) Press conference. Geneva. August.

23 P Enderwick, op cit, p 238.

CHAPTER 5

The Rise of the State and Science-Based Industries

INTRODUCTION

The application of science to production, which began in the nineteenth century, changed the requirements for economic and industrial growth and stimulated the expansion of the state in all advanced countries.

Where industrialization had previously depended on access to raw materials and unskilled labour, these needs were reduced by new forms of transport and communications, and synthetic materials. In their place were demands for an increasingly skilled workforce, for co-ordination of research and development across industrial sectors, and for technical standards to enable the interconnection and interchange of products to ensure economies of scale in manufacture. In varying degrees, governments responded by enhancing the powers of the state in the following areas.

Governments' responses to technological change have produced interventions in the economy, which range from educational measures concerned with creating new skills through policies for diffusing this knowledge by means of state research and development, to economic policy tools aimed at applying the new technology to production. The involvement of the modern state in industrial innovation, production and marketing is now all pervasive (see Table 1).

In this chapter, our concern is to show how the state has been obliged, or has felt itself obliged, to greatly extend its scope to include a range of services and programmes which would have been inconceivable to nineteenth century governments.

Many writers have stressed that the growth of the state is an indispensable adjunct to the development of capitalism.[1] For example, Galbraith maintains:

'Qualified manpower is decisive for the success of the planning system. The education on which it depends is provided mostly in the public sector of the economy. By contrast, capital, which was once decisive, comes mostly from the private sector. The market for the most advanced technology and that which best allows planning is also in the public sector. Much

Policy tool	Examples
1. Public enterprise	Innovation by publicly owned industries, setting up of new industries, pioneering use of new techniques by public corporations, participation in private enterprise
2. Scientific and technical	Research laboratories, support for research associations, learned societies, professional associations, research grants
3. Education	General education, universities, technical education, apprenticeship schemes, continuing and further education, retraining
4. Information	Information networks and centres, libraries, advisory and consultancy services, databases, liaison services
5. Financial	Grants, loans, subsidies, financial sharing arrangements, provision of equipment, building or services, loan guarantees, export credits, etc.
6. Taxation	Company, personal, indirect and payroll taxation, tax allowances
7. Legal and regulatory	Patents, environmental and health regulations, inspectorates, monopoly regulations
8. Political	Planning, regional policies, honours or awards for innovations, encouragement of mergers or joint consortia, public consultation
9. Procurement	Central or local government purchases and contracts, public corporations, R & D contracts, prototype purchases
10. Public services	Purchases, maintenance, supervision and innovation in health service, public building, construction, transport, telecommunications
11. Commercial	Trade agreements, tariffs, currency regulations
12. Overseas agent	Defence sales organizations

Source: R Rothwell and W Zegveld *Industrial Innovation and Public Policy.* F Pinter

Table 1. A selection of government policy tools

scientific and technical innovation comes from, or is sponsored by, the state or by publicly supported universities and research institutions. The state regulates the aggregate demand for the products of the planning system. This is indispensable for the planning. And still discreetly, and with infirmity of intent, somewhat in the manner of a conservative cleric viewing an erotic statue, the state provides the wage and price regulation without which prices in the planning system are unstable. Clearly the modern organized economy was designed with a perverse hand. For how, otherwise, could so many needs unite to make a system which rejoices in the name of free enterprise be, in truth, so dependent on government?'[2]

Both capital and labour have an interest in the extension of state intervention. 'Modernization' of the economy was undertaken by Labour governments in the UK after the Second World War. Labour benefited from employment creation and an expansion of the public sector. The sick, the poor, the elderly and the young benefited from a publicly-financed health service, higher pensions and social security payments, and grants for higher education. It required training and education provided by the state to fit itself for a technically more demanding industry. The progressive industrial state required a more sophisticated workforce, and neither of the two major UK parties believed they could afford to use large-scale unemployment as a means of achieving their policy goals. Thus, a common interest was fashioned between the state and labour which promoted the formation of skills and the maintenance of employment.

We have seen how these coalitions were formed on both sides of the Atlantic in the 1930s and 1940s. This coincidence of interest between labour and the state had its origins in the USA in the 1920s and 1930s, when the depression arrested tendencies for workers to identify themselves with their employers, in favour of an increased identification with their unions. As Galbraith notes:

'As they grew in membership in this favourable environment, the unions became a factor in politics; as their role was adversary within the corporation, so it was adversary in their influence on the state. What the unions lacked in financial resources they compensated for in voting power. They found an ally in the emerging educational and scientific estate with its longstanding alienation from the entrepreneurial corporation. This, with some support from the farmers, was the heart of the Roosevelt coalition. It was easy for business enterprise to imagine that it was about to pass under the political authority of a state permanently dominated by the unions and the intellectuals.'[3]

This coalition did not completely unravel until President Nixon attracted the support of a large section of organized labour in the late 1960s. The steady increase in state powers over the economy led to an impasse, with two 'solutions' possible within a pluralist framework. The first solution was a 'social contract' between government and labour, to raise the series of deals made between government, unions and employers to a fully public and conscious level — though the implicit assumption was that the employers would suffer a relative loss of influence. We describe this development in Chapter 6.

The second solution was to 'roll back' the growth of union power — or union/state power — by increasing the relative influence of employers. This the 1979 conservative government has done, and is continuing to do at the present time. In Chapter 6 we give a brief description of the measures it has taken to dismantle the social contract.

THE ROLE OF THE STATE IN THE CREATION OF A SKILLED WORKFORCE

Britain

Although the industrial revolution occurred in Britain 50 years before France and Germany, it lagged 50 years behind in the establishment of higher technical education. Britain has still not reached the present levels of those countries' general provisions. State involvement in production, research and development was similarly slow to develop. Periodically, national attention would be focused on the inadequacy of existing state activity as a result of trade depressions such as those that occurred in 1870, 1924, 1930 or during the war, or latterly because of developments in the Soviet Union and elsewhere.

Traditionally, national attention took the form of high level Commissions of Inquiry reports, concerned with education, industry or science. The initial concern of such reports was for the reform of secondary and post-secondary education, although they continued to reflect the narrow complacency of employers towards the need for state involvement well into the twentieth century. Such attitudes were responsible for the delay in establishing universal secondary education with a key role for science in the syllabus, which did not occur until 1902. As late as the 1930s the government was receiving contradictory advice. On the one hand, the Department of Scientific and Industrial Research (DSIR) found that: 'insufficient density of technically trained people in positions of control and authority', was an obstacle to the diffusion of new techniques.[4] On the other hand the Malcolm Committee on Education and Industry found that: 'the facilities offered by the colleges and other institutions . . . Would appear for the moment more than equal to the effective demand from industry and trade . . . we have heard little or no concrete evidence of an unsatisfied demand on the part of industry for the product of a full-time system'.[5]

Three factors contributed to the relative backwardness of UK education and training. First, early industrialization in Britain did not need scientifically trained manpower and its success bred complacency with existing arrangements. Second, there was considerable suspicion on the part of the authorities of the political consequences of extending education to the poorer classes. Third, the *laissez-faire* attitude adopted by employers, and their belief that practical training of workers by the state would interfere with the maintenance of commercial secrecy, led to public involvement being restricted to technical education rather than training. Employers considered that training was more appropriate in the office, factory or workshop.

The continuing bias towards science rather than technology in state education stems from this conflict. Higher technical education in Britain has never attained the status that it has enjoyed in other industrialized countries, thus creating a void which that unique Anglo

Saxon institution, the professional association, has filled. Many such bodies were formed in the nineteenth century with members who took on the responsibility for coaching and examining aspiring professional engineers. With the expansion of university technical education in the twentieth century, their constitutions were modified to enable graduates to be taken into membership without examination, and they continue to have a large measure of influence over technical education and training.

Lower levels of technical training were provided by polytechnics, which were technical colleges established by local, often private, initiative and taken under the control of local authorities in 1918. Prominent among these private bodies were the descendants of the Mediaeval guilds. They played a significant role in the provision of technical colleges when the City and Guilds of London established in 1879 an Institute to administer technical examinations. Similar private initiatives resulted in the establishment of the Regent Street Polytechnic in 1882 and by 1905 12 polytechnics existed in various parts of London. These bodies offered evening, day release and later sandwich courses for all levels, from craftsmen to technicians and foremen. Central to their work was preparation for the Ordinary and Higher National Certificates which the government had established with the aid of the professional bodies at the end of the First World War.

In 1951, the Labour government proposed a significant expansion of technology teaching in the universities and improved financial assistance for selected technical colleges, together with the establishment of a College of Technologists to grant national academic awards. The Conservative governments which followed abandoned the proposal for a College, and it was not until 1964 that the Council for National Academic Awards (CNAA) was established. Nine colleges of advanced technology were reformed as universities in the period 1960-1970, while the CNAA degrees were used as the basis of certification in the remaining reorganized polytechnics, which took responsibility for education to sub-degree level.

Reform of the training system was even slower. The Technical and Business Education Councils began their work in the late 1970s to replace the century-old pattern of training qualifications administered by the Royal Society of Arts, the City and Guilds Institute and the professional bodies. The new National and Higher Certificates still had to gain acceptance from employers who were reluctant in some areas (such as banking) to recognize the new qualifications.

The Conservative government of 1959-64 gave the responsibility for training provision to Industrial Training Boards (ITBs), composed of representatives of employers, trade unions and the state. In 1964, when they were founded, the Boards covered over 60 per cent of the workforce. They were funded on the basis of a compulsory training levy of around one per cent of an employer's payroll, 90 per cent of which was repaid in grants to those who conducted training to Board standards. Training facilities within industry were supplemented by new government facilities and programmes.

In 1973, this system was modified by bringing the ITBs under the control of a new body, the Manpower Services Commission (MSC), which was also given responsibility for the Employment Service.

France

State involvement with the provision of qualified engineers began in 1775, with the establishment of the Ecole des Ponts et des Chaussées. The French revolution of 1789, and successive revolutions ensured this early tradition of state involvement in the provision of qualified engineers by establishing a further 40 Grandes Ecoles, each quite distinct from the universities, coming under the control of the Ministry appropriate to the vocational area rather than the Department of Education.

State influence on lower levels of vocational training was also developed. Throughout the nineteenth century, schools were established to provide technical training for aspiring foremen, technicians and middle managers. Towards the end of the century, the state began to establish lower-level craft training at Centres d'Apprentissage, which have developed into today's Lycées Techniques and Colleges d'Enseignement Techniques. It is significant that these developments were accelerated after the French defeat in the 1870-71 War and again after the two World Wars.

The 1968 events in France led to a series of agreements establishing a framework for continuing education and training which later applied, by law, to the whole of the working population. The framework provided for compulsory attendance, without loss of pay, at vocational training courses of up to 40 days per annum for all young workers under the age of 18. Adults who lost their jobs through redundancy became entitled to paid educational leave from the time of receipt of notice. There is now a minimum entitlement for all workers with more than two years' service to take leave of absence of up to 1,200 hours in any eight-year period. Training is run at plant or inter-plant training centres which operate under joint management-union control. The state exercises financial and technical control over the centres and supervises training standards. Workers' representation is achieved by collective agreements with the unions on training policy, and statutory consultative arrangements.

Germany

In developing its education and training institutions, Germany followed a path between Britain and France. The first half of the nineteenth century saw the establishment of higher technical schools which, though quite separate from the university system, shared the same structure, rights and rank as the universities and, with state support, developed close links with industry. Often top management in industry consisted of the graduates of these technical universities, and board members held senior faculty positions.

In contrast with France and its emphasis on school leavers, Germany made early provision for special schools to train foremen and middle managers from the ranks of mature students with considerable work experience. A hierarchy of technical schools developed below the universities — Fachhochschulen — to give three years' training to middle management and Fachschulen to run courses for prospective foremen and technicans. This system was rationalized in 1969, with the establishment of the Federal Institute of Vocational Training Research. The Minister of Economic Affairs was given responsibility for drawing up lists of occupations requiring formal training, establishing job descriptions, model training syllabi and examination standards.

In 1976, a new body, the Federal Institute for Vocational Training took over the work of the Research Institute, and the related responsibilities of the Minister. It is funded by a collective levy on all companies above a certain size of up to one quarter per cent of their wage and salary bill. In 1977, more than 50 per cent of school leavers entered vocational training. The government also announced its intention, in its objectives for the 1980s, of moving towards a system of paid educational leave as in France.

Japan

The development of state education and training in Western Europe was highly influential in the later industrialization of Japan. Early engineers and scientists received much of their training from European universities and colleges. The Japanese government supported the training overseas of their students on a large scale, and imported European academics to establish their universities and technical colleges.

Japanese science and technology policy started as a part of the modernization programme undertaken by the Meiji government which came to power in 1868. Many of the then advanced industries, such as iron and steel, were started as government enterprises — and the Japanese government also introduced science and technology into the universities. A deliberate policy was followed of importing Western academics to establish new universities and technical colleges, most of which started with an engineering school or faculty.

The benefits of the longstanding co-ordination of education and training with industrial policy can be seen in the high level of qualifications amongst the Japanese workforce. In 1971 there were 200,000 engineers and science graduates with more than two years' experience, the third highest figure in the world, and higher in proportion to population than any Western European country. In 1973, 90 per cent of school leavers had received secondary education and 32 per cent post-secondary education, and a third of these were science and technology graduates. By 1980, Japan was producing more engineering graduates than America and many more technicians.

In addition to their teaching functions, universities undertook the major part of basic research. In the 1970s, this represented 90 per cent of all basic research, and was heavily weighted towards engineering (35 per cent) and medicine (43 per cent). In 1981, the government set out for the first time to ally this capability to industrial research objectives, in order to develop a range of fifth generation computer systems. The government was concerned to co-ordinate the strategic plans of the state and private sectors. They concluded that: 'if we want to control the next phase of worldwide application (of technology) . . . the state will have to intervene more in co-operation with the firms and laboratories of the private sector.'[6] Government is focusing resources into two key areas: education and health. In health, the emphasis is on the computerization of hospitals; aids for remote diagnosis; accelerated treatment of emergencies; and a general support for the oldest segment of the population.

America

In the US, the early nineteenth century saw various local initiatives for the promotion of science, which culminated in the establishment of the Smithsonian Institute in Washington in 1846, dedicated to the: 'increase and diffusion of knowledge among men'. The foundation of the US National Academy of Science followed in 1863 to: 'investigate, examine, experiment and report upon any subject of art', referred to it by government.

State involvement stimulated the activity of the largely self-educated engineers who opened up the American continent. The light engineering industry produced goods for the newly-enlarged domestic market, and developed rapidly in the middle of the nineteenth century following the invention of the sewing machine, typewriter, the Yale Lock and the bicycle. The requirements for skilled manpower generated by this rapid industrialization led to the establishment of three classes of scientific and technological education by the end of the nineteenth century. These were private schools, such as MIT and Rensseleur, based on the Ecole Centrale de Paris; privately supported schools, attached to established colleges and universities such as Union College, Harvard, Yale and Dartmouth; and State and Federally supported schools, such as the University of Michigan. Particularly important were the Land Grant Colleges, established in 1861 by the Federal government for the 'encouragement of agriculture and the mechanic arts'. Each state was offered a grant of public land in proportion to its population: 'to promote the liberal and practical education of the industrial classes in the several pursuits and professions of life.'[7]

THE STATE AND THE DIFFUSION OF TECHNOLOGY

Britain

As the pace of technological change accelerated towards the end of the nineteenth century, governments began to build on their earlier involvement in education by developing policies aimed at sponsoring research and development. This was to give British governments new responsibilities for directing both government research and research in industry, for setting technical standards, and for supervising standards as an element of trade policy.

State involvement in research and development began in earnest in response to the establishment in Germany of the Physikalisch Reichsanstalt, in Charlotenburg in 1895. The National Physical Laboratory, modelled on this establishment, was founded in Britain in 1909 to maintain standards of national importance, to test scientific instruments, and to undertake other similar tasks.

The experience of the First World War underlined the fact — to the British government and scientific and industrial establishments — that its technology lagged behind Germany. The government's response to the problem was to appoint an eminent scientist, Lord Haldane, to recommend an appropriate structure to encourage national research and development. Haldane's 'machinery of government' committee proposed a number of independent research bodies, funded by, but operating wholly separate, from government. These were funded by the Department of Scientific and Industrial Research (DSIR), which, as an historian of British science/state relations of the period, L Vig, notes:'. . . was for nearly 50 years . . . the most important government agency for support of civil sciences in Britain'.[8]

Quintin Hogg, the first and only Minister for Science, was to comment in 1961 that the Haldane principle and practice were:

> 'basically sound . . . the research councils are kept separate from, and free from control by, the executive departments in order to safeguard their integrity and maintain their independence.'[9]

The various research associations funded by the DSIR, together with other research projects in defence, agriculture and aviation, were kept very much in separate compartments; they were also given meagre resources. DSIR expenditure tripled between its inception in 1919 and 1939, but even in 1939 it still received only £1 million. This was not wildly out of line with the expenditure of other governments, but a critical weakness in the case of the UK was that corporate R and D expenditure had not caught up with levels reached by US and German rivals.

The Second World War graphically demonstrated the results of applied R and D. Radar, the jet engine, rocketry and the atomic bomb were strong arguments in favour of effective science, and the change in attitude they helped to foster was in part responsible for an increase in government R and D expenditure, from £6.5 million in 1945-46 to £30 million in 1950-51. The DSIR budget was doubled, and spending in the universities went up five-fold. The National Research Development Corporation was founded in 1949 with a capital of £5 million. Industrial working parties were formed and a tripartite committee on productivity was set up.

The 1950s saw two tendencies. Interest in science and technology increased, at least amongst MPs, while the Parliamentary Scientific Committee was successful in promoting interest in, and action on, the expansion of technical education.

Yet the pattern of R and D became firmly oriented towards defence and aviation on the one hand, and atomic power on the other — projects owing more to conceptions of 'national prestige' than trade policy. Defence and aviation were boosted by the onset of the cold war in general and the UK's participation in the Korean War in particular, while atomic power rapidly assumed the status of a national mission. Expenditure on the United Kingdom Atomic Energy Authority rose from £47 million in 1954-55 to £106 million in 1958-59, and while the programme resulted in the UK taking a clear international lead in atomic power research and development during that period, the technical leadership then held has not resulted at the present time in a sustained leadership in domestic nuclear programmes, nor in export opportunities for UK power plant companies.

As one of the foremost commentators on science policy, Chris Freeman, has noted, Britain tended to concentrate its research in precisely those areas in which the US also was concentrating its R and D resources; and the UK could scarcely hope to win such a contest. In addition, the problems of scale and of the high risk of failure in the projects chosen were exacerbated:

'by some extraordinarily inept public decision-making in relation to big technology throughout the 1950s and 1960s . . . commercial and market factors were frequently ignored, and even the most elementary project evaluation procedures were honoured more in the breach than in the observance . . . even the considerable British R and D work in military electronics did not provide the basis for exploitation of civil electronic markets to any great extent, although the potential here was and remains enormous.'[10]

With the election of the Labour government in 1964 much changed, but it is a mistake to see this new government as a complete watershed. First, the temptation to indulge in prestige projects was not confined to the Conservative Party, as witness the Concorde project. Second, as we have suggested above, forces for change had been gathering momentum for some time. Indeed, there had been an alternative ideology to the 'Haldane principle' since that principle had become practice. Third, although the Labour governments of 1964-70 did a good deal of administrative reshuffling, there was little change in the priorities of government support.

Among scientists and the 'scientific establishment', the 'anti-Haldane-ites' were considered to be of the left. Before the Second World War, socialist and communist scientists, of whom Bernal was the most out-standing, had advocated state support for science and high-technology projects, often using the example of the Soviet Union to show up the UK's policies in an unfavourable light. Many of Bernal's prescriptions, though part of a general critique of capitalism and a programme of revolutionary change (as he saw it) could be and were adapted later by social democrats as part of their programme of increased interventionism within the broad consensus of 1950s and 1960s politics.

Anti-Haldanites were also to be found in the Tory ranks. From 1956, government and company expenditure on R and D was increased. The DSIR began a number of studies, and stepped up its aid to industry. Two reports — the Zuckerman Report (1961) on government research and the Trend Report (1963) on the organization of civil science called for more expenditure. The Trend Report suggested the replace-ment of the DSIR with a Science Research Council which still retained the ethos of the Haldane principle of scientific autonomy.

Among the Tory 'radicals' were Edward Heath and Robert Carr, both of whom favoured increased centralization and supervision of scientific effort. Carr chaired a Tory backbench committee on science which recommended that: 'the government's influence should be recognized and deliberately directed to meeting the economic and scientific needs of the nation, and that the machinery of government should be adapted to this purpose'.[11]

Between these Tories and the Labour Party's mainstream of thought on the subject, there were few differences of substance.

Prior to 1964 the Labour Party received various bits of advice: a committee chaired by Robert Maxwell, the publisher, advocated American-style R and D support; a report by Lord Taylor called for priority to be given to expanding university places; while Richard Crossman, appointed by Wilson as spokesman on education and science and chairman of the Party's science and industry sub-committee, recommended a much-enlarged government stake in R and D, backed up by the NRDC.

Wilson put himself behind the last of these strains. In many speeches after assuming the leadership, he placed the issue on the top of a future Labour government's agenda. For example, in his keynote address to the Labour Party's 1963 conference, he said:

'The central thread of Labour's policy, the key to our plan to redynamize the British economy, is our plan to mobilize the talent of our scientists and technicians, redeployed from missiles and warheads on research and development contracts, civil research and development to produce the new instruments and tools of economic advance . . .'[12]

The major proposals of the Trend Report were implemented by the incoming Labour government. The new Ministry of Technology, Mintech, which took over the functions of Trend's proposed Industrial Research and Development Authority, was initially given responsibility for computers, electronics, telecommunications and machine tools, and later took on mechanical and electrical engineering, and motor vehicles. It was equipped with a range of policy tools to improve the performance of the industries it was to sponsor, from the use of the NRDC through development contracts with government laboratories to undertake industrial research to the creation of new enterprises.

Mintech introduced the principle of the 'market test' for industrially related government research, through its proposal to merge its atomic energy and industrial research establishments to form a British Research and Development Corporation (BRDC). Although the idea was lost with Labour's defeat in the 1970 election, the market test principle resurfaced in Lord Rothschild's report in 1971 'A Framework for Government Research and Development'. Rothschild's proposals, subsequently implemented, formalized the 'customer-contractor' basis for applied R and D. The structure was to involve a: 'series of broadly based requirements boards which would be given a direct customer responsibility for the R and D fields allocated to them and would be expected to play the leading role in determining the balance of government-sponsored R and D programmes within these fields.' Government laboratories would have to apply to these requirement boards for finance in place of the old system in which research programmes were effectively established within the laboratories themselves, only requiring endorsement by advisory committees and the chief scientists.

Two brief points should be made regarding Mintech. The first was that its Minister was largely responsible in giving the word 'intervention' a new meaning: that of being a systematic attempt, through fiscal and legislative means, but also through extensive demand management, state ownership, and a battery of formal and informal incentives and disincentives to achieve various economic objectives. These economic objectives under Labour governments were backed up with policies designed to promote public ownership as a *social* objective, conforming to Clause IV of the Party's constitution. Second, the 'White heat of technology' initiative was long overdue and inadequate when it came. The explanations for this have at their core the long-term relative decline of UK industry, its historic neglect of R and D and its reliance, especially in the electrical/electronics sector, on foreign innovation and entrepreneurship. Also, Conservative philosophy and practice was often inimical to state-directed industrial growth.

Labour's practice in 1964-70 was, to a considerable extent, an attempt to emulate the best practice of state capitalist economies elsewhere, and this remains a central concern of many in the labour movement. However, the instrument which was to have underpinned that attempt, the Department of Economic Affairs, failed to carry out its brief. Planning on the *supply* side of the economy — a vital corollary to any initiatives which might be taken by the Ministry of Technology — virtually collapsed back into demand management. 'Intervention' tended to be *ad hoc* rather than strategic, either as a response to pressures from capital (on bankruptcies) or labour (on unemployment). Bureaucracy grew, but its efficiency did not grow commensurately.

Labour's industrial policy in the 1970s attempted to break with this pattern. A new emphasis was put on strategic planning through the NEDC, with an executive agency, the National Enterprise Board (NEB) playing a key role in implementing government interventions. In Chapter 6 we will examine the circumstances behind this change of policy, and its practical implications, and we will briefly comment on its demise, and replacement by the policies of the free market.

France

The British approach to developing state research and development has not been shared by other governments, most of them to the Right of the political spectrum in other capitalist or mixed economies. The French have adopted an increasingly self-confident attitude towards the development of new technology since the war. During the 1960s, the Conservative government promoted the Plan Calcul, aimed at establishing an indigenous French computer industry. By the 1970s, its concern had broadened to include the modernization of the telecommunications network, and the need to bring the local industry under French control. Towards the end of the decade it published the influential Nora-Minc report (1980) setting out a basis for state control of the whole range of social consequences of the new technology.

French policy towards the electronics industry has been heavily influenced by what happened in 1966, when the US government vetoed the export of a Control Data computer for the national atomic energy programme. The French government was determined neither to be exposed to foreign suppliers of advanced electronic components, nor to have their domestic computer and telecommunications industries under foreign, or even European, control. It was for this reason that they pulled CII out of the EEC-backed Unidata computer manufacturing consortium and in 1975 arranged to merge it with Honeywell Bull with French majority shareholding. The amalgamated company was given a guarantee of state purchase of £475 million of equipment, or equivalent compensation over its first four years. A similar initiative was taken in minicomputers, where the government brought about the forced amalgamation of the two major French companies to create SEMS (part

119

of Thomson-CSF), while in computer terminals and peripherals 'growth contracts' were concluded with six selected firms.

It has been in the field of telecommunications that the last French government made its major efforts. As late as the early 1970s French telecommunications was regarded as something of a joke. In 1976, two interlinked initiatives were taken by the French government. It radically restructured French ownership of telecommunications, especially in exchange manufacture; and the VIIth plan identified telecommunications, together with computers, as the most vital sectors of the economy. The result has been to raise French-controlled sales of telecommunications equipment to the domestic market from 43 per cent in 1975 to 71 per cent in 1977 — and in the crucial area of telephone exchanges, from 31 per cent to 81 per cent.

Finally, the French government has sought to iron out the stop-go tendencies in telecommunications investment by setting up a tripartite planning structure between the Planning Agency, the Directeur Général de Téléphone (DGT) and the National Assembly, carefully separating out long- from short-range plans. The DGT is given responsibility for the implementation of agreed plans.

Various changes were made to the structure of industry to support the plan. Before the changeover to digital exchanges, the government forced the foreign transnational companies, ITT and Ericsson, to transfer key subsidiaries to Thomson, and directed orders away from the remaining ITT company CGCT. The French General Electric Company CGE's shares in CII-Honeywell-Bull were transferred to Saint-Gobain-Pont-à-Mousson and converted into a controlling stake.

Having rationalized the structure of the industry the government set out to establish an indigenous capability in electronic component research, development and production. FFr.600 million (£53 million) were allocated from 1979-84 to encourage various major research efforts, such as the extension of existing production of large volume integrated circuits and the creation of new manufacturing units for components not yet produced in France. Between 1975 and 1980 investments in telecommunications amounted to £8.3 billion and spending is continuing at a rate of £3 billion per annum. The task of the DGT is not only to modernize the French telephone service but to use its purchasing power to establish French industry as a world leader in information technology products. To this end, the DGT has become heavily involved in the promotion of view-data systems (in head on competition with the British), facsimile transmissions, satellite transmission and optical fibres.

In late 1982, the DGT took charge of France's first major initiative in cable TV. In sharp contrast to British intentions, the DGT was given charge of the installation of the cable network, at a cost unofficially estimated to be some £400 million.

The operation of the system is to be decentralized, but the initial cabinet announcement in November did not specify whether or not private capital would be allowed to participate. The installation is to coincide with the expected introduction of satellite TV in 1985. Satellite-beamed programmes will be distributed through local cable networks from collective receiving stations. It is planned that 1.4 million households will be wired up by 1985.

The French decision to use state power and finance to boost their information industries to a position where they are fully competitive with those of the US and Japan is one which originated in the VIIth Plan under President Giscard D'Estaing and has been carried further under President Mitterrand.

The Mitterrand socialist government has, since its election in 1980, demonstrated its willingness to strengthen state power to achieve its aim. Power has grown at all levels of government — central, regional and local; the most obvious accretion of central power has been the nationalization of the five major technically advanced companies, together with 36 banks and two finance companies and much of the steel industry.

President Mitterrand made it clear that he did not intend to allow French business to be dominated by centres of power in New York, Tokyo or London. Elsewhere, he has been quoted as saying: 'I am doing with nationalization what de Gaulle did for nuclear defence. I am giving France its economic strike force'.[13] Yet he and his ministers and advisors know that mere nationalization is not enough: and they have been careful, in their pursuit of a vigorous pro-EEC policy, to distinguish nationalization from nationalism.

In an economy used to central control (somewhat lessened since de Gaulle but still considerable under Pompidou and Giscard), the socialists operate as super-interventionists, unable or unwilling to strike a full-blooded 'contract' with their natural allies, labour.

However, the government is acting as far as possible in what it sees to be the interests of workers. It has taxed large accumulations of wealth and increased tenants' rights, and it has curbed the power of employers and enjoined both employers and unions to negotiate wages once a year. It has set a target of reducing the working week from 40 to 35 hours; it has proposed 'solidarity contracts' with companies, under which companies which create new jobs by work sharing or early retirement schemes would be favoured by state aid and contracts.

Mitterrand has also proclaimed his desire to: 're-conquer the domestic market' by aiding all companies in every sector to produce more, more efficiently. Naturally, this policy has raised fears of protectionism and feather-bedding clapped-out industries — though in practice, eg the steel industry, the government appears willing to let unused capacity go.

Foreign, particularly US, penetration of the French market has risen sharply in a number of sectors, as the table below shows. Over the latter half of the 1970s, French companies cut back their investment, thus exacerbating the problem. By boosting investment, partly through the newly nationalized key sectors, the French government hopes to reverse that trend. It will probably help the process by applying selective import ceilings in some of the sectors in the table. However, the second aim, of applying computer technology to all levels of French industry, is necessary for the 're-conquering' of the domestic and overseas markets.

	1970	1975	1981
semi-manufactured goods	21.9	22.3	28.8
household goods	27.5	38.2	51.7
capital goods	25.0	26.1	37.3
transport equipment	18.5	22.2	29.3
industrial products	17.4	20.5	28.7

Source: National Statistical Office/Financial Times

Table 2. Foreign penetration of the French market (percentages)

The French have taken a quite different line from the Japanese whose planning system they much admire and wish to copy. Not content with investing heavily in new sectors, such as electronics, they are attempting to modernize old industries as well — industries which other advanced countries have all but conceded to developing countries. M Alain Boublil, the influential Presidential advisor on industrial policy, told the *Financial Times*:[14] 'You can make shoes in old factories using out-of-date machines and traditional methods. Or you can use computer design, advanced numerical-controlled machined tools and modern methods. If you do the latter you can be competitive in France'.

The French government's policy towards R and D and technical change has been less noticed abroad than its commitment to fight unemployment. Yet funds deployed for R and D by the present Industry and Research Minister, Jean Pierre Chevennement, are considerable, exceeding $1 billion in 1982, a 30 per cent rise from the previous year. The aim is to raise expenditure on research and development from 1.8 per cent of GDP — a low figure for an advanced economy — to 2.5 per cent by 1985.

Transnational capital was clearly alarmed by President Mitterrand's victory. Though its stake in the French economy is not quite so large as in West Germany and the UK, it is still massive. In 1977, US companies had total assets (including minority holdings) in France worth $24.3 billion with sales of over $34 billion and nearly 500,000 employees.[15] Through their management of their foreign exchange portfolios they have been able to exert considerable pressure on the government, and the franc has been devalued twice since Mitterrand's election.

A survey in *Fortune*[16] soon after the election quoted Walter Hays, Vice President of Ford in charge of political affairs, as saying that: 'our export dollar value is greater than the whole Bordeaux wine industry. Mitterrand would be a fool to tamper with that'. Rand Araskog, Chairman of ITT, is reported as telling his board that: 'we expect the French government will act responsibly'.

Governments come and go, but Ford of France survives. It is a comforting nostrum and there are three reasons for believing this is so:

1. Investment is not all one-way. Renault, the state-owned car company, has a controlling stake in AMC, the number four US car maker. French investment, especially in the US electronic sector, has grown rapidly in recent years.
2. France needs US microelectronics skill, and its leading electronics companies have signed a number of deals with US companies to enable them to transfer their technology.
3. Companies with $24 billion assets and $34 billion sales cannot be treated in a cavalier fashion, especially as the largest — Ford, General Motors, IBM — all run increasingly integrated operations, of which France is a part. The two big car companies are moving rapidly along the 'world car' route, while IBM has been making 'world computers' for decades. It is pointless to nationalize plants which are making parts of products, assembled from the components manufactured all over Europe, a point which has certainly occurred to the companies which make them.

Nationalization of the leading companies will, if successful, allow France to deal on rather better terms with the TNCs because it will put more capital at the disposal of French companies and will aid their technological advance. It will also largely remove from them the possibility of being taken over. However, they will have to deal with transnational capital in both domestic and foreign markets. Mergers, joint ventures, joint financing deals and the like will continue to be an increasing part of French industrial and commercial life, as they are in all advanced economies.

Germany

The tendency towards increasing state intervention is not confined to France. Even in West Germany, government has steadily extended its concern with the promotion of technological change. West Germany has developed a range of institutions to promote the application of science and technology, initially at state level, and, since the mid-1960s, at federal level. By 1975, the budget of the Federal Ministry of Research and Technology, which excludes defence, and the science component of the Ministry of Education, exceeded $1.5 billion. This was channelled through industry-wide research laboratories in high technology such as nuclear power, advanced electronics and aerospace. In addition, via the Organization for the Rationalization of German Industry (RKW), a non-profit making organization with some 10,000 members, extensive managerial and technical advice was available to small companies.

Since 1967, the government has spent more than £1.2 billion in support of its data processing industry. The first programme, 1967-70, took the form of loans and grants for the development, production and sale of computer equipment and parts. In addition, funds were provided to assist small- and medium-sized companies with their first computer installation, and contributions made towards computer centres which would be used by groups of small firms. A second area of investment was through the Science Ministry, where £5 million was provided for research, regional computer centres, information exchange and the opening of training centres.

These schemes were considerably expanded in the second and third programmes, from 1971-79, during which time public sector purchasing was used to increase Siemens' share of the domestic market to 20 per cent. The programme aimed at covering all areas of fast growth, semiconductors, computer hardware, peripherals, software and applications, and covered basic research, applied industrial research, education and training. From 1980-83 a further £250 million is to be provided to develop an information technology industry, and enhance the country's communications infrastructure.

To disseminate knowledge of the new technologies the government established a centre in Berlin in 1978, to produce educational material, advise industry on new products and processes, promote products developed with government assistance, and carry out commercial studies. It is assisted in this work by the Chambers of Commerce, and the RKW.

Japan

Japan represents an illuminating case of the successful application of state science and technology policy. As A Singh remarked:

> 'It is paradoxical that at one level the Japanese government has very little direct control over output compared with that of other capitalist economies . . . however, in Japan the government has played a far more fundamental role in the post-war reconstruction of industry than in any of the other advanced industrial economies.'[17]

Japanese governments have regarded technology policy as a central area of state activity ever since Japan was forcibly opened to world markets in the nineteenth century. Initially, the government was concerned to build up an indigenous technical competence. This was achieved by the careful importing of selected Western technologies and their local adoption, often in state enterprises and laboratories, to the Japanese environment.

After the Second World War the government was instrumental in rebuilding Japan's economy with the explicit goal of relying heavily on science and technology to catch up with Europe and America. During the first phase, from 1945 to 1950, the major effort in manpower and resources was placed into reconstructing the coal, iron and steel industries, and re-establishing the basic economic cycle of coal feeding steel production, to create products for the coal industry. From 1950 to 1955, the objective was to shift the centre of gravity of Japan's industrial structure away from the older sectors towards advanced industries, namely machinery, electrical machinery, metals, chemicals and, somewhat later, electronics.

In the Japanese industrial strategy, technology policy was complemented by interventionist policies for commercialization, investment and marketing. Companies were encouraged to look for market share rather than short-term profitability. This meant developing low-cost high volume plants using the best available production engineering technology while limiting product variety.

Responsibility for industrial technology was vested in the Ministry of International Trade and Industry (MITI) through which the government developed a range of instruments to support its strategy. These included:

(a) Control of the import of technology, through regulations on foreign exchange.
(b) Control of investment through the Japan Development Bank and commercial banks.
(c) Protection of markets by import regulations.
(d) Tax benefits, special amortization provisions, allocation of raw material, land use, special laws for promotion of specific industries, etc.
(e) The granting of exemptions from cartel regulations.
(f) Restrictions on the export of capital.

Priority in the importing of technology was given to groups already developing indigenous technology. Company plans were required to conform with sectoral plans established by joint industry-government advisory committees, and they had to be consistent with the goal of transforming the industrial structure. Both government and industry developed supporting science and technology monitoring organizations throughout the world: industry through extensive trading companies, and government through Jetro, the Japan External Trade Organization.

Because of the scarcity of funds, government money channelled through the Japan Development Bank played a major role in financing industries, and commercial banks generally followed the government lead. Special temporary measures or laws were introduced to promote specific science-based industry, by allocating investment funds on favourable terms, tax benefits, or exemptions from the anti-cartel laws if industry agreed to follow the prescribed programme. The 1947 Anti-Monopoly Act gave the Fair Trade Commission broad powers. Following amendments in 1953 and 1977, exemptions from its restrictions can be authorized in a number of circumstances; such as when the price of goods falls below the average cost of production (and a great number of producers are likely to be forced to discontinue business); or where it is necessary to rationalize business in order to improve technology, quality of goods, efficiency or to reduce costs; or to prevent excessive competition between small- and medium-size enterprises.

Information technology has been at the heart of the latest phase of development of the Japanese industrial strategy. Since 1966, the government has provided financial support, including loans, of £1.6 billion. Ojimi, the then Japanese Vice Minister, outlined the reasons for the new policy in 1970:

> 'Industrialization in developing countries will stimulate competitive relations in the markets of advanced nations in products with a low degree of processing. As a result, confrontation between free trade and protectionism will become more intense . . . the solution of this problem is to be found according to economic logic, in progressively giving away industries to other countries much as a big brother gives his outgrown clothes to his younger brother. In this way, a country's own industries become more sophisticated.'[18]

Government assistance to the new technology area was granted in three major areas. First, the government gave financial assistance to Japanese manufacturers, to assist them to gain a larger share of the home computer market. It promoted the Japan Electric Computer Corporation, which was funded by the seven Japanese computer manufacturers and the Japan Development Bank, to purchase computers from the manufacturers and lease them to customers. By the end of 1978, the gross value of JECC's rented assets was over 400 billion yen.

Second, the government has attempted to maintain the home market through various restrictions. Until the mid-1970s quantitative restrictions were applied to the importing of both components and computer systems, and MITI continued, until recently, to dissuade Japanese companies from purchasing foreign-made machines where a domestic equivalent existed. Restrictions were also applied to the establishment of foreign-owned manufacturing operations in Japan, which were lifted only under pressure from the American government, in exchange for Japanese access to US rocket technology. In the public sector, an informal procurement policy exists, as a result of which 90 per cent of the computer market is taken by Japanese companies, compared to 50-60 per cent of the overall market. Similar policies are followed for telecommunications.

Third, the government provides funds for up to 25 per cent of all computer-related R and D in Japan. Two tax measures, the R and D tax credit and the accelerated depreciation of research and development facilities offer further assistance to the industry, amounting to five per cent of their total R and D expenditure. In practice, a system has emerged in which there is industrial co-operation in the funding of new projects, but continued competition in existing products.

As we have seen in Chapter 3, Japan has now reached the stage where its information technology companies can contemplate forming alliances with older transnational firms in exploiting new technology worldwide.

America

In America, the Second World War saw the creation of sophisticated government involvement in industry with the introduction of the federal research and development contract. This linked the government with industry in pursuit of scientific and technological development. D K Price has identified five new relationships which developed between government agencies and private institutions as a result of the contract system. In the first instance there were straightforward contracts placed for research leading to specific objectives such as equipment improvement. Secondly, master contracts were placed with an organization which allowed a continuing relationship to develop between the agency and the contractor with the minimum of formality. Thirdly, there were cases of tactical and strategic studies which had previously been carried out by the military being subcontracted. Fourthly, to meet the need for new large-scale laboratories to meet military requirements for scientific and managerial competence, the universities joined the government in establishing special off-campus laboratories. Finally, new private bodies such as the Rand Corporation were specifically established to undertake federal contracts. These funding mechanisms, which reached a peak of $176 million in 1968, coupled with government procurement policy, were to lead to the growth of new industries, in particular in aerospace, electronic components, and computers.

Although America still enjoys a considerable lead in the development of new technology, deficiencies in the rate of application and growing competition have led to further government initiatives in science and technology in the 1970s. Since the war, the scale of government spending, especially in space and defence applications, has contributed greatly to the technological strength of the country. Nevertheless, by the 1970s it was becoming apparent that the technological base of older sectors of the economy had fallen behind. Attention was drawn to this decline in American competitiveness in commercial technology intensive areas in 1971, when, for the first time since 1893, the country's balance of payments went into the red, by $1.5 billion. By the mid-1970s, anxiety was being expressed about the construction, railroad, metal casting, shipping and automotive industries, and by the end of the decade this anxiety had extended to the new technology industries themselves.

The government has recently returned to a more direct policy of intervention in new technology industry in response to the Japanese challenge. The Department of Defence established a $200 million microelectronics project to run until 1985, for the design and development of advanced integrated circuits. This represented the first direct grant to industry for basic research since the rundown of the space programme in the early 1970s, and demonstrated that government promotion of the development and application of new technology had become a permanent feature of the US economy.

Acting on the recommendation of the Science and Technology Office, the Commerce Department carried out a review in 1979 of the mechanisms for promoting innovation in industry. Their study proposed 32 measures to reform the environment in which research and innovation are carried out in order to facilitate economic growth. Comprehensive proposals were made in the areas of patents, anti-trust policy and federal regulations. The Labour and Commerce Departments were to establish a national labour/technology forecasting system to develop advance warning of industrial changes and permit timely adjustments, while the National Technical Information Service was to establish a new centre, with an annual budget of $2 million, to improve the flow of knowledge from federal laboratories and R and D centres to private industry.

CONCLUSION

The increasing involvement of the state with industrial innovation has led to many successes in the development of new products and processes, Governments, by directly stimulating demand, by subsidy, or by establishing technical infrastructure; or indirectly through the universities or through the climate of government regulations have made major contributions to the development of most new technologies. Rothwell and Zegveld have assessed these effects, starting from the initial investment of firms in research and development of products or processes and including subsequent 'improvement' innovations, such as colour television, or successive generations of computers and aircraft. They conclude that governments have made a major contribution to the developments listed below in Table 3.

State involvement has become increasingly self-evident, and the search for appropriate innovation policies has prompted a host of government reports in recent years around the world. This increasing intervention by the state is no longer confined just to advanced countries — whose policies we have described in some detail in this chapter — it is now a universal phenomenon.

Electronic devices and systems	television radar computers transistors integrated circuits NC machine tools electronic instruments optical fibres laser applications satellites	*Nuclear power*	gas-cooled reactors turbo-generators isotopes heavy-water reactors light-water reactors fast-breeder reactors
Synthetic materials and other new chemical products	polyethylene PVC polystyrene synthetic rubber synthetic fibres antibiotics insecticides fertilizers herbicides tranquillizers	*Mechanical engineering equipment and instruments*	shearer-loaders automatic looms potato harvesters cotton pickers bulldozers power tools tower cranes biro pens xerography optical instruments
Engines, motors, transport equipment and durables	turbo-prop engines large aircraft jet engines diesel engines passenger cars and components wankel engine diesel-electric consumer durables	*Processes for basic materials*	direct reduction continuous casting oxygen steel float glass process catalytic cracking gas reforming refinery processes Chorleywood bakery

Source: R Rothwell and W Zegveld *Industrial Innovation and Public Policy*, F Pinter.

Table 3. Some technical innovations arising from significant government intervention

REFERENCES

1 R Millibrand (1969) *The State in Capitalist Society*. Weidenfeld and Nicolson.
2 J K Galbraith (1978) *The New Industrial State*, p 220. Mentor.
3 ibid, p 274.
4 DSIR Report (1948-49) pp 15-16.
5 Final Report of the Committee on Education and Industry (1928) pp 201-202.

6 J J Servan-Schreiber (1980) *The World Challenge*, p 236. Simon and Schuster, New York.

7 G S Emmerson (1973) *Engineering Education*, p 147. David and Charles.

8 L Vig (1966) *Science and Technology in British Politics*, p 12. Pergamon.

9 Q Hogg (1961) 'Science and government'. Fawley Foundation Lecture, p 13. University of Southampton.

10 C Freeman (1979) 'Technical innovation and British trade performance in de-industrialization', p 70. Heinemann/NIESR.

11 Vig, op cit, p 97.

12 H Wilson (1964) Speech to Labour Party conference: 1963 Conference Report. Labour Party.

13 *Financial Times* (1982) 8 January, p 2.

14 *Financial Times* (1982) 8 January, p 15.

15 1977 Benchmark Survey of US Investment Abroad (1981) US Bureau of Economic Analyses International Investment Divisions.

16 *Fortune* (1981) 15 June.

17 A Singh 'The reconstruction of British Industry', p 217. Heinemann/NIESR.

18 I C Magaziner and T M Hout (1980) *Japanese Industrial Policy*, p 6. Policy Studies Institute. January.

CHAPTER 6

The First Social Contract and its Aftermath

INTRODUCTION

Social and economic life in the twentieth century has been increasingly regulated by agreements reached between the state and powerful groups within society. In this chapter we will be concerned with the most explicit of such agreements ever attempted: the UK social contract of 1974-79, and its influence on government policy with respect to the education and training of the workforce, and the diffusion of technology. We will describe the origin of these policies, their implementation by the Labour government, and their subsequent history after the Conservatives came to power in 1979.

SOCIAL CONTRACTS

In his brilliant study of the interaction of state, organized labour and capital in the twentieth century, Keith Middlemas observes that:

> 'while government in the future may well choose between progress towards socialism and reversion to the market order by taking some middle way in which "the state directs and controls predominately private-owned business according to four principles: unity, order, nationalism and success", it makes better sense to argue that the extension of economic management in post-war years on which this line of argument is based has only been possible because of the existing nature of the triangular system, and the power, inherent in corporate bias, of governing institutions to convey popular consent by means other than those of political parties. To imagine power as only positive is an illusion; without assessing negative power, the equation is incomplete.'[1]

(1979)

In the detailed evidence which he has amassed to support that remark, Middlemas has shown that twentieth century political life in the UK has evolved through a series of consensual manoeuvres by successive governments involving employers and unions; not, as many theorists in the 1960s claimed, resulting in the erasing of class differences, but rather ensuring that tactical compromises succeeded.

Within the past two decades these manoeuvres have crystallized round increasingly overt social contracts, though only one, developed between 1972 and 1974 and operational under the Labour government of 1974-79, bore that name. The Labour governments of 1964-70 at first sought TUC and FBI (later CBI) involvement in a National Plan. The NEDC, inherited from the tories, did not gain sufficient strength to act as a directing body, and while the government made it clear *it* defined the national interest, in practice, business interests predominated in the Plan's objectives which concentrated on income rather than price control. Ten years earlier, the government might have been able to rely on trade union support for these modest measures. By the mid to late 1960s, however, the changing political balance of the Labour Party conference's dominant component, the trade unions, meant that Gaitskellite policies could not command automatic support.

Lewis Minkin has catalogued how, after a decade of right wing control in the 1950s, long-term union affiliation, occupational changes, and amalgamations, shifted the balance of power within the Labour Party to the left between 1964 and 1970.[2] By the early 1970s, the left had achieved its strongest position since the formation of the Party, and had made its major priority industrial policy. This was to become the key divide between Left and Right.

On the Centre and Right, Britain's economic decline, relative to other Western countries, was explained by reference to a prevailing anti-manufacturing culture in Britain and the inadequacy of technical education.

The Left saw the roots of decline lying elsewhere: in the economic base. They argued that, as long as Britain could continue to draw rent and profits from overseas investments, the monopoly of overseas natural resources and markets in the old colonies, and its ascendancy in services, such as insurance and shipping, there would be no need to adapt to changing patterns of production. It was this absence of economic imperative, they argued, which was reflected in the weak will to change either education or the cultural atmosphere which was shaped by the educational system. Because of this, motivation for change had to come from the state, by its intervening directly through public ownership of a major company in each sector of the economy to speed up investment and technological innovation. Indirect intervention, through Mintech, had been tried and had been seen to fail.

The left wing rejected incorporation into what it saw as the structures of state capitalism on unfavourable terms. Its members worked with the centre and right of the TUC and with elements in the Labour Party and Cabinet to successfully defeat the Wilson/Castle legislation based on 'In Place of Strife' (1968) which was designed to contain voluntary collective bargaining within a statutory framework. Though 'In Place of Strife' held out the promise of a social contract, the ambitions and power of the trade union movement had run on.

The first social contract to bear the name grew out of the need for the political and industrial wings of the labour movement to re-establish their common purpose after the trauma of 'In Place of Strife'. The vehicle was the TUC/Labour Party Liaison Committee, a body on which the Parliamentary Liaison Party (PLP) and the National Executive Committee (NEC) had separate and equal representation. The Committee was first created in 1971 to discuss oppositon to Heath's Industrial Relations Act, and met only sporadically. It was granted a new lease of life the following year when the Labour Party managed to persuade the TUC of the need for co-operation on a future economic and industrial policy.

The first public fruits of the Liaison Committee's work were displayed in February 1973 in a document called 'Economic policy and the cost of living'. The document, rejecting a statutory incomes policy, was vague about a voluntary one, and promised price controls to help 'prevent the erosion of real wages — and thus influence the whole climate of collective bargaining'. More noteworthy was the very wide range of issues included within the terms of the deal: rents, taxation, increased spending on social services, more investment, full employment, industrial democracy, faster growth . . . the document promised far too much. Yet it was clearly founded on a new principle of explicit status bargaining over the policy of the next government. The document conceded a great deal to the power of the unions, yet it also demanded responsibility.

The struggle over policies within the party continued up to its victory at the polls in February 1974. New elements, such as the National Enterprise Board (NEB) planning agreements, public ownership of 25 major companies and nationalization of the banks, were toned down by Harold Wilson and others in the party leadership, a process which later fuelled much of Tony Benn's attack on the leadership (and his own bid for assumption of it) in the post-1979 period.[3]
tion of it) in the post-1979 period.[3]

The social contract's lack of effectiveness between 1974-79 was much criticized. In 1974-75, rises in earnings reached 30 per cent, with inflation following hard behind. Between 1975 and 1978, earnings were held down by a series of agreed norms. A fourth tentative agreement of five per cent did not gain assent, however.

Though inflation *was* brought down, real living standards also dropped and unemployment rose sharply to over one million. Monetary discipline became enshrined in Treasury practice under Denis Healey — though the strategy was agreed not only by Cabinet, but also by the General Council. Nevertheless, despite this lack of effectiveness, the TUC and Labour Party leadership have argued that the *form* of this social contract, which brought the TUC into a close and influential relationship with the government, represented a major gain for labour.

Indeed, the unions believe that an explicit contract between government and labour (and other groups such as youth, the elderly and the ethnic minorities) can form the basis for a governing alliance which can attract the conditional acquiescence of managers and professional sections.

PLANNING UNDER LABOUR

Manpower Services

Despite the social contract's promise of 'a massive expansion in training and retraining'[4] labour's training and education policies in the period 1974-79 developed as a series of *ad hoc* initiatives in response to the growing unemployment crisis. Although the period saw a vast increase in the resources devoted to training through the Department of Industry and the MSC, this only served to emphasize the existing fragmentation of state education and training provision, and did little to support other aspects of the government's industrial policy.

Under the MSC's direction, the Industrial Training Boards' (ITBs) concentration on craft level training was broadened to a concern for vocational preparation of all young people. The MSC drew attention to the fact that 60 per cent of the half million young people starting work before they were 18 received little or no training from their employers, compared to only 30 per cent in Sweden and 10 per cent in Germany. A 'counter cyclical' Special Training Measures programme was established by the government through the ITBs, under which 30,000-40,000 young people were helped to obtain apprenticeships between 1975 and 1979.

By the mid 1970s, rising unemployment led the government to extend the MSC's work in training unemployed young people and adults. Between 1978-79, 372,000 young workers passed through the Youth Opportunities Programme, and 70,000 training course places were made available to unemployed adults in 1979-80. Towards the end of the 1970s, the general preoccupation of the MSC and ITBs with initial training had given rise to calls for more attention to recurrent training and education.

A government Advisory Committee on Applied Research and Development Report called for: 'the public sector (to) accept much greater responsibility for training', and recommended introducing a service-related 'training benefit' similar to that in France.[5]

The National Economic Development Council

Wilson's moderation of the Party's programme of 1973 was embodied, as far as planning was concerned, in the device of the Industrial Strategy, which in part replaced the large role seen in the programme for the NEB and for the conclusion of planning agreements between major companies and government.

There were five elements in Wilson's new approach:

1. Better co-ordination of public policies affecting the efficiency of industry.
2. More efficient use of the instruments of industrial policy and financial assistance to industry.
3. Consideration of the need for sufficient profits for investment and innovation.
4. Effective manpower policies.
5. An improvement in planning both in industry and government.[6]

The government committed itself to expanding the tripartite Economic Development Councils (EDCs) by adding a number of similarly constituted Sector Working Parties (SWPs) to cover 32 major manufacturing sectors in all. By 1979, this number had reached 48. It aimed to establish a planning framework for each sector which drew attention to the prospects, strengths and weaknesses of the industries, which would take the form of a five-year rolling programme. This was to be discussed at national level at the NEDC, at industry level in the SWPs and EDCs, and at company level: 'primarily though not exclusively in the context of planning agreements'.

The attitude of both the unions and the employers towards the NEDC exercise had changed since it was first established in the climate of consensus of 1962. During the 1960s, the economy was expanding and the employers' side appeared to recognize that necessary industrial restructuring could not be brought about by market forces alone. The exercise was seen by the unions as opening up participation in a whole range of new questions: from finance, investment, manpower, production, government assistance, marketing, overseas sales, to the questions of the relationships between industry and their sponsoring Ministries.

By the 1970s, the enthusiasm of the previous decade was on the wane. The introduction of the 1971 Industrial Relations Act by the Conservative government had put a great strain on the operations of the NEDC. The participation of full-time officials delegated to represent the unions fell off as the demands of the new employment legislation and the developing systems of collective bargaining increased. The employers, too, revised their earlier approach and now sought to use the Industrial Strategy more as a way of lobbying the government on management-oriented questions.

It was against this background that Wilson's expansion of the NEDC's work took place. The unions changed the nature of their representation by appointing lay officers for the first time, while the new employers' representatives also tended to come from plant rather than national level. It was soon apparent, however, that the exercise was designed to by-pass any company-based discussions or planning agreements. The employers continued their tactic of bringing forward agenda items of immediate concern to them, such as steel requirements and export guarantee anomalies. The unions' response was to press demands related to import substitution and manpower problems and to try to push the discussions down to company level.

The TUC's gains from Wilson's NEDC exercise were extremely limited. By the end of four years of the Industrial Strategy, they had won only one regional conference for plant level representatives from each sector to come together to discuss the Strategy.

Import penetration targets had been established by less than half of the EDCs and SWPs. Indeed, over the period of the Industrial Strategy from 1975-78, 19 Sectors, covering in the main science-based industries, had reported a rise in import penetration. In manufacturing as a whole import penetration rose from 18 per cent in 1973 to just under 25 per cent in 1979.

The Strategy had, however, brought trade unions further experience of the industrial and economic policy-making by government, and of the strategic planning carried out by companies, at official (rather than merely general secretary) level. It pointed out the direction for the further development of the unions' own industrial policy. At the TUC Congress in September 1979 (after the fall of the Labour government) a resolution on industrial strategy and industrial democracy was carried, which stated that:

☐ Multi-union committees needed to be established at company and plant level.

☐ Pressure should be exerted to gain joint control over company strategic plans — especially because of the rapid development in technology.

☐ Links should be established between this activity and the TUC's work on the SWPs and EDCs.[7]

Planning Agreements

As conceived by Wilson, planning agreements would be drawn up between the government and major companies to cover the main areas of their strategic plan. Agreement would be a by-product of the annual corporate planning cycle, following government and company dialogue. Unions would be invited to take part in these consultations and they would be kept informed of any discussions whether initiated by management or government.

The Labour government's thoughts on the contents of planning agreements were set out in a Department of Industry Discussion Paper in 1975 (see Appendix 1, p 205). Essentially they were seen to be a reflection, at company level, of the sector discussions at the NEDC. The agenda would be similarly organized and the status of any agreed document which emerged would be akin to a voluntary NEDC Sector

Report. To reinforce this approach, the government took reserve powers in its 1975 Industry Act to compel companies to disclose information which it required for planning agreement purposes, and it announced the intention of restricting access to certain discretionary investment grants to companies who were co-operative.

In practice, the voluntary nature of the bargaining process was to prove to be its downfall. The CBI successfully held back its members from concluding agreements and, as we have seen, only one was ever signed. The government never followed through its intention to restrict investment aid, nor did it exercise its information disclosure powers.

The National Enterprise Board

The NEB, though not at the centre of the Industrial Strategy, was nevertheless an instrument of considerable power.

The Labour Programme of 1973 had seen the NEB as a:

> 'new and more flexible institution of national and regional planning. It will for the first time provide an instrument for exercising control in the area of profitable manufacturing industry. Its tasks include job creation, especially in areas of high unemployment; investment promotion; technological development; growth of exports; promoting government price policies; tackling the spread of multinational companies; the spread of industrial democracy; import substitution.'[8]

The Programme continued, however, to point out that: 'for the range of tasks suggested, some 25 of our largest manufacturers . . . would be required'. This was based on the reasoning that the government's industrial strategy would require the ownership of leading companies in every sector because: 'firms in every sector are strongly influenced by the investment planning, plant building and pricing policies of their most feared competitor'.

This last, over-ambitious, claim provided a battlefield for a resumed struggle between those who favoured public ownership and those who favoured mixed economies, which was won by the latter group.[9] When the functions of the NEB were set out in the 1975 Industry Act, Wilson's successful campaign against the '25 companies' commitment and his elaboration of the NEDC industrial strategy to fill much of the space reserved for the NEB ensured that its functions were rather more circumscribed than the Programme had originally promised. They were:

> 'to establish new industrial enterprises or assist existing enterprises, promote reorganization within industry, extend public ownership into profitable areas of manufacturing industry, promote industrial democracy in its subsidiaries and administer shareholdings and other property already in public ownership.'

As soon as the NEB was able to develop a plan of its own activities it identified the area of high technology — specifically computers, microelectronics and computer software — as key investment opportunities. In September 1976, the Computer and Electronics Division was set up to co-ordinate the activities of the electronic companies already in the NEB's portfolio, such as ICL, and to identify new acquisitions. The 1977 Annual Report noted that, in the past year, most progress had been made in that sector.

The years 1977-79 constitute the period of the Board's most self-confident expansion. Chairmanship of the Board passed, in July 1977, from Lord Ryder to Sir Leslie Murphy, a merchant banker, who had been Deputy Chairman of Schroders. Murphy worked hard, and successfully, at promoting the Board as an uncontroversial public sector entrepreneurial centre, seeking to work with the grain of British industrial life. In the 1978 report, Murphy spelled out his version of the Board's function:

> 'Our activities in the field of computers and microelectronics provide an excellent example. The evidence was that, left to itself, the private sector would not have secured an adequate place for the UK in this major technical and industrial revolution. The NEB is proving to be an instrument that is capable of working effectively with the managers and entrepreneurs upon whom success will ultimately depend and has found ways of motivating these people to achieve success.'[10]

While in opposition, the Conservative Party had always been solidly opposed to the NEB, and when back in power, quickly moved to kill off most of its ambitious activities. Murphy was replaced by Sir Arthur Knight, the former director of Courtaulds, as chairman. The Industry Act, passed in June 1980, commanded the Board to dispose of its assets as soon as possible and take up a more restricted role.

The stakes in ICL and Ferranti were sold off, as were Cambridge Instruments and Sinclair. Clearly, the role of the NEB is now negligible. However, it has not quite withered away. It has managed to ensure a minor presence for itself in the area which it picked up in 1978: electronics and high technology. Knight managed, in his brief tenure at the Board, to hold on to many of the information technology companies, including Inmos, Nexos and the Insac software consortium. He was much more concerned to bring in private capital to the Board's ventures, but he accepted that the NEB retained a function in starting projects unattractive to the market.

The appointment of the fourth chairman of the NEB in January 1981 signalled a transformation of the company. Sir Frederick Wood, former conservative candidate and chairman of the chemicals company Croda International, was also chairman of the National Research Development Corporation. In July 1981, he gained government approval to merge the NEB with the NRDC. The merged corporation (renamed the British Technology Group) was seen as a government-funded: 'spearhead (for) Britain's efforts in promoting the industries of the future'.[11]

Its three divisions deal with the public funding of research and the exploitation of investment; launching new products with a mixture of state and private funds; and the management of the hundreds of companies controlled by the group. Particular emphasis was placed on its catalytic role and its desire to turn companies over to the private sector as quickly as possible.

A Strategy for Electronics

The history of the NEB's electronics strategy provides valuable lessons on the limitations of a social democratic approach to state intervention — an approach which leaves key production planning decisions to the market.

The NEB inherited, or acquired in 1976, a number of holdings in, or full ownership of, companies in the advanced electronics sector. These included a 24.4 per cent stake in ICL (later increased to 25 per cent); a 62.5 per cent stake in Ferranti, full ownership of the scientific and medical instrument company Cambridge Instruments, the computer peripherals company Data Recording Instruments, Sinclair Electronics, which made various microelectronic-based products and 20 per cent of the industrial instrumentation company Brown Boveri Kent. In the years up to 1979, it also picked up the Burndept radio communications company; United Medical Enterprises (a medical equipment company); Automation and Technical Holdings, and Computer and Systems Engineering (both communications equipment companies) and ASR Servotron (an industrial controls manufacturer).

These acquisitions were not always an integral part of a carefully plotted strategy: many were just plain broke, and desperately needed help to stay on their feet. However, three new ventures were deliberately started up to be the cornerstones of an embryonic electronic industry strategy, and were of considerable importance.

Insac

Software — the programming of computers and computer-based systems — has taken over from computer hardware as the major element in automation. It is now software production, rather than hardware manufacture, which is labour intensive. The NEB saw software companies as an indispensable area for investment, and accordingly drew up a list of six companies in which it attempted to acquire a stake.

These were: Computer Analysts and Programmers, Systems Programmed Holdings, Logica, Hoskyns, Software Sciences and Scicon. It acquired shares in the first three and later added a fourth not on the original list, Systime. (The latter three were acquired by other companies.)

Acting as an umbrella marketing and services group over these companies was Insac, a company which NEB formed in February 1977. The board of Insac was made up of representatives of the software companies and from the Board itself. In June 1977, the NEB put up £20 million to finance Insac's marketing operation, especially in the US.

Insac and its member companies gave the Board command over nearly 40 per cent of the UK's vigorous software industry. The companies had considerable expertise in word processing systems, process control, commercial and systems software and applications for mini- and microcomputers. Their managers appeared satisfied with the Board's low-profile presence on the Insac board, and industry analysts generally conceded that the NEB intervention in the industry had been helpful. The Insac software group was sold off by the new Conservative government at a substantial loss.

Inmos

The founding, in July 1978, of the semiconductor company Inmos with an initial capital of £25 million and the promise of a further £25 million over the next five years, was more controversial. Yet the case for establishing such a company seemed, and still seems, indisputable.

US companies (Texas Instruments, Intel, Mostek, Fairchild and others) were the initiators of the semiconductor technology, and still remain at the forefront. In the latter part of the 1970s, the heavy backing provided by the Japanese government to its leading electronic companies has placed their companies on a competitive position with the US industry, and they are currently expanding production facilities in both the US and Europe.

The European response to this has been very largely to catch up by buying in. Most of the larger European companies now have formal co-operation with US companies, which provides the Europeans with access to technology and the Americans access to markets. However, as many commentators have stressed, the transfer of technology to Europe will only be successful if European companies can ensure that R and D is carried out in Europe, rather than merely shipped across from the US or Japan.

Semiconductor components provide what has been termed the 'fuel oil' of the electronics industry. It is in this sector that the UK lagged behind very badly, even behind the rest of Europe.

Inmos was, from its inception, to be a *mass* producer of chips, creating a synergy with other NEB electronic companies and with companies in the private sector. The Board rejected the original idea that the company should be a joint US-UK venture in favour of complete NEB ownership. Besides causing a number of Labour back-benchers and some leftists within the Cabinet to become enraged at the attractive terms offered to its three founders, it ran into substantial opposition from the Department of Industry bureaucracy which had become prejudiced against it by the established UK electronics companies.

Having surmounted these hurdles, and established an R and D

(and small production) plant in Colorado Springs, Inmos then found there was a change of government, from Labour to Conservative, in May 1979. Although it was ready to establish its UK base by late 1979, it was delayed by the new government's prevarication. The NEB estimated that Inmos was losing some $5 million a week expected turnover because of the inability of the government to decide whether or not to release its second tranche of £25 million. The government made the decision to do so in July 1980, on condition that the company sited its production plant in South Wales rather than in Bristol, the preferred location. Ironically, the choice of Newport meant that the company attracted another £35 million in regional grants, plus government cover for various borrowings and leasing arrangements.

In its three years of existence under a Conservative government, Inmos has experienced more government intervention in relation to its development than it experienced under Labour. It has also been pushed in the direction of the private sector: Sir Arthur Knight, said that: 'the objective now is to inject private capital as soon as is practical, that is sometime in 1983-84, if things go right' (*Financial Times* 25 September 1980). In July 1981, its management talked of entering into a partnership with a Japanese electronics company, possibly Matsushita.[12]

Although Inmos has not yet completed its start-up phase, and has not therefore reported a profit, it has had some commercial success. Its first memory chip, a 16K RAM produced in America, has taken three quarters of an estimated $30 million market. Its 64K RAM is competing in a far larger market, estimated to be worth $1 billion. It has recently announced its first microprocessor, the 'transputer' which it intends to bring into production in 1984.

By the second half of 1982, Inmos had swallowed £100 million in grants and government-backed loans, and was asking for a further £10 million — which it appeared certain to get. Wood declared himself to be sitting on the fence regarding its future: 'If no other source of funds could be found, and if we felt that the company was going in the right direction, then I would be prepared to make a case for recommending more government funds'.[13] However, the explicit intention remained to sell it off.

Nexos
The third large-scale electronics venture the NEB made was into office equipment: their vehicle was Nexos, founded in February 1979 with a capital of £45 million and a Director, Muir Moffat, hired from IBM. Nexos, like Inmos, was long overdue: no UK-owned company had a significant presence in electronic office equipment.

Such was the shortage in the UK that Nexos at first had to put together its office equipment package almost wholly from Japanese and US sources. However, from the beginning the company formed a close association with Logica, with which it developed a word processor, launched in early 1981. The product was extremely important for Nexos. It was widely described as the 'make or break' element for the company, its success guaranteeing the availability of all its £45 million in funds (it had spent nearly half that by early 1981), and its failure ensuring its closure.

Yet Nexos' business was only partly involved with developing and marketing hardware. It has staked much of its future on the rapid maturing of the 'office of the future' concept, where information of all kinds, from telephone conversations to graphs, can be stored in computer files and reproduced at will. One of the company's earliest marketing agreements was with Delphi, the Exxon subsidiary which manufactures a highly sophisticated communications control system, designed to handle the mixed data and voice streams in such an office.

Nexos' plans were never given time to mature. At the instigation of the Conservative government, it was sold off and broken up.

Telecommunications Equipment

The only major sector of the civilian electronics equipment industry in which the NEB was unable to establish any presence was telecommunications equipment manufacture. The Post Office was an independent entity, while its three main suppliers, GEC, Plessey and Standard Telephone and Cables (STC) were wholly private companies. In the latter part of 1978-79, the Board began a round of confidential talks with Plessey and STC. What appears to have been mooted was a merger between STC and Plessey's telecommunication business, with the latter under the effective control of the former and the chairmanship of the new creation passing to STC.

Under the plan (as far as we can tell) ITT would either be required to divest itself of STC, or be content with a minority holding. As a result of ITT's opposition, the NEB's initiative failed. Ironically, ITT subsequently decided, in 1982, to divest itself of STC.

WHAT WAS ACHIEVED?

The first social contract set out ambitious targets for training, under the control of the tripartite MSC, and for state intervention to promote a modern industrial structure through the tripartite NEDC and NEB. The training initiative proceeded largely independently of the government's technology strategy, and was soon overwhelmed by having to cope with the problems of mass unemployment. Wilson's Industrial Strategy based on planning agreements and the NEDC produced little economic benefit, while he converted the NEB from a socialist into a social democratic institution.

Under Wilson there were three broad alternatives open to the NEB in

1976. It could have become a centre for greatly extending public ownership in all sectors of industry, able to command investment and labour policy. The nearest Western equivalent is the Italian state holding company, IRI. This would have required a set of policies more radical than had been attempted previously, policies for which the Labour leadership were not prepared. Lacking the traditionally close involvement of state and industry which have characterized the French and Italian systems, the Labour government would have been required to restructure not only industry, but financial institutions as well. Both industrial and financial sectors would have been hostile to such a policy.

The second alternative, which was the one adopted, was to try to occupy the high ground in the emerging new technology industries which had been conceded in advance to the NEB by private companies who were not prepared to take the necessary risks. By adopting this strategy, the NEB had, by late 1978, put itself in a position of being the governing body for UK civilian electronics. It controlled the largest single part of the software market, had founded the only mass producer of microprocessors and memories in the UK and had finally laid some foundations for an advanced office equipment industry. Its share in ICL guaranteed it a say in the direction of Europe's most vigorous computer company, while the historically inefficient telecommunications industry seemed ripe for change. The building blocks were in place for a coherent strategy: UK companies, guided by the Board, by co-operating with each other and by judicious agreements with advanced companies abroad, could find a place in advanced world electronics which would not be swamped when IBM made a wave. British research and development could find an outlet in British production; public funds could fill the investment gap; while public purchasing could provide a start-up market and a base from which to look for export orders.

In this way, with the passage of time, the NEB's economic power and influence would have grown naturally. It did not mean that the NEB had to conform with the views and plans of UK industry, nor, indeed, with those of the civil service. As we have seen, the Board's innovations and projects ran up against fierce opposition which was, at times, successful. The plan to restructure the telecommunications industry was aborted. The large electronics companies outside the NEB's ambit, especially GEC, remained scornful of many of its endeavours. A closer relationship with ICL and the other parts of the NEB's electronics portfolio was not achieved. This approach meant that the spread of the NEB's influence was generally measured and that, at the end of Labour's term of office, it had not tackled large sections of its brief.

The third alternative is roughly what the Board had become by the early 1980s: a stimulator of (predominantly private) investment in certain areas of new technology. Its extremely modest role has meant that even those executives appointed to oversee its activities under terms of reference set by a Conservative Industry Secretary have been unable to find a useful role for themselves.

NON-INTERVENTION UNDER THE CONSERVATIVES

The cement of the social contract, never wholly set, began to loosen as early as September 1976, when the pound crashed. As a result of hectic talks between TUC and government, cuts in public expenditure and higher indirect taxes were reluctantly agreed and a third stage of incomes policy (following the 1975 and 1976 limits) was loosely agreed.

By 1978, the pressures to return to free collective bargaining, however disorderly, had become too great to be ignored. Both the Transport and General Workers Union, whose leadership passed from Jack Jones to Moss Evans, and the National Union of Mineworkers were committed to free collective bargaining. Equally significant was the determination on the part of shop stewards in *all* unions, not to endure a further year of powerlessness. This unstoppable force met the government's immovable objective of keeping wage rises to five per cent. In the 1978-79 winter of discontent, health and other public service workers, together with lorry drivers blew away not only the social contract but also, in the May 1979 elections, the chance of Labour returning to power.

The Conservatives came back under Margaret Thatcher, to curb both unions and the public sector. Despite the hankering of some senior Tories for an armistice with the TUC (the chief among whom, James Prior, was Employment Secretary for the government's first 20 months) the government as a whole set its face against such a heresy to their free market faith. In particular, Sir Keith Joseph, a close Prime Ministerial adviser and Industry Secretary in 1979-80, held it as an article of faith that pay settlements and inflation were wholly unconnected, and that social contracts in which a national deal had to be struck to achieve wage moderation were undesirable and unnecessary.

'I do not believe in pay policy,' he told the *Sun* just before the 1979 election. 'It has never worked in Britain and has been shown not to work. Other countries do not need it, so why should we? I cannot conceive the circumstances in which a wage freeze would be good for the country.'[14]

Sir Keith staked out what was an extreme position in justifying private wealth amid mass poverty (set against a liberal-tory-social democratic middle-ground of 30 years' standing). 'Redistribution is unwise. But it is also morally indefensible, misconceived in theory and repellent in practice.'[15]

The government, however, was to deviate from Sir Keith's purist line.

By 1980, the Chancellor, Sir Geoffrey Howe, was appealing for moderate settlements and enjoining employers to stay within government pay guidelines. However, he did not attempt to strike any kind of a deal with the unions. The government's main, and very effective, weapon against high wage settlements and industrial disruption was unemployment, which rose from over one million when labour left office, to over three million in 1982. This unemployment would be enough to undermine any basis for a contract between the government and labour. The squeeze on public expenditure, which has forced down private and public pay settlements, has also beaten every attempt at industrial militancy, except that of the mine workers, who successfully defeated a pit closure plan in early 1981. The government has consolidated its position by bringing in sweeping changes in employment law which have restricted secondary action, picketing, and the closed shop, laid union funds open to confiscation and greatly cut back trade union immunities.

The government's stance of non-intervention in the economy has extended to its policies for training and education, and the diffusion of technology. We have seen how, with the NEB, the steady progress of state intervention in these areas which has taken place since the war has been set back. Conservative policy with respect to training provision by the state has had a similar objective. Nevertheless after three years of Conservative rule, government expenditure on training is higher than it has ever been, while a U-turn in industrial policy has led government again into attempting to play an active role in stimulating industrial change.

Training and the Unemployed

The influence of free market thinking has been strong on training policy, as the government has attempted to use it as an adjunct to the working out of its economic theories. The rapid growth of unemployment especially among the young, has forced the government to devise schemes to alleviate the situation. These schemes also have another purpose which is to lower wage rates and 'price workers into jobs'.

Training in the UK was generally recognized to be in a critical state by the end of the 1970s. In that decade, some 600,000 unskilled jobs had been lost; by the mid 1980s, projections showed that white-collar jobs would outnumber manual jobs, which would require an increasing amount of technical sophistication. Without large-scale training programmes, structural unemployment appeared certain to rise rapidly.

In Britain 44 per cent of those seeking work have no qualifications. Around 60 per cent of school leavers never take any full-time education again. Two-thirds of Britain's workforce has no formal qualifications of any kind.

Apprenticeships in the UK ran around 100,000 until the early 1980s, when leaping unemployment made employers cut back: in

145

1981, the apprentice intake was only 80,000, of which 12,000 were taken on by engineering companies — little more than half the number estimated to be necessary.[16]

A major vehicle for training the country's young were the statutory ITBs which, when the Conservatives took office, covered 24 industrial sectors. The numbers were sharply reduced, in 1981-82, to seven, covering clothing, construction, engineering, hotel and catering, road transport, rubber and plastics and petroleum products. The 17 sectors relieved of their statutory duties were persuaded by government to take on voluntary arrangements — not always successfully.

Meanwhile, the universities' contribution to technical training was also being reduced: places had to be cut back by 12,000 by 1984. In schools there had been a decline in capital spending too: in many areas, expenditure in 1981-82 was less than 60 per cent of its 1974-75 level. These cuts are leading to shortage of science equipment and text books: many secondary schools can no longer offer all the sciences (physics, chemistry and biology) to O and A levels.

Under the Conservatives, the organization of training provision in the UK in the late 1970s and early 1980s went through a series of profound changes. Changes were much needed, but the expansion which took place was for the wrong reasons. Vocational training grew out of schemes designed to assist unemployed youth,[17] because that group has been the worst hit by the present recession.

The first large scheme in the training area was introduced by the Labour government in 1978. The Youth Opportunities Programme (YOP), which was catering for nearly 250,000 young people by mid 1982 at a cost (in 1982-83) of £750 million, gave its clients some on-the-job experience and training, mostly for a six-month period. Business, unions and government all agreed as to the value of the scheme, but, by 1982, two in three of YOP graduates were leaving the scheme to join the unemployed.

Two other schemes were brought in during 1980-81 to mop up more of the young and the long-term unemployed. The first was the Community Enterprise Scheme, which paid voluntary organizations and local authorities for employing workers to do community work. Secondly, a Young Workers Scheme was formed, which was run directly by the Department of Employment under the prompting of Professor Alan Walters, the Prime Minister's personal economic adviser, which subsidized employers to take on young people — as long as they paid them less than £45 a week.

The dichotomy between the need to increase training and to cope with massive numbers out of work, and the drive to reduce wages meant that the government's new training initiative, embodied in a white paper in December 1981, was launched into a hostile environment. Its scope was ambitious: it planned to offer training to all 16-year-olds and 17-year-olds who became unemployed, with a scheme costing over £1 billion a year; it proposed to develop an 'open tech' along the lines of the Open University; to reform apprentice training by 1985; and to co-ordinate better skill and vocational training at national and local level.

By 1982, the MSC had become the most overworked public institution in the country (though, perversely, its staff numbers were still being cut). It was estimated that its schemes would cost £1.5 billion by 1984, and it had also to grapple with such difficulties as apprenticeship reform. Ahead of it was its gravest problem: what to do with the more than one million long-term unemployed, of whom the under-45s were the larger proportion.

An Industrial Policy U-Turn?

High technology industry and a highly trained workforce go together. Present government policy has been to attempt to withdraw as far as possible from responsibility for ensuring that industry is technically competitive with its main rivals — indeed to deny that such a responsibility exists.

As with its training policy, the government found that a policy of total withdrawal was not practicable. Industry may have welcomed the destruction of the NEB on ideological grounds, but it lobbied long, hard, and successfully, both behind the scenes, and publically through the NEDC for a national strategy for electronics.[18]

The outcome was that after a period in which the new government ostentatiously refused to have anything much to do with new technology, it changed course sharply and appointed an Industrial Minister — Ken Baker — with special responsibility for it. Baker extended Labour's Microelectronic Awareness Programme to 1985. Under this scheme, the government mounts exhibitions and pays consultancy fees and up to 25 per cent of new product development costs. 1982 was declared 'Information Technology' year. A new £25 million scheme was established to extend support to the optical fibre industry, and elaborate plans were made to use the public sector as a test bed for new machinery. To this end, a number of projects concerned with office automation, electronic mail and internal viewdata have been set up. On the education and training front, the government has announced plans for the establishment of community centres to introduce the young unemployed to computing techniques, and plans for the introduction of a microcomputer into each secondary school.

However, these extended industrial support schemes are to be funded not with new money, but with money taken from other resources. For example, the funding of research associations for the wool, textile, hosiery and furnishing industries has been cut back by the ending of statutory levy arrangements. The influence of public purchasing over the direction of the technology is being reduced by a policy of treating foreign owned TNCs as being, to all intents and purposes, British.

147

The change in government policy was marked by an avalanche of new measures, none of which appeared in the Conservative Manifesto of 1979, which set out to open up the UK market for information technology services. The essence of the Conservative's revised industrial policy was that the government would put up 'winners' and invite the private sector to back the government's judgement with its money. The most dramatic changes were those planned for broadcasting and telecommunications.

Broadcasting

Alongside Ken Baker's appointment, the government established an 'Information Technology Advisory Panel' (ITAP) whose first report 'Cable Systems' was published in March 1982. The report recommended the lifting on existing controls on cable television, and called for an expansion so that it could reach 50 per cent of the population. A host of other studies followed after its publication, including the following:

☐ A Home Office Inquiry, to consider questions affecting broadcasting policy which would arise from such an expansion.
☐ A Department of Industry technical working group to recommend design standards consistent with commercial viability.
☐ Further examinations by ITAP of the relative roles of the Home Office, the Department of Industry and British Telecom in regulating the convergence of wireless and wired services.

The emphasis on broadcasting policy stemmed from a particular coincidence of circumstances: two commercial lobbies and an approaching election. The first lobby consisted of the UK cable companies, who had been held back for some time from investing in their networks which reached only 14 per cent of the UK population, the lowest penetration in a major Western European country. The major factor holding them back from what seemed like US style boom was government regulation. In particular, the requirement that, for social reasons, the existing networks, for the most part capable of only four channel operations, must carry the existing three national services. The Hunt Report (October 1982) recommended that this requirement should be dropped, just before the fourth national channel came into operation in November 1982. Restrictions on cable had to be maintained according to the Annan Committee report in 1977 in order to ensure that a proliferation of incompatible networks would not evolve. The result was that there had been a slow decline (140,000 over five years) in the number of subscribers to commercial systems and the profitability of the cable operators was poor.

The second commercial lobby was that surrounding the putative direct broadcast satellite (DBS) industry. They needed an expanded cable network to carry their TV signals into mass markets, and with present technology this can only be achieved economically by cable. ITAP's recommendation that early approval be granted to DBS services was taken even before the publication of their report.

Thirdly, the government badly needed to demonstrate its belief that the private sector could successfully accomplish structural change in the economy and create new jobs. ITAP claimed that the private sector would provide the £2.5 billion required to cable half the country with the promise of revenue from entertainment and interactive services. This claim, and their belief that the new industry would generate a £1 billion turnover per year, was music to the government's ears, especially in a pre-election period.

The Department of Industry group was set up to look at the vexed question of reversing the position of the 1977 Annan Committee which had opposed the deregulation of cable in order to prevent the proliferation of technically incompatible local networks. Strong technical arguments were advanced by British Telecom and others for the adoption of a network structure which could evolve into a universal broadband network by the end of the century. British Telecom outlined one such design which involves multi-channel services being carried by optical fibre to a local switching centre from which home subscribers would select the services they wished – the 'star' system.

ITAP had regarded this as 'over engineering' and have preferred the adoption of proven 30 channel non-switched US 'tree and branch' technologies, which deliver every channel to each home by coaxial cable.

Telecommunications Services
Telecommunications services formed the second plank of the government's new industrial strategy. After British Telecom began to receive close attention from the government it underwent a confusing number of switches in policy – in the general direction of deregulation, and denationalization, of the network. By mid 1982, that programme was well advanced:

☐ The British Telecommunications Act of 1981, split the old Post Office into two corporations – the Post Office now covering postal services and Giro, and British Telecom covering telecommunications services.

☐ The Act allowed the progressive deregulation of equipment supplied. Private suppliers can now supply handsets, later all kinds of terminals, later still switchboards.

☐ Competition was permitted with British Telecom trunk services. By February 1982, Mercury – a consortium of Cable and Wireless, BP and Barclays Merchant Bank – was given a license to lay its (optical fibre) lines beside British Rail tracks.

In November, BT and Mercury agreed a network integration

149

programme, allowing the new service to operate from Spring 1983. The agreement allows Mercury subscribers access to the BT network via a local call, and connects subscribers' equipment to Mercury through lines leased from British Telecom.

☐ British Telecom was encouraged to enter joint ventures with other private companies as well. In March 1982, it announced a joint venture with GEC-Marconi and British Aerospace in a direct broadcast satellite capable of carrying TV and telecommunications signals across an area of several thousand miles.

☐ A white paper of July 1982 announced the sale of 51 per cent of British Telecom by November, together with the creation of an Office of Telecommunications — along the lines of the Office of Fair Trading — to supervise the new private sector corporation.

CONCLUSION

We have seen in this chapter how Labour's first social contract attemped to democratize state intervention in the economy, yet failed to win it either political dividends — in the form of continued political power, or economic benefits. Little remains of the government reforms of this period. Since 1979, employment in the UK engineering industry has declined by over 25 per cent, and output is down by 12 per cent. Protected markets for computers and telecommunications equipment and services have been thrown open to overseas competition and the NEB electronics strategy has been dismembered.

The momentum of trade union advance has however been maintained within the Labour movement itself. The unions, through the TUC, now regard the business of striking a high level bargain with the Labour Party as a central part of their collective purpose, one which, at least potentially, lends great weight and importance to their programmes, debates and divisions — provided that this potentially governing coalition can be appointed by the electors to govern.

The revised statement of the social contract which emerged from the Liaison Committee in 1981 demonstrated that the TUC's influence over joint policy-making was now the dominant one, and that it expected to play an even more central role under a Labour government of the future than it had done in 1974-79.[19] The document called for a 'new national understanding' involving working people in decisions which affected them, and an agreement on: 'such crucial issues as social reform and distribution of income and wealth'; a return to full employment linked to a programme of investment growth; controls on the import of manufactured goods; reintroduction of exchange controls; a much larger flow of finance for the public sector through a new national investment bank and control of the lending institutions; and an increase in training and retraining.

Complementary to these measures are to be fresh proposals on planning and industrial democracy, which are now seen as integrally linked so that planning at national level can be articulated with planning at company level, in both of which organized labour would have a large say.

In Part 2 which follows, we examine the form and content of this new social contract, and assess its likely effectiveness against the background of recession and other social implications of the STR.

REFERENCES

1 K Middlemas (1979) *Politics in Industrial Society.* Andre Deutsch, London.

2 L Minkin (1978) *The Labour Party Conference*, p 330. Allen Lane, Harmondsworth.

3 For a good narrative account of the policy battles in this period, see M Hatfield (1978) *The House the Left Built.* Gollancz, London.

4 The Labour Party (1973) *Economic Policy and the Cost of Living.*

5 ACARD (1979) *Technological Change: Threats and Opportunities for the UK*, p 31. HMSO.

6 H Wilson (1973) *The Governance of Britain.* Weidenfeld and Nicolson, London.

7 TUC (1979) Conference report, p 544.

8 The Labour Party (1973) *Labour's Programme.*

9 M Hatfield, op cit, pp 188-90.

10 National Enterprise Board Report and Accounts (1978).

11 *The Times* (1981) 21 July.

12 *Financial Times* (1981) 3 July.

13 *The Observer* (1982) 4 July.

14 P McHugh (1979) 'Sir Anti-Freeze'. *The Sun*, 20 April.

15 Sir Keith Joseph and J Sumption (1979) *Equality.* John Murray, London.

16 'Sorcery among Britain's apprentices' (1981) *The Economist,* 12 December.

17 ibid.

18 NEDO (1982) *Policy for the UK Electronics Industry.*

19 TUC/Labour Party (1981) *Economic Issues Facing the next Labour Government.*

Part 2:
A New Framework for Agreement

CHAPTER 7

Data Agreements

INTRODUCTION

The development of computer-based information systems was transformed in the 1970s by the activities of the Scandinavian labour movement. In Northern Europe, traditional methods of systems development came under a concerted attack by a combination of collective bargaining pressures, and union-inspired legislation. The international labour movement was able to draw on this experience and incorporate it into the programmes of national trade union centres, when, in the late 1970s, the microprocessor triggered a second automation debate throughout Western Europe. In this chapter we will be examining why and how the North European unions came to play such an influential role.

LABOUR'S INFLUENCE ON TECHNOLOGICAL CHANGE

Scandinavian unions were the first to recognize the significance for workers of the development of computer-based information systems. This stemmed from the peculiar form that corporate collective bargaining had taken in the Nordic countries. Firstly, although the system was based, as elsewhere, on central bargaining with legal restrictions on the right to strike which discouraged shop floor level collective bargaining, the third party to the negotiating process for most of the post-war period was a Labour government. This meant that the unions could negotiate a continuing 'social contract' arrangement with the government in which they could rely on the country to uphold pro-labour legislation to open up areas of management decision-making to local unions, while they also gained access to the state's research resources. In addition, the general debate on individual privacy and the freedom of information, which had led to the Swedish Data Statute, made union members sensitive to employers collecting personal information in their growing data bases. Furthermore, some unions, concerned to establish

155

a shop steward network, saw negotiations on the introduction of computer systems as a means of stimulating its development.

In a recent paper, Jostein Fjalestad of the Norwegian Computing Centre has described various activities which have been developed as part of a long-term strategy to improve trade union influence on technological change.[1]

AGREEMENTS AND ACTS

Partly in response to research commissioned by the Iron and Metal Workers Union in the late 1960s, the Norwegian Labour Movement pioneered data agreements to regulate the introduction of new technology. The first agreement was reached in 1974, and by 1982 most of the working population was covered by these agreements. National data agreements have established a framework within which local technology bargaining takes place. These state that:

☐ Employees, through their unions, have the right to all relevant information about systems which may affect their interests. The information should be given sufficiently early to allow the unions to exercise real influence upon the decisions made, and be given in a language understandable to non-specialists. System descriptions should also include information about the effect on the interests of employees.

☐ Employees and their unions have the right to participate in systems development.

☐ Unions may elect an additional shop steward (data steward) with systems as his special field of responsibility. He has the right to receive education for this job.

In 1977, these collective agreements were put into legislation, known as the 'Act relating to Worker Protection and the Working Environment'. The Act lays down general requirements for the planning and organization of work. It specifies not only the harmful factors which should be removed from the working environment, but also physical, social and psychological factors which should be introduced. Like Equal Pay and Opportunities legislation in other countries, this law has been useful in establishing a new environment in which the unions can manoeuvre. It is being followed up by codes of practice covering the use of VDUs and procedures for system design.

LOCAL TRADE UNIONS

The Norwegian national data agreements have been supplemented by local agreements which spell out in more detail the procedures to be

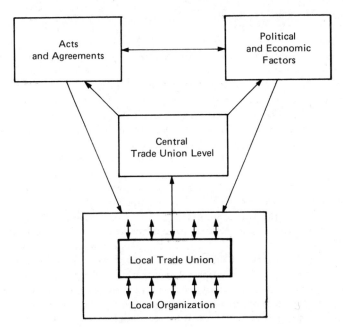

Source: Jostein Fjalestad (1981) Arbeitstagung über 'Partizipation bei der Systemtwicklung', GMD, Bonn. (Unpublished paper)

Figure 1a The context of trade union intervention

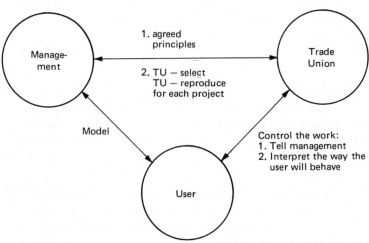

Source: Tør Haug (1977) Office of the Future. Diebold Research Program-Europe

Figure 1b Social relations in project implementation

Figure 1. Information system development in Scandinavia

adopted on implementing computer systems, and the uses to which data may be put. Figure 1 shows how the system development process has been modified as a result. For example, the local agreement at the State Educational Loan Institute requires each feasibility study to investigate not only technical feasibility but also the employment situation in each affected department, and the impact of the proposed system on job content and work organization. The investigation is required to produce estimates of the economic benefits of the proposed system, while the new national agreement for the public sector requires the management of the Institute to consult on how these liberated resources might be used.

Similar provisions are found in the agreement reached with the Co-operative Retail Society, which also specifies that the union will have access to the test system to check on its properties before the system goes live. It also requires prior agreement on how modification in the system will be carried out. In the paper industry, the Chemical Workers have negotiated an agreement at Borregaard Fabrikker which requires the company to prepare long-term plans for the development of computer systems and discuss them, at least once a year, with the union, before plans are finalized. The agreement provides for the unions to propose alternative solutions. More recent agreements have contained 'status quo' provisions, providing for no change to be made to existing systems before the procedure has been exhausted.

A typical personal data agreement covers all information, directly or indirectly traceable to individuals, irrespective of the method of collection or storage. The gathering of this information must be agreed in advance with the union, likewise the computer programs which would have access to it. Both programs and data are restricted, so that they may only be used by a mutually agreed group of people. Individuals named on the files have the right of access to their own data, which they can amend. The only exceptions to this provision might be access to medical information where, in the opinion of the doctor, this was considered inadvisable. All information in existence prior to the agreement being reached, and not covered by its provisions, would have to be destroyed. Other clauses might cover the time data would be kept on the system, and there would be special provisions for deleting records of those who had left the organization.

These new procedures have substantially enlarged the agenda of collective bargaining. Unions have become concerned with the impact of the new systems on social contacts, job availability and the power structure at work, and have resisted attempts at increased surveillance, work pressure and deskilling of jobs.

Problems of job availability have been tackled within a context of a no-redundancy agreement. Special provisions have been made for older workers, and, where jobs are changing, appropriate training programmes have had to be agreed as part of the feasibility studies.

To overcome any isolation of work groups with resultant negative consequences for union solidarity, demands have been made on systems design so that the new systems can support the expansion of the range of social contacts at work. This special characteristic of the new systems is called 'cross contact'. An information system was said to provide cross contact between a group of people when it made it possible for them to exchange information they themselves selected as relevant to furthering their own interests. This required bargaining over what data would be recorded and the language in which it would be stored. For example, the chemical workers made a claim on the Institute of Occupational Health in 1977 concerning the design of a data bank of hazardous chemicals. They stated:

> 'Firstly, the data must be present in such a way that safety shop stewards and other shop stewards are able to use them . . . The data must include any subjective experience from our shop stewards and safety representatives which might indicate problematic chemicals and possible health hazards . . . and should also include a register of safety representatives, shop stewards and local unions who have reported on these "problematic chemicals" in order to enable those who experience problems in the future to contact unions with experience.'

At the Educational Loan Institution the unions have negotiated access to the organization's computer hardware and software for their own use, and similar developments have taken place at the Kongsberg Weapons Factory where one of the early Iron and Metal Workers projects was carried out. There, the union's demands were related to the production planning and control systems — the IBM system CLASS, and the KVPOL system then being developed within the company. KVPOL is an information system based on a central data bank and two-way terminals located on the shop floor. It collects information on the state of production and distributes control information. The union's work produced new insights into the effects of the CLASS system. The analysis of the KVPOL system resulted in a number of proposals for changes, some of which were later negotiated with the management.

By 1980, the union had concluded agreements on the regular provision of information from the system on overtime, absenteeism and changes in the planned time for jobs. The latter was inserted at the demand of the union in order to enable them to monitor any tendency towards speeding up the pace of work. A new transaction had also been introduced into the system to enable operators to examine their wages earned to date so that they could regulate their output. An associated change, which gave operators the freedom to record the end of a job some time after it had actually been completed, had the added bonus of undermining the value of any statistics collected on the time taken to complete jobs, and thus any use they may have had for individual work monitoring.

CENTRAL TRADE UNIONS

Trade union centres have had to adapt their own organizations to support the extension of collective bargaining into these new areas. In the first period of policy development the unions took the unusual step of commissioning their own research into the impact of information systems. The 1970 National Congress of the Iron and Metal Workers called on its Executive to start up its own research in the area as the employers had been doing for some time. Once a framework of policy had been established the unions had to expand their training programmes to disseminate knowledge of both policy and practice among the membership.[2]

Funds for research were supplied by the Norwegian Council for Scientific and Industrial Research, and an interdisciplinary research team was provided by its Computing Centre. The work was carried out under the supervision of a steering committee, composed of representatives of the central and local trade union organizations involved, together with an equivalent number of academics drawn from various research institutes. Four case studies were established:

1. Kongsberg Weapons Factory (government-owned, technologically the most advanced company in the job shop industry, producing computers and control systems).
2. Norsk Electricity and Brown Bovari (NEBB, the Norwegian branch of the Swiss Brown Bovari, producing electric generators, etc).
3. Jonas Øglaend (a bicycle factory with assembly lines and batch production).
4. Hydraulik (a company producing precision hydraulic equipment for ships and off-shore activities).

This pioneering Norwegian work led to further projects at home, while stimulating similar programmes in Sweden in 1975 with the Demos Project, and in Denmark in 1976 with the Due Project. In Denmark, projects were undertaken at the Post Giro, at a shipyard, and in a manufacturing company. The Office and Shop Assistants Union carried out a study of the introduction of a point-of-sale terminal system, while the Nurses Union looked at medical automation. In Sweden, the work was incorporated by the TUC into an Action Programme on Industrial Democracy and Data in 1976 which stated in part that:

> 'The workers and the trade unions are not content with managers and their
> experts who say they develop systems for planning and control which take
> human beings into consideration, by paying attention to the needs for

self-realization and the social impact of technical systems etc. On the contrary, the unions must work for a situation that makes it possible for workers to develop their own resources of organization and knowledge.'[3]

Central union activity concerned with new technology did not end with the establishment of research projects, data stewards, and bargaining over systems design. The unions were aware that their freedom to negotiate on aspects of system design, especially in the area of production planning and control systems, was heavily constrained by the nature of such systems on the market. They therefore sought to extend union influence into research and development carried out on all computer-based systems. As they had achieved representation on State research committees, they were in a position to lay down a policy to guide the work of their representatives in this area. Representatives were brought together under the General Council's Research Committee to propose a rolling programme for endorsement at each National Congress to control their work. Demands for a research policy for computer technology were incorporated in the programme adopted by the Executive Board of the Council of Nordic Trades Unions (NFS), in April 1978. The NFS called for research into how computer technology could be used for improving the work environment, democratizing working life and developing democracy in society as a whole. This would be achieved by giving:

☐ 'union aims . . . the same importance in state research as aims of an economic and technical kind;
☐ union organizations . . . a large influence over research within the computer industry, computer service companies and in other institutions and companies that are today under the control of the employers;
☐ increased resources to be at the disposal of the unions for research on the effects of computers on conditions in working life.'[4]

As the union's experience of technology bargaining increased, an educational programme was started for data shop stewards. In Norway, course development is funded from the industrial levy of 1½ per cent of salaries, paid by employees (half per cent) and by employers (one per cent). Control of this fund is split equally between employer controlled vocational training and union-run training. Paid leave is granted for stewards attending the trade union courses which are divided into two parts: one designed jointly by representatives of the employees' union and a government training institution which runs the course, and the other designed and run by the union.

LABOUR'S POTENTIAL FOR SUCCESSFUL INTERVENTION

Trade unions have negotiated agreements at both national and local levels which guarantee them a right of intervention in the development of new computer systems, a right of access to management information, and a right to specify other areas of information to be collected in order to protect workers and the workforce.

Reviewing the unions' experience with their strategy, Jostein Fjalestad listed five key conditions which have determined the extent to which the unions have been able to gain real influence over technological change at work.[5]

Power Base

A necessary condition for influencing technical change is the extent of the union's power base. In part, this is a function of the solidarity existing between union members which can be used for collective sanctions. The traditional power base has had to be extended in order to deal with complicated technical matters and to even out the distribution of power between strong and weak unions. In Scandinavia, this has been achieved by Acts and agreements which define both the socially desired properties of computer systems and the rights of employees in the system development process.

Consciousness

In order that union power can be successfully applied it is necessary that those who are to realize its potential are conscious about possible areas of influence and what can be achieved. The Norwegians found two barriers here. On the one hand, there was the attitude represented by an older worker who commented that: 'Automation is like the sun, there is nothing we can do to influence its coming and its course.' On the other hand, there was the problem of a series of isolated technical changes with limited consequences, adding up to an unforeseen development of serious proportions.

While externally produced information and training could, to some extent, overcome these difficulties, it became apparent that it was necessary for consciousness to be developed out of practice. This awareness would then be expressed in the particular union objectives set for the system development process, since it was difficult to rely extensively on external guidelines. Without such locally agreed objectives it was not possible to relate the different action options to the interests of the employees.

Action Options

To exercise influence, it is necessary to have a choice of options for action. A considerable potential for influence was found to exist, despite the constraints of designs on the market and the abilities of the systems designers.

Generally speaking, packaged software, which is bought on the open market, is a problem as it may not be easily modifiable. However, given the state of systems development it has been found to be often more predictable than in-house developed systems where the local union organization is weak. Even the limitation of having to adopt centrally packaged systems (because the organization formed part of a larger economic or administrative unit) might be exploited by a sufficiently strong union in order to extend its influence over the work process as a whole.

Information

It was found that three types of information were needed for effective union intervention. In the first case there was information relating to the proposed system, which data agreements specified should be provided in non-specialist language, and should include details of the social consequences of automation. This information had to be provided early enough to enable plans to be influenced. In practice, conflicts developed over the definition of relevant information, the completeness of the material on the social consequences, and the meaning of 'understandable form', which was frequently reduced to a simple concern to translate English terminology into Norwegian. Furthermore, the information was often given too late to the union for it to influence events owing to bad management and project organization. Documentation might only be produced after a lengthy informal management process in which key decisions had already been made.

A second type of information related to the collective knowledge and experience of the local union concerning the impact of new technology on working conditions and negotiating strategy. Here it was found that the knowledge needed to be made explicit in order for it to be useful. Having been made explicit this information has to be systematically distributed through publications, seminars, etc. A third type of information related to the use of outside experts who had a knowledge both of computer systems and trade union values and problems.

Organization

Union organization needs to satisfy two objectives: procedures need to be developed to exploit the possibilities of influencing system design; while, a learning process has to be promoted to develop consciousness and objectives. It was found to be very difficult to start and maintain this organizational process. The most effective method has involved recurrent seminars for groups of local trade unions who share similar activities. It is important that the data shop stewards report regularly about their activities to a supporting group of representatives within the firm. At the same time, the opportunity should exist for conflicts which occur to be taken up at a higher level within the established negotiating machinery.

CONCLUSION

Scandinavian trade union work on new technology developed from the need to respond to the two management techniques of system design which were described in Chapter 1 as participation or coercion. In the absence of union intervention in this area members would either be co-opted as isolated individuals into the development process or be excluded altogether from the process of systems development. Neither alternative seemed likely to protect the particular interests of the unions and their members.

REFERENCES

1 J Fjalestad (1981) 'Some factors affecting participation in systems development'. In Arbeitstagung über 'partizipation bei der systemtwicklung'. GMD, Bonn.

2 K Nygaard (1979) 'The "Iron and Metal" project: trade union participation'. In A Sandberg (ed) *Computers Dividing Man and Work*, p 94. Arbetslivscentrum, Stockholm.

3 LO (1976) Action Programme for Industrial Democracy and Data. Stockholm.

4 Council of Nordic Trade Unions (1979) *Guidelines for Nordic Trade Union Work with Computing Issues*, p 27. Stockholm.

5 J Fjalestad, op cit.

CHAPTER 8

Technology Agreements

INTRODUCTION

Data agreements, as developed by the Scandinavian unions, provided other union movements, including the British, with a model. The theory and practice of new technology agreements, were some of the most significant developments in collective bargaining since the Second World War.

By the time the British unions began to develop such agreements and bring them to the bargaining table, there was a very bleak economic and political environment. The most rapid restructuring of work ever undertaken was taking place in a period of deep recession. When considering the response made by labour to the introduction of new processes, it is essential to bear this context in mind. Labour's response is conditioned by many elements, but above all by the state of the labour market. In recent years, that market has shown a steadily rising labour surplus, and it is inevitable that policy on new technology will be subsumed into the over-riding aim of trade unions to better their position in relation to both employers and government by tightening up the market. That is, by reducing the time worked (reducing labour supply) and/or by arguing for reflation (increasing labour demand).

The unions have fought hard for these demands in the UK, where the trade union movement is numerically and politically strong. Here, the recession has been intensified by government policies designed to cut back the proportion of GNP used up by public expenditure, and by high sterling and interest rates. Unemployment has climbed to over three million (mid 1982) and is expected to reach at least three-and-a-half million by the end of 1983. We have seen in Chapter 2 how, as a direct result, unions' membership, at a peak of around 12 million in 1980, fell back to around 11 million by 1982. Those unions with the largest proportion of their members in manufacturing industries, and in the private sector generally (the TGWU, the AUEW, and GMWU) suffered heavily.

Because of these pressures, the early efforts of the UK unions to comprehend the nature and effects of automation in their members' industries have tended to be pushed to one side. In aggregate, these efforts were impressive and, as a number of commentators have noted,[1] of a higher standard than equivalent responses from the employers' side.

In spite of the severity of the UK recession in manufacturing, workers have shown little inclination to indulge in Luddism. Interestingly, the most hostile formal response to new technology came from the National Union of Journalists — a union which is presently under little threat from its effects and whose numbers have remained relatively stable over recent years at around 30,000. In contrast, unions with their bases in manufacturing and service industries (the AUEW, the EETPU, AUEW-Tass and Apex) are opting strongly for increased investment in automated systems, basing their position on the recognition that lack of investment in advanced technology will cause the UK to lag even further behind other modern economies than it is at the moment. The EETPU's statement that it: 'recognizes the need to enthusiastically foster the introduction of new technology in all sectors of the UK engineering industry'[2] is typically unequivocal, but not out of line with the pronouncements of other unions.

It should also be borne in mind that unions in the UK have generally co-operated with large-scale rationalizations over the past five years, and many of these rationalizations have been intimately associated with the introduction of new work processes. There have been very large manpower reductions in the following sectors: British Steel Corporation, BL, British Shipbuilders, International Computers, the consumer electronic industry, the telecommunications manufacturing industry, the paper industry, the chemicals industry and the textiles industry. (In only one sector — construction — have large layoffs been the result of factors other than technological change.) These layoffs have rarely been achieved through the medium of a formal agreement with the workforce, and in this respect, the employers have acted in a manner which accords well with their short-term interests.

New technology agreements potentially open the way to union involvement in corporate planning and to the type of industrial democracy which the Bullock Report[3] outlined and against which the CBI fought most successfully. Unlike wage bargaining, new technology bargaining from the outset requires at least consultation on working practices and thus, logically, company strategy. David Lea, the TUC Assistant General Secretary who chairs its employment and technology committee, put the issue succinctly at a Rome seminar:

> 'the trade union response to technological development is clearly linked to the area of industrial democracy. We are seeking both to widen the agenda on which bargaining takes place and to exert influence at a much earlier stage in decision-making.'[4]

On such a basis, managers with an aversion to bilateral planning and industrial democracy will scarcely find the prospect of new technology bargaining appealing at any level. Our description, then, of the early experience of such bargaining in the UK is one of limited success, and of potential rather than actual achievement. Yet it is in the potential for securing a leverage over new technology that the labour movement possesses one of its greatest opportunities for future development.

OPPORTUNITY OR THREAT?

New technology has always been two-sided, and has thus provoked ambivalent responses from people involved in the process of change. Above all, in a period when the UK's share of world trade has continued to shrink, including its share of high technology products, it was generally recognized by the labour movement that the process of industrial restructuring would be both painful and that it had to be accepted — on the best terms possible.

In December 1978, Eric Varley, the Industry Secretary, launched a programme of government support for microelectronic technology, including an 'awareness programme' aimed particularly at industrialists and trade unionists. This was coupled with government support for applications, measures for training and education and public purchasing of microelectronics. The government's package was announced in ambiguous terms. James Callaghan, then Prime Minister, told the NEDC meeting at which the package was unveiled that there would be 'crucial job losses' but that other jobs would be created. The inter-departmental paper announcing the measures pronounced that micro-technology evoked a:

> 'mixture of fear and excitement... The excitement is about the possibilities of dramatic increases in productivity, for saving resources of all kinds (especially energy), and for improving working conditions. The fear is of increasing rapid change, especially in employment patterns . . . But as a trading nation we only have one realistic option — to seize the opportunity provided by this new technology to catch up with our industrial competitors and to adopt and develop it at least as fast and comprehensively as they do. To opt out will lead to the very worst fears being realized.'[5]

The theme of 'catch-up' was imperative: the main reason why the medicine had to be swallowed. Though at other points in the paper the more hopeful formulation, that the UK 'must not fall behind our competitors' was preferred to the slightly desperate 'catch-up', the government knew well enough that catching up *was* the name of the game, and that it would be a very difficult one to play. A memorandum by Geoffrey Chandler, issued by the NEDC at the same time as the inter-departmental paper, noted that the rate at which microelectronic technology was being taken up in the UK already lagged behind Japan, the US, West Germany, France and Sweden. Enormous changes would be required by companies and unions, bringing fears and misunderstandings, but vital opportunities too.

There is no doubt that the Labour government's sponsorship of these memoranda and other measures to support the manufacture, use and understanding of microelectronics deeply affected the response of the unions. Thus when, in 1979, the TUC produced its influential report 'Employment and Technology', it was not surprising that the first paragraph should reiterate the perceived central dilemma:

> 'Technological change and the microelectronic revolution are a challenge, but also an opportunity. There is the challenge that the rapid introduction of new processes and work organization will lead to the loss of many more jobs and growing social dislocation. Equally, however, there is the realization that new technologies also offer great opportunities − not just for increasing the competitiveness of British industry but for increasing the quality of working life and for providing new benefits to working people.'[6]

THE TUC AUTOMATION DEBATES − TWENTY FIVE YEARS ON

'Employment and Technology' marked something of a shift from the report of the TUC on automation presented to the 1955 Congress, as did the content and tone of the debates in 1978-80 compared with those in 1955. However, there was no absolute discontinuity. Many of the concerns expressed in the 1950s came up again, and many of the lines of argument remained fundamentally the same. The major differences lay in other factors. One was the context surrounding the two debates. The first was in a tight, the second in a slackening, labour market; another was the depth of experience and perception of computerized technology. The first debate was carried on with unions whose members had experienced almost no job loss directly traceable to computerization, and its capabilities and potential were largely guesswork. The second took place when it was becoming clear that the capacity of automation to destroy large numbers of jobs was immense.

Another difference was the greater emphasis in the latter debates, and in 'Employment and Technology', on the need for government planning and intervention, on the explicit linking of new technology with industrial democracy and planning at company and national level. This reflects, to a very considerable extent, the close links forged between the Labour Party and the unions in the 1970s, especially through the crucial medium of the TUC-Labour Party Liaison Committee, which had the effect of encouraging unions to think of themselves collectively as a key component of a present or future government. Lastly, there is the, perhaps curious, fact that the later debates have a much greater degree of unanimity about them than have the earlier ones. Indeed, the 1955 technology debate was largely subsumed under the broader struggle between left and right-wing led unions on public ownership. The debates of the late 1970s, in contrast, showed divisions only between the degree of pessimism as to the employment effects of the new technology (and thus the stance which should be adopted).

The resolution which was carried on 4 September 1978 at the TUC Congress became, together with the government's announcements, the main 'official' texts for the labour movement on the subject. The dualism of challenge and threat is clearly contained within it, but it was debated in a year in which the Labour government had overcome many of its problems and in which the thrust of the NEB into high technology was still relatively strong. It was an ambitious and self-confident programme which the resolution set out. Brian Stanley, General Secretary of the Post Office Engineering Union who moved it, said:

> 'As trade unionists we have to strike a responsible balance. On the one hand, we do not want to be latter-day Luddites, blindly opposing all changes in technology and insisting on the maintenance of existing equipment and skills, however inefficient and irrelevant they become. On the other hand, we cannot accept all the changes in technology at the time, in the form and on the terms proposed by the scientists, the economists and the managers. Unless trade unions intervene in the most positive and in some cases the most determined way, unless detailed and realistic agreements are negotiated, the introduction of new technology will wipe out many jobs and reduce others to boring routine.'[7]

Harry Smith of AUEW-Tass followed Stanley. He highlighted the problems more vividly and stressed the inappropriateness of market forces:

> 'Nowhere in our society can anyone really predict the number of new jobs which may be created by the new products and new standards of information, but I suggest that all the experience of our movement proves one thing, and it is that if we leave it to market forces there will be massive unemployment alongside every sort of waste and social rottenness. Then when we react in the only possible way we shall be called Luddites or worse.'[8]

Though all the speakers made significantly different emphases, broadly definable as 'tending to the optimistic' and 'tending to the pessimistic', there was no repetition of the split in the 1955 debate. The resolution already represented a consensus before it reached the floor, and that consensus was consolidated by a debate in which each of the two potential sides could satisfy the other. Smith's complaint about 'market forces' did not go so far as to call for the public ownership of key sectors. In a large part, this unanimity was due to the supportive role played by the TUC during the 1974-79 Labour government. The motion debated explicitly welcomed the NEB's initiatives. It also, in the list of demands for future government action, reflected a certain confidence born of four years of a 'social contract'.

The 1979 debate followed the publication of 'Employment and Technology', which the 1978 motion had called for. Introducing that report, Lord Allen, the retiring General Secretary of the shopworkers' union Usdaw, said that the General Council, rejected both easy optimism and easy pessimism in favour of an acceptance of the need for change coupled with 'agreement on the direction and speed of that change', and a recognition by government of its role in stimulating growth, training and 'protecting those most at risk'.[9]

Terry Duffy, president of the AUEW's dominant engineering section, followed Allen, and moved a long resolution which concluded that trade union action on the lines proposed by 'Employment and Technology': 'can mean the difference between tremendous improvements in leisure and living standards or massive impoverishment of the masses of workers'. Duffy was, at that time, leading an ultimately successful strike aimed at reducing the 40-hour week in the engineering industry to 39. He linked the union's campaign to the motion, claiming that the AUEW was: 'in the spearhead of an attack to reduce working time'.[10]

Later in the debate, Campbell Christie, Deputy General Secretary of the Executive Civil Servants (SCPS), rose, to voice for a second year his reservations about accepting the new technology:

> 'I believe that the trade union movement, in regard to job loss, must be pessimistic. We cannot afford to bury our heads in the sand and believe that new technology will result in the improved markets, the improved production, that will produce the extra employment for those jobs that are destroyed.'

In the following year, 1980, the tone of the TUC Congress was sombre, and, at times, confused. The walls of the Brighton conference centre were hung with the latest unemployment totals. The outgoing leader of the Labour Party, James Callaghan, asked the delegates, with visible bitterness: 'What can you offer? Can you offer anything? Can you offer anything to a new partnership?' The Congress adopted contradictory motions on incomes policy and indulged in much anti-Tory rhetoric. The resolution on new technology, moved by Bill Whatley, the successor to Lord Allen at the shopworkers union, was a composite which tied in new technology's effects with general job loss, and with the need to reduce the working week to 35 hours. Whatley, whose union could see automatic checkouts and computerized stock control slashing down its 470,000 membership, placed significantly greater stress on the side of pessimism than had been customary among centrist union leaders in the previous two years. He voiced fears that found an echo in all quarters of the movement:

> 'We are concerned that some employers are getting away with murder, that they are fooling all but the most sophisticated by claiming that the job losses are due only to the recession. What they are keeping from us is the

fact that they are using the recession as an excuse to avoid discussing with their workpeople the way that new technology should be introduced, the way that benefits should be shared, the protection that needs to be built in. I do not want to be over cynical but in many cases I believe that employers are quite deliberately reducing their labour force before new technology is introduced, so that they can say that the job loss is minimal because of new technology.'[11]

The 1978-80 debates reflected the general mood of organized labour in these years: new technology was clearly seen as linked to employment, and to be very largely the responsibility of government. Where unemployment was rising rapidly and the government, after a general election, reduced its commitment to subsidize the technology's adoption and to provide buffers for its shocks, the trade union movement reacted, rationally, with greater pessimism and hostility.

EMPLOYMENT AND TECHNOLOGY

The TUC report is of great importance and also stands at the peak of a serious and substantial attempt to introduce new technology and the concept of bargaining to a very large number of officials and ordinary members. The report began by setting the theme that: 'whether technology will prove to be friend or foe will depend, not on the technology itself, but on its application and the policies adopted by governments, trade unions and employers'.[12] It continued by demonstrating a correlation between high productivity growth and low unemployment rates; then argued for an expansion of the services sector and of R and D effort. It briefly explained the development of microelectronics and its applications, then got down to its main task which was discussing the possible employment effects and laying out policy.

Its 'Programme for Trade Union Action' was the centrepiece. Here, the TUC put its imprimatur on the concept of new technology bargaining: 'the first principle of which would be that no new technology which has major effects on the workforce should be introduced unilaterally'.[13] Bargaining on new technology should have the reduction of working time as its main aim, and work on the understanding that it should extend where possible the frontiers of industrial democracy. A long list of further recommendations picked up on aspects of previously-formulated TUC policy (on education, manpower, training and redundancy and unemployment provisions) while a final chapter committed the TUC to a microelectronics awareness programme among its member unions.

The most important policy recommendation of 'Employment and Technology' was that of the establishment of new technology agreements, where possible. A framework for these agreements laid out as a 'checklist for negotiators' formed the last chapter of the report. Their 10-point checklist is set out below.

1. *Objective of 'change by agreement'*: no new technology to be introduced unilaterally; status quo provisions recommended.

2. *Challenge to union organization*: inter-union collaboration in negotiations; build up of technical expertise by unions; technology stewards.

3. *Access to information*: all relevant information to be provided to union representatives before decisions taken; linked to regular consultation on company plans.

4. *Employment and output plans*: preferably no redundancy agreements or improved redundancy payments if impossible; planned approach to redeployment and relocation of workers; pursue commitment to expanding output.

5. *Retraining*: provision of retraining, priority for those directly affected by new technology; principle of maintained or improved earnings during retraining.

6. *Working hours*: scope for reducing working hours and systematic overtime.

7. *Pay structures*: avoid disruption to pay structures and polarization of workforce; ensure income levels maintained and improved; move towards single status and equal conditions.

8. *Control over work*: union influence over systems design and programming; no computer-gathered information to be used in work performance measurement.

9. *Health and safety*: stringent standards for new machinery and processes including visual display units.

10. *Review procedure*: joint union/management study teams to monitor developments and review progress.

THE EMBODIMENT OF CAPITALIST VALUES?

The core argument of the unions for accepting microelectronic technology is that rising productivity through technical progress has been progressive. It is maintained that it can continue, despite serious dislocations resulting from the rapidity of its introduction, to be progressive, provided the process is agreed, planned and underpinned by state aid at a number of levels. This has been the subject of a series of criticisms. There is the assumption implicitly or explicitly made by the unions that technology is neutral and that the important issues for struggle are the way in which it is applied and the effects which flow from its application. These are, as we have seen, common themes, and ones which some radicals have sought to challenge.

Mike Cooley, an AUEW-Tass past-president and main author of the

Lucas Aerospace combine committee's corporate plan, has been among the best known of these critics. In his book, *Architect or Bee?*[14] Cooley, quoting Robert Jungk,[15] argues that:

'the organization of work, and the means of designing both jobs, and the machines and computers necessary to perform them, embodies profound ideological assumptions. So, by regarding science as neutral, we have failed to recognize as anti-human, and consequently to oppose the effects of values built into the apparatus.'[16]

The theme is echoed by the late E F Schumacher, when he claims that:

'the basic aim of modern industrialism is not to make work satisfying, but to raise productivity; its proudest achievement is labour saving whereby labour is stamped with the mark of undesirability. But what is undesirable cannot confer dignity; so the working life of a labourer is without dignity.'[17]

This critique has most recently been powerfully restated by Tony Manwaring,[18] who has sketched in an attack on the unions' responses as being archaic, conservative and passively acquiescent in the management's push for new technology. Manwaring argues that:

'The technology is not socially neutral, but *embodies*, and is developed within, antagonistic relations of production . . . the union movement has recognized the "challenge" posed by new technology, in terms of the threat to jobs and their consent, but believes that an extension of traditional collective bargaining relationships will ensure that the era of the chip will not be characterized by the "collapse of work" but by widespread benefits to union members. The "silicon dream" is of increased leisure and higher material standards of living brought about by shopfloor bargaining over the introduction of new technology and sympathetic government action.'[19]

Are unions guilty, then, of conspiring with management (unconsciously) to strip their workers of dignity? Are the new technology agreements which have been signed employers' charters? It is to these agreements we now turn.

NEW TECHNOLOGY AGREEMENTS

A new technology agreement is an agreement made between union(s) and management in a given company or plant at a given time. Much more than the relatively abstract aims of achieving certain goals, it is determined by (i) the relative strength of the two sides; (ii) the company trading position and ownership structure; (iii) the knowledge and ambitions of the negotiators and the workforce; (iv) the level of technology already in use in the company and of that coming in; (v) the general climate of industrial relations in the company, and in the country.

173

Job Security

Many agreements stipulate that there shall be no forced redundancies: a very few guarantee no redundancies; others contain clauses allowing redundancies as a last resort; some do not mention the subject at all.

In the past, it was usual for these features to be found, if at all, in general procedure agreements, such as that between Prudential Insurance and ASTMS in 1970. This agreement says that: 'the manpower required for any purpose will be determined by the company' but later states that 'it is agreed that the company's policy of no involuntary redundancies shall be maintained'.

In technology agreements, these generalizations are avoided. The C A Parsons/Apex (1979) agreement specifies:

> 'no redundancy as a result of VDUs or their associated systems. Should an excess of labour develop in any area there will be a full discussion with the Apex joint negotiating committee with a view to redeployment.'[20]

(This clause, and the agreement in general, is unusually favourable to the union, and has been described as 'pacesetting'.)

In a curiously-worded clause, the *Observer*/Natsopa Clerical chapel agreement (1980) lays down that:

> 'any suggestion that new operating procedures will create non-jobs will result in discussions to ensure a realistic sharing of job functions to retain meaningful jobs . . . in relation to the introduction of computerized technology the company will guarantee a minimum chapel size of 141 staff (the present numbers) occupied in meaningful activities.'

As a rule, new technology agreements with insurance companies are better from the unions' point of view than the average. For instance, the Norwich Union/ASTMS (1980) agreement guarantees full employment for all existing staff members and for staff recruited between March 1980 and December 1982. The Zurich Insurance/ASTMS (1980) agreement specifies that 'no employee will become compulsorily redundant as a result of the introduction of new technology'.

Consultation and Disclosure of Information

Most new technology agreements contain clauses guaranteeing consultation or provision of information on the new processes. In a review of its agreements drawn up in mid 1981, Apex — which, with ASTMS, is the union with most experience in this area — commented that: '*all* agreements guarantee to provide detailed information. It is not clear in many cases, however, when and how this information is to be disclosed nor how the Apex representatives propose to assess the information and monitor developments'.[21]

The type of clause to which the Apex review refers is exemplified in the Rolls Royce (car division)/Apex (1980) agreement, which says that 'management will continue to provide the Apex new technology working party with all relevant information to enable it to monitor developments, extensions to existing systems and further introduction of computer-based systems'. There are clear drawbacks here, where one side has control of the flow of information while the other may lack the detailed knowledge required to assess the implications of the material provided.

Many agreements refer back potential disputes to already-existing disputes procedures. A reasonably typical example is the clause from the CPC(UK)/ACTSS and ASTMS (1979) agreement:

> 'It is the intention of the company to discuss with the trade unions each stage of its plans for investment and the introduction of electronic data processing equipment on to the Trafford Park site . . . matters that are not capable of resolution . . . will be pursued through the normal disputes procedure.'

Health and Safety

Health and safety is the most constant and by far the most detailed element in the technology agreements so far signed. Almost all the agreements we have seen contain a relatively long section on the subject, and some are almost wholly concerned with health and safety. It has been frequently suggested by officials that this is because there exists legislation on the matter (the Health and Safety at Work Act 1974) which brought into existence health and safety representatives who have built up some experience, also because health and safety, especially in relation to VDUs, is a quantifiable matter with scope for precise bargaining.

Further, the central health and safety issue is that of eyestrain for VDU operators. Many agreements specify a certain time away from the screen — the most generous appears to be the Underground Mining Machinery/Apex (1980) and C A Parsons/Apex agreements, which allow 20 minutes each hour. Others — such as the British Rail/TSSA (1979) agreement limits aggregate time on VDU work to four hours a day, while the Coventry Climax/Apex (1979) agreement calls for a variation of: 'visual tasks by taking short relief periods . . . during the relief periods employees will carry out other duties . . .'

Sharing Benefits

Few agreements incorporate a reduction in hours — a bargaining objective stressed in the TUC and other union guidelines. The Express Lifts/Apex (1979) agreement contains a clause in which: 'the management agrees to negotiate with the union on the union's target of a reduction in the working week and improvements in holiday arrangements in the light of increased productivity as a result of the use of the [new] systems': Provident Finance/ASTMS (1980) allows a cut in the week from 37½ to 35 hours as a result of technological change.

Few, too, agree to increases in pay, though there is often a recognition that increased skills should attract extra payment. C A Parsons/Apex says that: 'full use will be made of the job evaluation scheme to recognize both changes in responsibility and increased flexibility which may result from the introduction of VDUs'. The Plessey Telecommunications/Apex (1980) and the Ford/Tass (1979) agreements contain similar formulae.

Individual Liberty

Much has been made, especially in leftist writings on office technology[22] of the threat to individual liberties by the ability bequeathed to managements by automated equipment to monitor office workers' performance and work rate. Interestingly, this concern has found its way into new technology bargaining, and has resulted in a few clauses where managements have guaranteed not to secretly monitor work. The TI Accles and Pollock/Apex (1980) agreement says simply that: 'any work measurement elements of equipment installed will not be measured by computer-based systems', while the London Borough of Islington/Staff side agreement (1980) says that: 'any work measurement elements of equipment installed will not be used without the knowledge of the operator concerned'.

Summary

Our survey of some 70 agreements bears out comments by trade union research departments and academics that the achievements — judged by the unions own standards as laid out in the TUC congresses and union conferences and detailed in the model agreements and reports — are modest. Health and safety is the most strikingly precise of the issues agreed: the others, such as job security, consultation and disclosure, and sharing benefits — are usually either tentative or vague, and all depend heavily on the maintenance of considerable strength and vigilance on the part of the unions.

There has been one striking omission in our examples — there are no technology agreements in the heart of white collar work, the civil service. Such agreements have been under discussion since 1979. From the beginning of these discussions, the civil service unions, coming together in the Council of Civil Service Unions, had linked the acceptance of new systems to a shorter working week, and had declared as a basic objective a no redundancy clause. In the course of some nine meetings in 1980 within a special joint committee of the Whitley Council, the civil service negotiating machinery, progress was made on health and safety and other issues, but none on shorter hours or a no redundancy clause. The Civil Service Department would not concede either principle. In March of 1981, following a meeting in January between the Civil Service Minister Mr Barney Hayhoe and the unions, the CSD clarified its position. A letter to the CCSU said that: 'it has not been the practice to buy improvements in the efficiency of the Civil Service with extra pay or improved conditions'. By that time, a dispute had occurred over pay; a three-month period of disruptive action followed, during which, at successive union conferences, the unions withdrew any intention of co-operating with the introduction of new automated systems.

In discussions with government officials later that year and early in 1982, the unions did come round to initial acceptance of a limited, two-year deal introducing new systems. However, the two largest unions (the Civil and Public Servants Association and the Society of Civil and Public Servants) then overturned the agreement at their conferences, and all nine unions agreed to withdraw.

TECHNOLOGY IN MANUFACTURING

Manufacturing industry has a history of technological change. For that main reason, there have been few new technology agreements.

Manufacturers, however, do consult their heavily unionized work-forces over the introduction of new systems, and have done so in a variety of ways. It is unlikely that major new systems have been introduced into UK industry, even at a time of relative trade union weakness, without such consultations which, in many cases, would amount to bargaining. The fact that they have not resulted in specific agreements based on new technology need not necessarily be seen as a point of weakness — though when unions redress the balance of power again, many will feel it to be in their interests to sign such agreements.

We take one example of the introduction of new systems in the late 1970s-early 1980s, crucial to an important UK industrial sector.[23]

BL

BL, the former British Leyland, has pinned much of its future on the success of the Mini Metro, built, since June 1980, in a custom-made plant at Longbridge. The company chose to wholly automate the Metro's production, with robots welding the body shell and sub-assemblies. Warehousing, painting and quality control also are all fully computerized.

The workforce was consulted about the plans from 1976, when the new car was first mooted, through a technology joint committee, part of the BL participation system. The committee included convenors and stewards from Longbridge and from the Swindon body shop, together with management representatives. It made a number of key decisions, including commitments to break down tedious work routines and reducing demarcation.

However, the collapse of BL's participation plan in September 1977 ended the life of the technology committee as well. Union hopes for a special pay deal for Metro workers were dashed on the achievement of pay parity between the plants, and a demand for *ex gratia* payments to buy out old working practices was not met. A technology agreement has not been negotiated.

The Metro has been a successful model for BL, and there has been little disruptive action associated with it. There have been no redundancies at Longbridge, though far fewer workers make the Metro under the new conditions than would have been required under previous production systems. For example, only 38 workers are employed on car body assembly compared with around 140 on a conventional line. On the other hand, the requirement for maintenance workers has increased, though not by a compensatory amount.

BL, like other manufacturing companies, operates in a sector with well-publicized problems. Workers, especially stewards, knew the problems and had well-founded fears for their future. They believed that they had no alternative but agreement with management's plans. Having accepted that, agreement was a relatively straightforward matter of detail. Technology agreements were not seen as necessary because the bargaining was contained within existing structures, while issues such as individual liberties and eyestrain did not arise.

THE TUC-CBI TALKS

It was largely because of the experience of these and other large companies in bringing in extensive new systems that a national understanding between the TUC and the CBI was aborted after it had reached an advanced stage in negotiation. The decision to attempt to negotiate such an understanding was taken at the January 1980 meeting of the NEDC. That meeting considered the TUC's 'Employment and Technology' and the CBI's 'Jobs: Facing the Future',[24] and it was felt that there was some common ground.

From the beginning, the TUC appeared the more keen of the two organizations to achieve a deal — though a significant minority of leftist General Council members baulked at the idea. There were two reasons for its enthusiasm. First, the TUC had more to gain at that juncture from an agreement than the CBI. The recession was biting hard, and rapidly rising unemployment was giving employers more power than they had enjoyed in at least a decade. An umbrella code of practice setting agreed standards, and guaranteeing consultation, would clearly set a valuable precedent for company and plant agreements. The TUC began with much more ambitious objectives: to secure a no redundancy clause and a shorter working week as a *quid pro quo* for acceptance of technological change.

Secondly, the TUC had developed a strategy of limited co-operation with the CBI on certain objectives. Under this strategy, the TUC and the CBI would find agreement on new technology, then procede to broader areas of agreement on matters such as trade and investment, pricing and possibly even incomes. Implicit in this joint approach, and explicit in the drafts was a muted criticism of government for its lack of encouragement for investment and its more doctrinaire free enterprise ideas: a criticism in which the TUC hoped for CBI support.

In both of these pursuits the TUC proved to be over-ambitious. Employers now could usually achieve change by a mixture of persuasion and threat, and the CBI was not prepared to be used as a pawn in the TUC's anti-government tactics. While both sides could agree on relatively modest measures such as the need for more effective manpower planning and training, the provision of information, extra payment for extra skills and consultation on health and safety, the bulk of the CBI membership felt that a national agreement on technology (see Appendix 2) would be a nuisance, and not something necessary to concede.

Thus, though the TUC Congress in September 1980 endorsed the draft agreement reached between officials of the two organizations, the CBI's council turned it down later that year. In a speech on 9 April 1981, Len Murray recalled bitterly that:

> 'We reached agreement with their [CBI's] senior representatives, then the backwoodsmen of the CBI threw it out. . . clear evidence of their lack of vision and lack of understanding of national and institutional realities . . . the British employers . . . stand condemned as insular and myopic.'[25]

NEW TECHNOLOGY AGREEMENTS IN OTHER EUROPEAN COUNTRIES

This chapter is largely concerned with the experience of British trade unions. However, for purposes of comparison, it is useful to glance at the parallel efforts of unions in other major European countries.

Patterns of work are being changed in every advanced society in similar ways. The same types of machines are replacing the same types of labour in the same types of enterprises manufacturing the same types of products or offering the same types of service.

Thus, it is to be expected that other West European labour movements have also 'discovered' new technology agreements, or an equivalent mechanism. With the exception of the Scandinavian unions, who are in many respects the trail-blazers, few have approached the issue in ways similar to those taken by the British unions. The reasons for this lie in the different traditions and practices of the various national labour movements and their perceived need of formal agreements and other structures to regulate technological change.

Many other European labour movements – such as the West German, the Italian, the Austrian, the Finnish and the Scandinavian — have greater regulation of their activities by statute. This is a practice that is looked on with suspicion by the UK (though there is a recognition in some quarters that some laws, for example on minimum wages, can serve their interests).

In spite of wide variations two common major elements emerge across the Western European industrial relations scene. First, the scope of collective bargaining is continuously expanding to cover issues beyond pay, encompassing the content and structure of work; and second, local bargaining is becoming more important. Both of these developments have assisted the spread of new technology bargaining, especially as it is often seen as a direct threat to jobs. Thus, a number of demands occur in agreements in various countries: joint control over new technology, the provision of information on a routine basis, no compulsory redundancies due to new technology, no work measurement by computerized equipment, and monitoring of health and safety.

Unions in West Germany

Unions in West Germany have protested against the effects, or the presumed effects, of technological change. As early as 1973, members of IG Metall, the engineering union, took action over the rights of their works councils to play a major part in the 'humanization of work'. Action was also taken by German printers (members of IG Druck und Papier) in the winter of 1977-78 against technological change in the industry. The settlement finally arrived at containing job guarantees for skilled workers for eight years, six years of which would be paid at wages comparable to those enjoyed in their former grades.

Much of German industrial relations is handled by the works councils, the main forum for the day-to-day practice of the co-determination principle. Technological change is one of the issues on which the councils have the legal right to negotiate, and it has been estimated that more than 60 works councils agreements on the introduction of new technology have been concluded. These agreements usually contain clauses similar to those concluded between UK management and unions, but often (as in the case of that signed by workers at Volkswagen's Wolksburg plant in July 1979) with a heavier emphasis on disclosure of personal records (whether computerized or not).

At a national level, agreements were signed in 1980-81 covering 800,000 of West Germany's 4.5 million engineering and metal workers providing for retraining and salary protection of workers made redundant by technological change. Collective agreements in the chemical, textile and leather industries cover older workers made redundant or otherwise displaced in this way, while banking and insurance companies have concluded agreements which cover the operation of computer terminals.

Unions in France

In France, both the relative weakness of, and political divisions in, the trade union movement have meant that the ability of unions to bargain effectively in large areas of the economy — including, crucially, parts of the expanding office sector — has been limited. In the area of new technology, this relative weakness has been compounded by the exceptional importance placed on information technology — 'informatique' — by recent governments. While initiatives taken by the government, and the very large presence of the state in the 'information industries' does not obviate the need for independent trade union responses, they have paved the way for French society, (including the unions) to accept new work processes.

At the same time, the new Socialist government has, since taking office in mid-1981, moved towards implementation of a shorter working week regulated by statute, explicitly designed to assist in the fight against unemployment caused, *inter alia*, by the effects of the new technology.

In 1980, the CFDT published nine propositions to cover the introduction of 'l'informatique'. These included a commitment to consult, and covered information on investment, on effects of new technology, on the use of experts and reviews of the systems once installed.

The CGT-FO believes that the issues thrown up by the computer technology should be dealt with in one forum, where the problems are reviewed regularly by the social partners. The union also believes that computerization will greatly increase unemployment, and has consistently argued for increased aid to the regions and investment in socially useful production to counter its effects.

There are few examples of new technology agreements in France, and these are largely confined to the printing industry and to the insurance sector. For example, the country's third largest insurance company, Assurances Générales, has negotiated a job security clause and a commitment to consultation.

NEW TECHNOLOGY AGREEMENTS: FOR OR AGAINST?

The technology agreements so far signed have been modest, and largely limited to the white collar sector. There has been resistance by employers, both individually and collectively, to agreements and there is clear evidence that, in the short term at least, the adoption of new systems does cause redundancies. Is this evidence that, as Manwaring puts it: 'the silicon dream . . . of increased leisure and higher material standards of living brought about by shopfloor bargaining over the introduction of new technology and sympathetic government action . . . is more likely to become a nightmare?'[26]

Has the new technology borne out the prediction that it 'embodies capitalist social relations' and thus discriminates against workers whenever and wherever it is brought in? The assumption is fatalistic because it assumes that new technology can only be accepted on 'employers' terms, or rejected on 'workers' terms — the latter action logically leading to the maintenance of 'old' technology.

Where Manwaring, and others who follow (or precede) him are misleading is in their confusion between the embodiment within the technology of certain relations, and its introduction and use within relationships whose relative power changes over time. Manwaring writes that: 'the technology itself is not socially neutral, but *embodies*, and is developed within, antagonistic relations of production . . .'[27] Here, the two processes of 'being embodied' and 'developing within' are presented as being naturally consecutive, where in fact they are practically opposites.

Automated equipment, as we have noted before, introduces logic and memory into production, displacing those previously uniquely human qualities. That displacement takes place on terms set by the balance of power among the various social forces and institutions which are concerned with the process. In short, automation possesses no *inherent* quality which marks it out from other, earlier technologies.

The conditions which governed the introduction of the new wave of automated equipment into plants and offices are less mysterious than embodied forces. In the UK, these are a recession, rising unemployment and a government committed to reductions in public spending and set against planning for industrial and economic expansion. These factors have made one side of the bargaining process much stronger than the other. The limitation of technology agreements, and their absence from large areas of UK industry, stand alongside the low wage settlements, the abortive industrial actions, the often-hopeless factory occupations and mass redundancies as evidence of trade union weaknesses. As the ETUI put it in a recent report:

> 'Recessional elements mean, among other things, that a widespread restructuring process is taking place and, if it gains strength without being checked in any way, it could undermine union efforts to defend and improve job content.'[28]

At the same time, lack of growth in the Western economies means that most manufacturers are interested in rationalization rather than expansion. The introduction of new technology is primarily seen by employers as a *labour saving* device. This does not simply mean redundancies; it also means widespread changes in work organizaton, union organization and traditional demarcation lines.

CONCLUSION

The early experience of workers in the UK, and throughout Western Europe, confronted with rapid technological change has been uneven. Many have been untouched. Others have known technical change in a relatively small way, change which has been absorbed in working practices with little dislocation. Still others have been greatly affected in their particular industry or trade, though these changes have not been seen within the wider society to be particularly significant.

We have been concerned with the area within which debate has focused: automation. Here, we see two broad trends. In offices, automation is bringing in equipment which reproduces some of the elements of the manufacturing production line. This has been met with attempts by white collar unions to control the speed and manner of its introduction, with limited success.

In manufacturing, technological change has been commonplace. The rate of its introduction has been fast and the restructuring of work has proceeded very rapidly. There are clear signs that those managements determined to innovate are now being able to do so more easily than in the recent past, and they have successfully resisted ambitious attempts by the trade union movement to control the process. In manufacturing, the effect of new technology may be, in some plants at least, to 'de-Taylorize' production and to restructure work among more decentralized units, by turning over much mass production and mechanical work to robots. The best-known example of this trend is Volvo's Kalmer plant in Sweden, where teams of around 20 work almost autonomously. Siemens and Olivetti have both adopted similar systems, and it is clear that advanced production methods will increasingly lend themselves to such arrangements.

The way such restructuring will take place will clearly vary considerably from sector to sector. Unions in the UK have yet to come fully to grips with the process which has been largely dominated by management initiatives. The CBI, in discussions on the national technology agreement, emphasized that management must have the right to adopt and apply new technology in ways it sees fit, and in 1980 managers were strong enough to beat off a trade union challenge to that view. Whether the unions can gain sway over the new processes in the future will depend on a variety of economic, political and social factors which, in the early 1980s, are highly volatile.

REFERENCES

1 P Bassett (1979) 'Labour and the Microchip'. *Financial Times*, 23 October; and National Computing Centre (1979) 'The impact of microprocessors on British business', para 14.1. Manchester; and K Robins and F Webster (1980) 'The trade union response in the UK, p 2. Oxford Polytechnic Paper.

2 Electrical, Electronic Telecommunications and Plumbing Union (1980) *The EETPU and Technological Change.*

3 Report of the Royal Commission on Industrial Democracy (1977) HMSO.

4 D Lea (1980) Address to the IRES-CGIL International Seminar on Industrial Democracy. Rome. May 22-23.

5 Departments of Industry, Employment and Education and Science (1978) Joint Paper on microelectronics. December.

6 TUC (1979) *Employment and Technology*, p 7.

7 TUC (1978) Conference Report, pp 478-9.

8 ibid, p 480.

9 TUC (1979) Conference Report, p 538.

10 ibid, p 541.

11 TUC (1980) Conference Report, p 475.

12 TUC (1979) *Employment and Technology*, p 9.

13 ibid, p 59.

14 M Cooley (1980) *Architect or Bee?* Langley Technical Services.

15 R Jungk (1973) *Qualitats des Lebens*. EUA, Cologne.

16 M Cooley, op cit, p 47.

17 E F Schumacher (1979) *Good Work.*

18 T Manwaring (1981) 'Trade union response to new technology'. *Industrial Relations Journal*, p 7. July.

19 T Manwaring, op cit, pp 20-24.

20 Industrial Relations Review and Report (1979) June.

21 Association of Professional, Executive, Clerical and Computer Staff (1981) Internal Review of New Technology Agreements. Unpublished.

22 CSE Microelectronics Group (1980) *Capitalist Technology and the Working Class.* CSE Books.

23 This case study is based on Incomes Data Services Study (1980), 202. June.

24 CBI (1979) *Jobs: Facing the Future.*

25 L Murray (1981) Speech on Unemployment and Working Time. TUC Consultative Conference. 9 April.

26 T Manwaring, op cit, p 22.

27 T Manwaring, op cit, p 27.

28 European Trade Union Institute (1981) *Redesigning Jobs: Western European Experiences*, p 37, May.

CHAPTER 9

A New Social Contract

INTRODUCTION

In the UK, since losing the 1979 election, the Labour Party has reconstituted the TUC — Labour Party Liaison Committee, which has taken over the major policy formulation role for the Labour movement. Labour's programme, it may be assumed, cannot move far from Liaison Committee policy.

Great claims have been made for the new social contract which has emerged from the Liaison Committee. Roy Green has described it in a recent issue of *New Socialist* as heralding:

> 'a new form of mass politics of the labour movement . . . implicit in the TUC statement that the 300,000 shop stewards and union officials constitute a nationwide network capable of influencing decision-making within enterprises and changing their plans. The creation of a form of political activity which is immediately related to the everyday economic activity of union members must contribute to the overcoming of that alienation from political processes which reflects the separation of the state and political life from society.'[1]

PLANNING AND INDUSTRIAL DEMOCRACY

The relative success of the unions' technology bargaining policies, compared to the Labour government's efforts at industrial planning, has heavily influenced the efforts to reconstruct a social contract. The Liaison Committee's interim report 'Economic Planning and Industrial Democracy: a framework for full employment' which was published in July 1982 is evidence of a radical response at the centre of the labour movement to the difficulties which led to the breakdown of the earlier social contract, and the failure of the attempts at planning in the 1960s and 1970s. Its main objective, as its title suggests, was to reconcile: 'strategic issues agreed at the centre' with accountability to workers and to society.[2]

The report rejected the attribution of failure of previous policies to a lack of political will, and recognized that the central problem was the limitations of government powers over economic activity. It proposes that the major factor in this has been the lack of company level involvement by workers, and concludes that such involvement, through industrial democracy, is a necessary agent of the planning process.

The Structure of Industrial Decision-making

As we have noted, trade unions have been relatively successful over the post-war period in securing joint control over operational decisions in the enterprise. Although progress have been uneven, they have extended the frontier of negotiation beyond terms and conditions of employment to include issues formerly within the employer's prerogative. Among these issues are the organization and pace of work; staffing levels; recruitment and deployment of labour; demarcation and labour flexibility; quality; inventory and financial control; grievances and discipline; and health and safety.

The report explains how workforce influence in these areas has been enlarged through developments in the scope of collective bargaining. Much of the impetus has come in recent years from the negotiation of new technology agreements. These have been accompanied by significant changes in trade union structure. The shift to plant and company bargaining has led to the growth of joint committees which have strengthened the ability of workforce representatives to put pressure on management on an ever widening range of issues relating to the organization of production.

Employers have been able to limit the scope of workforce involvement at all levels by making long-term strategic planning their sole prerogative. But the growth of plant and company bargaining in recent years poses a challenge to the employer's prerogative even at this level:

'The case for extending worker influence over the major strategic decisions of enterprises is therefore firmly rooted in the actual development of collective bargaining and joint control. While this development has been temporarily held back by economic recession, it will resume with greater vigour as our expansion plans get under way.'[3]

The Liaison Committee relate the need for extended worker influence to their central concern to find a method of effective planning. Their argument goes something like this: planning is essential in Britain to revitalize industry and sustain a return to full employment; the market cannot fulfil these objectives; the way our economy is organized and run must be changed, but how?

This is an analysis which lies at the root of Labour's reassessment of the promise of science and technology. The party noted in another recent report that in the past:

'there was a widespread belief that the "white heat of the technological revolution" could transform the lives of working people in terms of material improvement. But in the late 1970s and in the 1980s we have seen Britain becoming a de-industrialized country . . . One of the reasons for this decline relates to science and technology . . . In the absence of a planned socialist economy with comprehensive training and re-training, people are being put out of work with the introduction of new methods of production based on technological advances.'[4]

The Liaison Committee bases its argument for planning on the evidence that the market is not the decentralized ideal of economic orthodoxy. The decisions which shape the economy are taken in TNCs, without any accountability to their workers or to the community. These decisions are seen to be responsible for Britain's poor economic performance over many years. The report therefore argues that planning can improve economic performance and can co-ordinate production to meet social needs only if it changes the nature and direction of company behaviour. It is argued that: 'increased influence and control by workers through their trade unions will be the key to making concentrations of power accountable to society'.[5]

Why Labour Failed

The Labour Party's past experience is less than encouraging. There are two episodes in the post-war period which provide some lessons. The first was the 1965 National Plan. This set detailed targets for growth and investment but: 'failed to change the various strategies being pursued by companies. In particular, the relation between the national growth target and the targets for individual sectors was vague, while the relation between companies' plans and sector plans was vaguer still'.[6] The Plan was subsequently blown off course by the Treasury response to balance of payments pressures.

The second episode was the attempt by the Labour movement in the early 1970s to learn from the failure of the National Plan. The new approach was explicitly designed:

'to link the corporate strategies of companies with the development of a national industrial strategy through the proposed system of "planning agreements". Negotiations between government planners and large companies were to lead to joint agreements on such basic issues as investment location, import substitution and product development.'[7]

This approach also came to very little for a number of reasons listed by the Liaison Committee: 'most crucially, the role envisaged for workers and their trade union representatives was not clearly formulated'.[8] The impetus and leverage which industrial democracy might have given to planning negotiations had been recognized only as an afterthought.

The industrial strategy provided no structure through which workers could exercise greater control over the organization of the individual enterprise, let alone project their influence into the wider planning system. To sum up: 'Two lessons stand out. First, there must be firm links established between national planning and company planning; and, second, workers must be involved at all levels of the planning system. These lessons are central to our thinking'.[9]

The report therefore seeks to build on the well-developed systems of voluntary collective bargaining by calling for an extension of rights to information and consultation, including the representation of workers on joint union committees and on company boards — these rights to be triggered by workers when they wish to take the responsibility for exercising them.

A Third Attempt at Planning

Planning machinery envisaged by the report rests on the extension of industrial democracy, rather than being imposed by the state upon society. It assumes the widening of collective bargaining into areas where it is only partly present, or entirely absent: especially in the direction of the enterprise itself. Thus, the limited form of consultation between government and trade union leaders which characterized the previous Labour government is extended to representation of the shop floor, in an attempt to pre-empt the gap which always existed between them in the 1974-79 period which was ultimately instrumental in destroying the old social contract.

The mechanisms proposed by the report are summarized below. They are:

☐ A new *Department of Economic and Industrial Planning* to act as a central focus for planning in the machinery of government. This Department will conduct a 'national economic assessment' covering the broad allocation of resources, and negotiate 'agreed development plans' with companies.

☐ An independent *National Planning Council* to channel and develop the trade union role in planning at sector and national levels. This body will be 'stronger' than the National Economic Development Council, which it will supersede.

☐ New *statutory rights for workers* to information, consultation and representation in the enterprise and in wider planning. Workers themselves will decide how and when to use these rights through their joint union committees, backed by new facilities and rights to time-off.

☐ New *regional planning bodies* to give planning a regional focus and encourage and co-ordinate local initiatives. Trade unions and local authorities will have a representative voice on these bodies.

☐ A *National Planning College* to provide education and training for trade unionists, managers, public servants and all those who have the job of making planning work.

The new proposals seek to spread economic democracy in a more radical way than ever before proposed by a Labour party. Their challenge may have to wait some years before they are matched with a response — but they already represent a significant advance. Yet, although the TUC and Labour Party have gone beyond the position of the first social contract in many aspects, they remain within the tradition of corporate collective bargaining. The stress on the role of the state in planning technological change is also firmly within the Party's Bernalist tradition. As we have seen in Chapter 2, both strands are firmly rooted in the political thought of the 1930s. How adequate will this be in the last decades of the century?

THE NEW SOCIAL CONTRACT AND THE STR

In its current form, the new social contract lacks a vision of the form a socialist society might take in the social and economic environment of the 1980s, and 1990s. It also lacks a policy for the development of information systems to link planning and industrial democracy which would be a prerequisite for bringing about a socialist society.

The new social contract is clearly open to the same problems which beset Labour in 1974-79. The new Planning Department could, when wrestling with the familiar British problems of low growth and low productivity, choose to ignore the consultative and representational mechanisms, especially where the latter were badly supported by workers. Under the proposals, unions are given an enormous task to which they may not prove themselves equal. The sectarian divisions within the Labour movement may once again guarantee immobility.

Even if these problems could be overcome, the new strategy does not come to terms with the social consequences of the STR, in particular the long-term economic impact of the shift in the technical base of the world economy which we have described in Chapter 2. We saw there how corporate collective bargaining emerged as scientific managers and organized labour became increasingly concerned with what they regarded as the negative social consequences of the productive forces unleashed in the 1920s. The scientific managers and their political allies proposed to control these forces by institutionalizing the sharing of political and economic power. Three distinct groups concerned with the management of technical change were recognized: trade unions, governments and large employers. They regulated production through negotiated agreements which have established the contemporary working environment.

Since the Second World War, each of these groups has become aware of the increasing challenge which technological change still poses to their interests. Unions, having gained extensive rights of veto over changes to domestic working practices by their industrial strength, now

189

seek to preserve these gains in the emerging world of transnational production processes. Governments, who have made increasingly sophisticated interventions in public purchasing, education, research and development are now needing to define their relationships with manufacturing industries. Large employers have evolved into transnational companies, concerned with controlling the accelerating application of new technology worldwide.

All this is consistent with Bernal's view of the social aspects of the STR. Its origin has been located in the theoretical advances which led up to the splitting of the atom in 1932, from which developed the twin disciplines of nuclear engineering and electronics. We have called the technology based on its electronics component, Dieboldism. As Bernal envisaged, some feature of the STR, such as the extension of government economic activity and the rise of the TNCs, differentiate it sharply from earlier periods of the industrial revolution. Science and technology have been central to this process. Science-based companies were, as we have seen in Chapter 3, not only initiators of planned research and development in corporate laboratories, but also pioneers of a form of direct overseas investment which has come to dominate the world economy.

We have seen how labour built up on the framework of collective bargaining to exploit the new possibilities which opened up for extending its influence; notably by democratizing the necessary state interventions in the economy. This process of socializing the economy has proceeded fitfully since the war. As Mr Len Murray, the General Secretary of the TUC, put it in a Guildhall lecture in 1980:

> '. . . unions see themselves as democratizing forces concerned with decentralizing power. Governments of both political parties have tended to move, though slowly, in this direction, for example in creating new tripartite bodies and agencies such as the National Economic Development Council, the Manpower Services Commission, and the Health and Safety Commission . . .'[10]

This general progress has continued with both Labour and Conservative governments largely because the growing strength of trade unions has been progressively accommodated within government, and their organization in the civil service, local authorities and nationalized industries encouraged. Trade union leaders have become increasingly involved in the affairs of state, while shop stewards have extended their influence.

At a time of mass unemployment, with the former gains by the labour movement under attack on all fronts, such changes in the pattern of politics seem to be marginal at best. Some on the Left maintain that this bleak prospect follows naturally from Bernalism in practice since:

> 'the essence of Bernal's argument was that science had become an ideologi-

cally neutral force of production and, as such, it now possessed an internal logic whose workings were best understood by scientists.'

Since his socialism was based on 'the same sort of productive forces as are found in capitalist society,' their social aspects were bound to be similar.[11]

This explanation represents yet another form of technological determinism – an attempt to explain socio-economic change as following completely from technical change. However, the source of the weakness of Bernalism is, the authors believe, to be found in an altogether different direction: in its failure to take account of those characteristics of the STR which are features of earlier periods of industrialization. It is this weakness which undermined the effectiveness of the old social contract and which threatens to undermine its successor. In the debates about the significance of the STR in the 1960s and 1970s, technological change was portrayed as an ever-accelerating process which, with some minor qualifications concerning the need for Mintech and indicative planning, can lead to an ever-increasing economic expansion.

In practice, shifts in the technical base of the economy have followed an altogether different pattern since the industrial revolution, a pattern which the STR does not yet appear to have broken. While little attention was paid to this in earlier debates it may be that this aspect of continuity with the earlier revolution may be equally significant in determining the social and economic implications of the new technology. We have, therefore, attempted to demonstrate that Dieboldism is following a pattern of development common to previous transformations in the technical base of the economy, associated with steam power, the railways and electricity. We expect that it will be seen to progress through two major phases: a prosperity phase in which old and new production techniques co-exist while the new technology is perfected, followed by a recession phase in which the old technology is superceded. The prosperity phase of Dieboldism, concerned with standardizing production techniques, establishing an infrastructure of supporting industries, and appropriate scientific and engineering disciplines may be said to have extended for a quarter century from 1945. The changeover to the recession phase took place during the 1970s, when, for the first time, the majority of new products were electronic-based, and the recession phase proper, in which the new technology is diffused throughout the production process, will last until the end of the century.

It is only now, as we enter the recession phase proper, that Labour's ability to defend and advance its interests with its traditional strategy, albeit packaged in a new form, is being sharply challenged. The old policies are particularly weak when dealing with the needs of a growing unorganized group of working people, the changing pattern of industry, and the narrowing options for national planning in the context of an evermore integrated international economy.

INDUSTRIAL DEMOCRACY AND THE UNORGANIZED

The first major weakness for Labour lies in the emergence of a two-tier democracy. A strategy of social negotiation, designed for an expanding economy, begins to look distinctly shaky when faced with growing numbers without work. To some observers it seems that a distinct tendency towards a two-tier system of democracy is emerging in the West. Those inside trade unions, perhaps just the active members, will have access to economic plans and be able to influence them. Those not in membership, either because they are pensioners, unemployed, or employed in occupations which are not represented by trade unions, will be cut off from influence. This in turn could lead to the emergence of a global class structure with a transnational managerial class at its apex, a large class of established labour enjoying relatively secure employment through the success of its strategy, and a third group of social marginals who find employment, if at all, in secondary labour markets not protected by collective agreements.

Corporatism
This tendency towards a close identification of organized labour with the large employers and the state, which some call corporatism, has distinct dangers for Labour. Although it is morally untenable, corporatism is not inconsistent with the interests of a labour aristocracy if the corporate state can protect its allies from the consequences of long-term economic decline. A sophisticated policy of accommodation related to industrially powerful groups of workers alongside the coercion of weaker groups might be an attractive proposition for both government and workers who seek to mitigate the social consequences of the short-term fluctuations of the business cycle. It is an altogether different prospect for the state to take measures to protect putative allies from the implications of a chronic decline in economic activity.

Dismantling the Welfare State
Yet that is precisely what the transition to electronic-based production appears to mean. As a consequence of the recession phase of new technology many millions of working people will be displaced from their present employment. Whether the economic system left to itself will ultimately create compensating job opportunities will depend on new sources of profit being found which are labour-intensive, and this

must remain an open question. In the meantime the economy of the advanced world will be depressed by the consequences of fairly long-term mass unemployment.

Many of those displaced through new technology may never work again, adding to the demographic problems of the industrialized world. Medical improvements, the low birth rates of the 1970s and progressively earlier retirement, will significantly shift the balance of the population between those in and out of work. In an ageing society the demand for certain public services, such as health, will intensify at precisely the same time as the public and private means available to satisfy this demand is reduced as a growing proportion of the population comes to rely on pension income. The proportion of those aged over 75, the largest single group of users of the social services, is set to double by the year 2000, and there are already signs that the complex system of pension provision, based on a combination of state and private schemes, which was established in the 1970s, may be brought into question.

The Chancellor of the Exchequer, Geoffrey Howe, has recently noted that the cost of providing pensions could become 'an unsustainable burden' on the working population. He cited the situation in the US, where similar guarantees had been made on minimum pensions, and where the social security system could face bankruptcy early in the next century. With respect to the private occupational pension schemes he asked: 'We must ask if private employers are not offering too generous pensions, in the sense that the real resources needed to meet them are placing too heavy a burden on the companies concerned. Is two-thirds of final salary after 40 years too ambitious?'[12]

The Politics of Reflation

It is a lesson which follows from the crisis of the 1930s (which was only ended when war brought full employment) that a market-driven decline of today's magnitude can only be ended by government action to expand the production of public goods. That is, goods not produced because they use technologies which are not patentable, or because there is insufficient income among users, or the technology is not obsolescent, or because existing investments are threatened. Under this heading are many potential services concerned with telecommunications, finance, health, housing, education and community care.

Any government which attempted to embark on such a course would find itself in need of substantial political support, which a corporatist Labour movement would be unable to deliver. Attempts to expand government activities within international markets such as telecommunications or funds transfer, or even self-contained national markets such as housing and medical services will be inevitably opposed by transnational manufacturing and service companies, as the French have found. 'Corporatist' Labour would not be able to provide the necessary political support, since the restricted democracy of an elite inevitably leads to a distancing of the elite from its base. Ultimately, the restriction of membership involvement, which corporatism implies, puts at risk the democratizing gains of which Len Murray has spoken, opening the way to sectarian manoeuvering by vested interests within party and union bureaucracies. In the end, this is a recipe for alienation not only of whole groups of unorganized workers, but of large sections of the trade union membership themselves. The first challenge to Labour's strategy is the need to adapt its approach to industrial democracy so that it becomes accountable to the needs of those without work, and increasingly accountable to those in work.

TECHNOLOGY CHOICE AND POST-INDUSTRIAL SOCIETY

The second major weakness of Labour strategy concerns the poor data on economic and technological options which the movement has to support its decision-making. As Veblen remarked, trades unions are ill-suited to the management of technical change since they represent today's workers rather than tomorrow's. If their knowledge of the available alternative technologies is to go beyond the collective intelligence of their members, and limited speculation on future technologies which ultimately stems from their bargaining opponents, a new and independent source of economic and technological information must be available.

The new social contract, like its predecessor, relies on the use of computer models of the economy for planning TUC policy and government interventions, and nationalized industries to provide the options for investment.[13] As Stafford Beer has noted, the models have major defects. In the first instance, the collection of statistics by the state reflects its own structure which in turn is based on an outdated reality. Secondly, the statistics which are collected are aggregated in order to keep secret the performance of individual enterprises and, as a result, they cannot be used to detect trends. Thirdly, the static input/output models of the economy used by government's economic modellers are based on a past relation between production factors, whereas, in fact, reality is dynamic, and, as we have seen, these relationships are now changing rapidly. Finally, the delay in collecting and processing statistics means that the picture of the functioning of the economy on which the government bases its key decisions is out of date. These delays, when added to the time required for the government's own actions to come into effect, means that when they do take effect there is a grave danger that they might be totally counter-productive.[14]

Using nationalized industries to provide investment options also creates difficulties. As Schumacher has put it: 'if the objectives pursued by nationalized industries are as narrow as those of capitalist production the same consequences will follow'.[15] In practice, nationalization opens no new technological doors and the state continues to receive advice little different from that emerging from the TNCs. In this way, future Labour governments will be at a permanent disadvantage in negotiations over 'agreed development plans'.

None of this would be a serious problem if industrial advice from the TNCs was less restrictive. In essence, the choice, according to Robert Noyce, is simple: 'we should stop worrying about declining industries, industries of the past, and put our energies into telecommunications, semiconductors, robots and training'.[16] It is a call which has found a ready response from the UK Conservative government, ever anxious to scale down public commitments to British Steel, BL and British Shipbuilders. According to Patrick Jenkin, the Industry Minister, the government wants to see: 'a progressive switch of resources from the rescue and nationalization of older industries to the encouragement and support of the new'.[17]

Bernal believed that the danger of the state's technology policy being formed in the boardrooms of monopoly companies could only be averted by first formalizing the liaison between the scientists and organized Labour through the establishment of a permanent joint Science Advisory Committee. The SAC was, as we have seen in Chapter 2, intended to give the movement an independent source of scientific and technological advice concerning long-term industrial trends, at the same time as it expanded its influence over the level and direction of state sponsored industrial research. In Chapter 7, we have seen how the Scandinavian Labour movements, aided by Labour governments, have succeeded in establishing just such a lever over the direction of state research, and been able to use it to effect in developing their Data Agreement policy.

The absence of such a research base is a weakness in the British labour movement which cannot be attributed to the inadequacy of Bernal's theory. It is a measure of the extent to which sectarian inertia still immobilizes the heart of the TUC.

THE NATION STATE AND THE INTERNATIONAL ECONOMY

A third major problem with Labour's strategy concerns its apparent inability to come to terms with the nature of the world economy. The emergence of a single world market in major products has ensured that business cycles of the advanced countries have become increasingly synchronized, where before they were out of step. In the 1920s when Europe was in a slump, the US economy boomed. Now this is no longer possible. The activities of the TNCs are an example of this interdependent world economy. In practice this means that it is no longer possible to build indigenous power, electronic or steel industries. New technology, applied on a world scale, has been at the root of the decline of national industries, such as the US car industry, or the German watch industry, and it can be anticipated that this process will accelerate in the future.

As we have seen, there are already signs that the post-war pattern of international free trade is breaking down under these pressures. Western countries are building up a pattern of inter-governmental co-operation agreements amongst themselves and with Eastern and Southern governments, and in the process even Conservative parties have become concerned with planning external trade at the level of industrial sectors. Often this work is carried out at arm's length from local industry, and with little relationship to wider industrial, fiscal or trade policies. In the Third World in particular, governments have demanded, as part of the New International Economic Order that the advanced world transfers not just technology but assists the South to develop the means to carry out its own autonomous technological development.

Government concern to influence global technological developments is apparent in advanced countries too. The Japanese CBI and MITI Group of Sixty have argued that: 'it will be necessary to apply these [new] technologies on a global scale; the old notions of nationalism and division of labour will no longer have any meaning in a world in which all work, creative energy and information can be readily available'.[18]

Any policy for planned industrial development against such a background (such as the proposed new social contract in the UK) which does not have an international dimension as well as a national component seems doomed to failure.

THE BREAKDOWN OF THE MARKET ECONOMY

Bernal's optimism that human reason, and the systematic and planned application of science to human problems, can effect radical improvements in the lives of people in the advanced and developing worlds no longer commands widespread acceptance. On the political Right, the previous belief that planning in national and international bodies could achieve the necessary redistribution of resources has been gravely weakened, if not wholly shattered, by two powerful right-wing governments in the US and the UK.

On the Left, especially in the UK, rapid rises in unemployment which have weakened trade unions, the political reversals suffered under a tide of right-wing advance, and the tendency to infighting and fragmentation have given birth to two contrasting attitudes: resigned pessimism as to the effectiveness of radical action, and a dogmatic and abstract insistence that all problems are soluble in the cleansing fluid of pure socialism.

The difficulties which confront any reforming government — for example, the Mitterrand administration in France — are certainly formidable. The basic problem is the growing weakness of the market mechanism in sustaining growth, even when it is still supported by traditional forms of state intervention. This weakness can be seen at every level of the economy, from the international to the local community and the workplace. At the global level, as the *Financial Times* has noted:

> 'rows of gaily-coloured DC-10 jetliners now stand empty on some distant airfield, just as lines of rusting supertankers float in Norwegian fjords and, indeed, the silent hulks of half-finished chemical plants are dotted about Poland. All of them are testimony to the failure of the international banking system to link up capital with consumers and match money with management.'[19]

At the national level, as we have seen in the UK, there is a withdrawal of the state from investment, public service and training in the so-far mistaken belief that needs once served by the state will be catered for by the private sector. At local and individual level, the steady rise in living standards since the Second World War has ended, throwing into vivid relief the inefficiency of the market in matching the needs of producers and consumers, and the growing inability of under-funded state or local government services to plug the gaps.

As in previous depressions, the burden of the fall in living standards has fallen on those least able to bear them. In Britain we have seen how young people have had to bear the brunt of unemployment, and how their schools have been deprived of teaching facilities. The unemployed have lost the protection of earnings-related unemployment benefit, and the value of their redundancy payments has been cut back by subjecting them to taxation and offsetting them against unemployment benefits.

Women have had many of their social and economic gains of the 1960s and 1970s taken away from them. Inflation and unemployment have reduced the value of household incomes and have increased the pressure on women to seek work. Yet automation and redundancy have eliminated many traditionally female clerical and semi-skilled jobs, and have reduced job opportunities elsewhere. At the same time, the reduction in state provision for pre-school children and the elderly has increased the demands at home.

Yet, as Bernal reminds us, there is an alternative. At no time since the onset of the STR has society had as great a range of alternative paths for development as it has today. As the optimistic model of the impact of technological change, which we outlined in the Introduction (see p 12), demonstrates, new technology has enormous potential for meeting many outstanding material needs and for creating new and effective means of social action. The key to its realization lies in applying labour's economic and political power to create an information technology, which, by opening up new communication channels in society, supports the full development of human resources.

A TECHNOLOGICAL AGENDA FOR LABOUR

The Decentralization of Power

The potential which the market possesses for pushing forward technological advance is formidable — our concern has been with its inefficiency in *applying* these advances to needs. The forms which the new technologies are now adopting, in market conditions, point to the range of choices which the developing and merging worlds of computer and communication technology now offer. That potential embraces both the more productive and effective use of human and material resources and the multiplication of options in modes of communication and sources of information.

We are now developing new means of telecommunications which are interactive, allowing us to give as well as to receive. Computer conferences, audio conferences and video conferences are already possible; the implications of further developments in tele-conferencing include the reduction in the need for travel, and thus in energy use and airline fleets; the growth in education media of the Open University type; and the inclusion of a range of social groups into a communication network which is able to cope with the complex communication needs of organizations, as well as the relatively simple transmission of voice from one individual to another. Cable TV and satellite networks are now growing rapidly; data networks using the same satellite and optical fibre cable are burgeoning; and knowledge engineers working on fifth generation computers are promising to construct 'super intelligent' machines.

How then might these technologies be developed by Labour to compensate for weaknesses in the market economy? The answer lies, we believe, in harnessing the technology to support an ever-widening process of democratization. This will both facilitate the articulation of new public demands on production and, at the same time, will assist the necessary education and organization to successfully prosecute these demands.

According to Michael Margolis, a critic of traditional state socialism, Labour should aim to build up cheap and open computer networks linking all computerized databases: 'providing equal opportunities for every citizen to gather information'.[20] The networks may be used, with safeguards for personal data, to facilitate direct access to the documentary information on which media reports are often based, to computerized records held by government or industry, and to current legislative proposals, administrative regulations and court cases. Once in place, the networks could be used as a decentralized communication system, so that any citizen could send messages to his or her representatives in local or national government, in unions and in voluntary organizations.

The opening up of existing computer networks in this way has implications which go far beyond assisting the functioning of official union or state organizations. They may also be used to support the wide range of informal information flows and consultations necessary to sustain any healthy democracy. Community and local groups could be encouraged to gain access to information in the databases of research bodies, government departments and local industry. This will considerably strengthen the grass roots of democracy, which is at present stimulated only by restricted local media. The explosive growth, in the 1960s and 1970s, of a variety of pressure and special interest groups structured along professional, geographic, sex and age lines, have created, and will continue to create, tension and contradictions to which solutions must constantly be found. Information flowing to and from these groups assists in expanding the conscious decision-making area enjoyed by them, and in allowing for a more complete — though never final — resolution of the tensions among them, and between them and government and other authorities.

National Co-ordination

Socialist politicans in both East and West have been concerned for some time with the question of how the new technology might be applied to support a decentralized planning system, based on social negotiations. In 1968, in Czechoslovakia, this took the form of concern over the manifest failure of the centralized planning system. The Czechoslovak Academy of Sciences, putting forward a programme on which Alexander Dubček based his reforms, argued that:

> 'Technologically advanced socialist society is indubitably faced with the task of working out, on the basis of a developed structure of interests, with the assistance of an integrated computer network and mathematical modelling, a *scientific system* of time economy. This is the only way to provide the exact picture of the effectiveness of different productive forces that will be indispensable in the future; then it will be possible to guide the mechanism of economic levers and instruments of management, to manipulate them in a rational way through rapid movements and universal transformations, while harnessing productive forces that — as in the case of science — possess entirely divergent economic characteristics. Failing this, disproportions will ensue and the opportunity to bring the future nearer to the present will be missed.'[21]

Czech scientists and planners were unable to put into practice the theories which they had proposed; nor was Czech society allowed to experience the development of divergent interests and social groupings which were latent in the Prague Spring and appeared to contain the embryo of pluralism.

In Chile, under the Allende government there was the desire to move beyond traditional free market economics which appeared to trap the country into a permanent state of economic and technological dependence. Stafford Beer proposed, and partially implemented, a reform of the methods of collecting and displaying economic statistics in his work for Allende on the Chilean planning system:

> 'We need to see how the parts (of the economy) are interrelated on a virtually continuous basis . . . instead of the lawyers' and shareholders' balance sheet model . . . the accountants' and the managers' profit and loss account model . . . or the input/output matrix beloved by economists.'[22]

International Development

In the 1980s and 1990s, any attempt at government planning needs to be supported by a system for extending its scope beyond national boundaries, since the effects of the economic long-wave on the pattern of world activity will be even more dramatic than its direct national consequences.

National labour strategies will need to have an explicit international dimension to exploit the developing framework of international regulation of transnational companies as proposed by Vredeling and the international trade union centres. Thus, international data agreements should allow for communication between members of national bargaining groups. Unions should exploit the potential of public data networks to provide increased opportunities for informal international co-operation outside formal structures. 'Agreed development plans', with indigenous transnationals, should cover international operations, and the form technology transfer agreements should take with the Third World. Bilateral government arrangements should be extended between governments of advanced countries to harmonize national plans in new technology sectors.

KNOWLEDGE ENGINEERING OR ENGINEERING KNOWLEDGE?

To make the development of human resources the objective, rather than a by-product, of economic activity requires a different type of information technology — a technology concerned with supporting the decentralization of power. As Stephen Boddington has noted, this should be the context in which labour's technology policy is made:

> 'The possibility of a self-directing community implies a much greater

awareness of function and social relationship. This is not just a matter of facilities and techniques for information transmission and handling. It implies an interest and a concern that is absent at present in Britain and in most other countries. The percentage of people who care or know what is currently being done by national government, local administrations or the management of whatever organization they work for, is very small. If this is so, why should it be different in the future? There is a very good reason for lack of interest in public affairs: it is pointless to waste time on something you cannot do anything about. That the man in the street can do nothing is not, of course, strictly true; but the impact on public affairs of anything he can do is so remote and intangible as to seem, if not nothing, then next to nothing. Social atomization — a society of isolated individuals — is a natural corollary of social relations expressed as commodity relations.'[23]

Technical Requirements

Key technical characteristics of such alternative information systems would include the following:

- ☐ Cheap and universal voice data and video networks.
- ☐ Software to support the rapid collection of economic data and its distribution to decision-making centres at every level.
- ☐ Job and profession-oriented computer languages, to enable data to be manipulated easily, supported by appropriate computer literacy training.
- ☐ Graphical and animation facilities, so that dynamic systems can be easily visualized.
- ☐ Simulation facilities, so that the data collected may be used as a basis for modelling alternative organization of production, distribution and exchange.
- ☐ System development techniques, which ease the construction and evolution of decentralized computer communication networks.

Manpower Requirements

Unlike most contemporary new technology, it will not be possible to develop these systems in isolation from the ultimate user, as the market place cannot be relied upon to provide signals relating to what is and what is not appropriate. A new engineering discipline concerned with the development of open information systems will be needed to support trade union data and technology bargaining. The scheme will require national union, and scientific and technical infrastructures to be strengthened.

As Veblen noted, the problem of running an advanced industrial economy is increasingly concerned with developing and extending the skills of engineers as part of the general effort to raise levels of technological literacy. This requires an extension of statutory paid training time, opportunities for exposure to foreign technical developments, and participation in the international scientific and engineering community. Indeed, the UK government may need to sponsor scholarships for long-term study abroad, thus reversing the direction of flow in the last century.

This process should go hand in hand with a positive response to the increasing pressure (exemplified in the UK's Finniston report) for engineers and technologists to play a larger role in national political life. It may require new sources of funding from government, and other sources for learned societies, the encouragement of trade union organization, and reform of existing methods of control and organization of state scientific and technical research to enable the direct representation of the scientists and engineers involved.

The Disclosure of Planning Information
Government needs to play a key role in stimulating the production and use of new public goods. In the UK, the state's purchasing decisions may need to be co-ordinated by a new central agency (such as the French Informatique Commission) represented in all departments of state. Similar initiatives may be required in other public sectors such as health and social services.

Special requirements for public tendering at present affect international organizations, such as the EEC, and particular industrial sectors such as the UK Offshore Suppliers. In these areas the prospective purchaser is obliged to post a notice of his intention in a journal or a publically accessible database. This principle may be usefully extended to other key areas of procurement in public and private sectors.

Just as public disclosure of operational intentions may be of value in stimulating economic activity, so the disclosure of strategic planning and investment models may be necessary to facilitate the co-ordination of corporate plans.

Institutional Reform
A provisional checklist of institutional reforms required to support the emergence of these new information systems as part of a process of decentralizing power would include:

☐ *Multiple sources of locally controlled funds*, for research and development.
☐ *Technology planning institutes*, concerned with developing alternative planning and information systems.
☐ *Technology development centres*, applying new technology to the design of new public products, as in education and medicine.
☐ *Long-range research centres*, concerned with the preparation of studies relating science and technology to industrial policies.
☐ *Technology transfer institutes*, concerned with the transfer of experience gained in the new technologies between public and

private sectors, by consultancies of various kinds.
☐ *Trade planning centres*, concerned with the external aspects of national planning, such as monitoring the development of world markets.

CONCLUSION

There needs to be a far greater awareness in Labour's debate on a new social contract of the structural changes in the economy which took place in the 1970s. These lessons are as important to Labour as its concern for the evolution of collective bargaining that was evident during the same period.

It must be recognized that we are in an era of scientific-technical revolution in which profound shifts in the structure of employment and unemployment and in the nature of industrial power are taking place. The expansion of public and private sector services in the 1960s and 1970s served to mask these tendencies. Structural change has undermined both the effectiveness of post-Second World War Keynsian methods of economic management, and the impact of traditional labour interventions in the economy. In particular, the nationalizations carried out by the Labour governments of the 1970s, such as aerospace and shipbuilding, and the setting up of the NEB, failed to take root sufficiently to prevent their reversal.

Any return to economic growth will therefore require state intervention of a new type — intervention that recognizes that growth requires motivation. Monetarism, whether practised by Callaghan, Thatcher or Reagan has manifestly failed to provide either individual or collective motivation. The only realistic alternative to monetarism, with the promise of sufficient power to rekindle optimism and motivate growth, is a 'Keynes plus' reflation which stimulates the desire for local democracy and social justice. This should be directed at creating an expanded public sector with new services, and encouraging the emergence of new forms of social and economic organization.

Only in this way can technology transfer, and development created by public demand, become self-sustaining. Under the impact of technological change, the old tertiary or service sector will split into an employment-contracting area in finance, transport and distribution, with an identifiable fourth sector, based around expanding public health, welfare, education, telecommunications and planning services. The emergence of this new sector is essential to pull the economy out of recession.

The depth of the Western recession, and the ascendancy of right-wing governments suggests that this fourth sector will not grow spontaneously as some pundits have maintained. Its emergence will require a period of acute political struggle.

If the labour movement takes on the ambitious objectives outlined above, it will be taking up the challenge posed by Bernal. It will be setting itself apart from those who prophesy that our children will inherit a bland world and that their major problem will be to find distraction, and from those who predict that medium-term stagnation and even decline is irreversible.

The realization of Bernal's optimistic vision is more possible now than at any time in the past. The political challenge to labour is clear.

REFERENCES

1 R Green (1982) Bridging the industrial divide. *New Socialist*. September.

2 Labour Party-TUC Liaison Committee (1982) *Economic Policy and Industrial Democracy*, para 41.

3 ibid, para 31.

4 Labour Party (1982) Interim Report on Science and Technology. In NEC Report to 1982 Labour Party Conference, p 155.

5 Labour Party-TUC Liaison Committee, op cit, para 21.

6 ibid, para 62.

7 ibid, para 63.

8 ibid, para 64.

9 ibid, para 9.

10 L Murray (1981) Guildhall lecture. Unpublished.

11 G Werskey (1978) *The Visible College*, pp 319 and 335. Allen Lane, Harmondsworth.

12 Sir G Howe (1981) *Financial Times*, p 36. 8 May.

13 TUC (1982) *Economic Review*; Labour Party (1982) *Programme for Recovery*.

14 S Beer (1974) *Designing Freedom*. Wiley, New York.

15 E F Schumacher (1974) *Small is Beautiful*, p 253. Abacus, London.

16 R Noyce, quoted in J J Servan Schreiber (1980) *The World Challenge*, p 236. Simon and Schuster, New York.

17 P Jenkin (1981) *Financial Times*. 8 May.

18 J J Servan Schreiber, op cit, p 142.

19 *Financial Times* (1982) Editorial, 6 February.

20 M Margolis (1979) *Visible Democracy*, p 161. Pelican, Harmondsworth.

21 R Richta *et al* (1969) *Civilization at the Crossroads: Social and Human Implications of the Scientific and Technological Revolution*, p 85. M E Sharpe, New York.

22 S Beer, op cit, p 40.

23 S Boddington (1973) *Computers and Socialism*. Spokesman.

Appendix 1
A Review of the Subject Matter of a Planning Agreement

UK Department of Industry, 1975

INTRODUCTION

This . . . makes proposals on the issues that might be covered by Planning Agreement discussions and outlines the information the government would need for them. But individual items will of course vary in importance according to the situation of the company; in particular cases some of those suggested may not be appropriate.

In the first year of an Agreement an Agenda of 12 subject matters outlined here might well be too extensive; and although decisions could only be taken company by company, perhaps in the first year discussions should concentrate on the first seven items with the others being reviewed mainly within the context of their relevance to them.

THE GENERAL BACKGROUND

Item 1: Economic Prospects
The Planning Agreement discussions, might begin with a review of economic prospects in this country and abroad.

This exchange of views, in which the government input would be the central feature, would include a review for the UK economy of:

1. prospects for the year ahead;
2. sector forecasts;
3. medium-term projections for the economy over a five-year period.

The government would contribute an assessment of the world trade picture in aggregate, and of economic prospects and policies in the major industrialized countries, including imports. It would also review with the company the effects of possible change in the national economy on its future prospects.

This exchange of views, about general economic and sector prospects would provide a framework within which the company would have an opportunity to discuss issues of government policy and to make its case

205

for changes. But while it may be possible for the government to take an immediate initiative on matters of particular concern to the company that do not raise issues of wider application, the Agreement document would obviously not be the place for recording changes of government policy of general significance.

Item 2: The Company's Broad Strategy and Long-term Objectives

Information

The government would invite the company to provide a substantial note on its long-term objectives and its broad strategy for achieving them. This would be set in the context of the company's past results and an appraisal of the problems and opportunities facing it. It would include a brief quantification of the important changes in the envisaged balance of company activities in the longer term and the broad implications for investment, productivity, employment, exports, and product and process development. It is with the direction and main lines of company policy, rather than the detailed figuring in long-term plans, that the government would be primarily concerned.

This material would be basic to the Planning Agreement discussion and should lead to general agreement on the strategic issues for particular attention. Bearing in mind the government's proposal that in general Planning Agreements should be introduced on a sector basis, this material when aggregated with similar information from other companies will also be valuable to the government in formulating policy for whole sectors of industry as well as contributing to the development of government policies for the management of the economy as a whole.

PARTICULAR ASPECTS OF PLANS FOR DISCUSSION

Item 3: UK Sales

Information
Information would be sought on past and future levels of:

1. sales for each main product line;
2. the company's market share;
3. the basis of the company's forecasts and how they relate to any forecasts made by trade associations or by NEDO;
4. the way sales are affected by government policies and the economic climate;
5. in appropriate cases, the prospects for import saving.

Discussion and Content of the Agreement
The government is generally concerned about the overall level of

imports, the scope for import savings, and inadequacies in the supply of particular materials and components that may cause supply bottlenecks for other sectors of industry. There may be occasions therefore when the government will wish to consider action in support of an investment programme specifically to increase the level of production for United Kingdom consumption. For these reasons the aggregate levels of sales and levels of sales for particular groups of products might form an appropriate part of an Agreement.

Item 4: Exports

Information
The company's views would be sought on export prospects for its main products to the main current and potential overseas markets. Forecasts would be helpful, in so far as they are available, covering, say, the next two or three years, together with an indication of the company's long-term objectives and marketing strategy.

Discussion and the Agreement
It is a central objective of government economic policy to increase the level of exports and, in particular, to increase the proportion of output exported. In the Planning Agreement discussions the government will wish therefore to give particular emphasis to exports and, while recognizing all the uncertainties of sales targets and the overriding need to respond to market changes, it would seek agreement with the company about its export performance.

The government would be anxious to identify what further action they could take in support of company plans to expand exports. The Agreement would refer to any specific action decided upon by either side, and the company's main objectives within the export field.

Item 5: Investment

Information
The government is concerned that industry should have sufficient resources for worthwhile investment, that the general level and quality of investment is increased, and that within the total, appropriate opportunities are taken to promote the expansion of industry in the assisted areas. In the light of these considerations and the relevance of investment to levels of employment and exports, government departments will wish to receive information about the company's investment plans in some detail but concentrating on:

1. the level in investment, identifying projects of major significance and the aggregate level of investment in each of the company's divisions and major plants;

207

2. the proportion of investment in the assisted areas;
3. investment related particularly to exports or import saving where this is a specific objective;
4. comparative information on investment per employee, and on constraints to investment.

Discussion

This would be a central issue in the Planning Agreement discussions, in which the government could have a specific role in financing certain investment, and considering industrial development certificates. The key issues will be the removal of constraints to desirable investment, and the location of investment.

The Agreement

Apart from understandings about the level of investment and on major projects, the Agreement could cover:

1. selective assistance under the Industry Act in support of investment schemes which yield an adequate return to the company and the nation;
2. applications for industrial development certificates; the scope for transferring particular proposals to assisted areas; and planning issues generally;
3. guarantees of rates of regional development grant for specified projects discussed during the Agreement negotiations which the government considered of particular importance;
4. support for measures leading to economy in the use of resources.

Item 6: Employment and Training

Information

Employment would form one of the major sections of the Planning Agreement discussions in which the government representatives would be concerned to know the present numbers in employment, prospective major changes, the possibility of substantial future redundancies and the scope for increasing employment in assisted areas. There would be a need for some information about the occupational and regional composition of the figures, and where major changes were envisaged, more detailed information would be sought.

This information would be of particular concern to the Department of Employment Group in the future planning of its work to meet the needs of Industry. The Group includes the Manpower Services Commission and its executive Agencies, the Training Services Agency and the Employment Service Agency. It is hoped that firms would agree to the Commission and the Agencies being involved in the relevant part of the discussions leading to a Planning Agreement.

Discussion
Any substantial redundancies would be discussed in depth, with a view to identifying what appropriate action might be taken by the firm itself and by government. The Department of Employment Group representatives would be ready to discuss with firms any existing or expected problems in such fields as recruitment, wastage and training, or any problems arising over particular categories of workers including disabled persons, with a view to their solution. Additionally the Department of Employment Group would be able to provide firms with information about the present situation and the future prospects for the local labour markets in which they operated.

The Agreement
This section of the Agreement might contain statements of intentions about:

1. the company's main plans and proposals for handling any expected changes in the labour force; training plans and the assistance which the Department of Employment Group could provide;
2. the handling of major redundancies, which might involve action by the company, trade union, and the Department of Employment Group and the Department of Industry;
3. undertakings about changes in the level of employment in assisted areas linked perhaps to government action in support of investment programmes and decisions on particular applications for industrial development certificates.

Item 7: Productivity

Information
As a background for discussion of this central issue, information would be sought, through the use of convenient measures of productivity, on levels of performance in the company, how they had changed in recent years, on planned improvements, and on comparative performance both in this country and overseas. It would be desirable to cover labour productivity, but also the productivity of capital investment and management.

Discussion and Action
Government Departments lack the skills needed to advise industry on specific action to improve productivity. But the relative performance of British industry, the specific reasons for its strengths and weaknesses are central to an understanding of the means of economic progress and it is a matter of major national concern to increase the productivity of all the factors of production. It is proposed therefore that an attempt should be made during the Planning Agreement discussion to identify

constraints to increased productivity and what action might be taken to overcome them. Specific issues that could lead to action within the framework of Planning Agreements include investment, output and training.

Item 8: Finance
This section would be concerned with financing the company's business. In present circumstances the following three issues may be the most important:

1. the finance of the company's investment programme;
2. meeting the effects of inflation;
3. providing early warning of any threat to levels of employment or the continued operation of particular plants as a result of financial stringency.

The discussions of this item would normally be of a background character.

Item 9: Prices Policy
This section of the Agreement would need to be related closely to such arrangements as might be in force at the time for the control of prices and margins. In examining the feasibility of achieving approved company plans, particularly in relation to investment, it may be necessary on occasions to consider whether existing rules for price control are the most appropriate.

Item 10: Industrial Relations and Arrangements for Negotiation and Consultation
As a background to discussions on this matter, information would be sought on current practice in the company in relation to that of the industry of which it forms part and its future plans for change.

Item 11: Interests of Consumers and the Community
This is a very wide area which will need to be specific to the sector concerned. Possible subjects include:

1. whether any officer or branch of the company is charged with the specific responsibility for considering the interests of the community (eg for considering equal opportunity policies and other interests of the community such as employment of disabled persons, noise levels and effluent disposal), as opposed to a section responsible for handling consumer complaints;
2. whether, where appropriate, the company gives any public account, other than its statutory Annual Report, about the effects of its activities on the community;
3. what evidence is there that the company's procedure for handling

customers' complaints is satisfactory? Has the NCC been asked about it?

4. whether the company's plans conflict with the requirements of competition policy.

Item 12: Product and Process Development

This section does not lend itself to standard treatment and companies will be involved in far more projects than could be discussed. But subject to the need for confidentiality about secret company projects, there should be scope for discussing the main lines of technological development within which the company will be working, the possibility of using the resources of any of the government's Industrial Research Establishments in support of particular lines of development; and the possibility of government financial support under the Science and Technology Act. In the event of an important technological development affecting a whole industry becoming apparent from discussion with several companies, wider scale government action might be appropriate, for example in anticipation of needs for new skills or in support of research programmes.

This is therefore an aspect of the Planning Agreement discussions that could lead to specific commitment in the Agreement document, but one which, apart from estimates of future expenditure on research and development, will not readily lend itself to handling through the provision of standardized information.

PRELIMINARY WORK FOR THE FOLLOWING YEAR'S AGREEMENT

The first Agreement with any company is likely to be limited in its coverage and achievement. Neither the company, the workers nor the government are likely to regard it as fully satisfactory but rather as a beginning. It may take two or three years before an Agreement reaches a full stage of development and it will be desirable therefore at the end of the Agreement discussions to identify issues which should be dealt with more fully in the following year's discussions.

Arrangements would also need to be agreed for modifying the Agreement as the year progresses in the light of developing circumstances. The arrangements would need to be flexible and swift if consultation was to be effective and company action not delayed. Such consultations should however be limited to issues that have been the subject of specific agreement or commitment or to changes that have major implications for the company's general plans, including in particular levels of exports, investment and employment.

Appendix 2
Technological Change:
A Joint TUC-CBI Statement

The text of a statement agreed in July 1980 by the TUC and CBI representatives at the NEDC and endorsed by the 1980 Trades Union Congress. The statement was subsequently rejected by the CBI's Grand Council.

INTRODUCTION

Technological change is a continuing and familiar feature of our modern, industrial society. The development of new techniques, their application to existing methods of production and products, and their use in developing new products and services has been, and can be in the future, a major force for economic and social progress. Several key innovations in the continuing process of technological change and adaptation — such as the development of the steam engine, the internal combustion engine and electronics — are readily discernible, and these have been associated with major changes in the structure of the economy and increases in our standards of living. Certain industries have risen in importance, others have declined; and there have been shifts in activity between whole sectors of the economy. New skills have developed, old skills have faded away. The organization of work has undergone many radical changes.

Such a major advance in the process of technological change is now imminent with the development of microelectronics and its associated technologies. Reductions in cost and increases in performance, reliability and productivity mark the growth and impact of microelectronics, and in its wake come even newer technologies such as fibre optics and biotechnology. More is involved than changes in individual pieces of equipment and machinery, and there are many variables in the process of change.

For the UK the major advances of microelectronics and the other new technologies offer the prospect of modernizing industry and commerce, keeping them competitive with countries which are already well advanced in such applications. In the past, productivity increases resulting from new technology have been associated with growth in output and thus in employment. But there is no room for complacency with regard to the effects of new technology on future employment and no certainty that we will succeed in taking advantage of the opportunities that new technology will present. There is no automatic mechanism linking improvements in productivity to increases in

212

employment or to increases in general social welfare. Fears concerning the impact of rapid technological change on employment levels, and indeed on the skill content and quality of jobs, are real ones — particularly in a period of already high unemployment. In the absence of positive action the risk would be great that technological innovation would either not occur — thus further weakening the competitive position of the UK in world markets — or would be based solely on the aim of cutting manpower and costs without any corresponding increase or diversification in production.

THE NEED FOR A JOINT APPROACH

It is clear therefore that the need for a rapid development of these new technologies, their introduction into the productive process, and their application to products and services, is paramount. It is equally clear that the successful exploitation of the opportunities offered by technological development requires positive action.

A period of rapid and major technological change is increasing the need for a common understanding of such factors as world market requirements, investment and research and development as well as the implications for employment. A joint approach is clearly the best way to develop such an understanding so that the fears and suspicions attendant on this process can be allayed, and the opportunities grasped.

The challenge of technological change places great responsibilities on everyone concerned with the management of the economy. Governments around the world have played an important role through, for example, public purchasing, investment, and research and development, in stimulating the development of microelectronics and hastening its application. The demands, in terms of training, education, manpower policy and the industrial and regional infrastructure which rapid technological change will pose require an active and strategic response from government. These changes are also more easily carried out in an environment of rapid economic and employment growth and low inflation.

Many of the key decisions which will determine the success or failure of adopting new technologies will be taken at the level of the enterprise and individual plants within it. It is at these levels that trade unions and employers have the responsibility to establish mechanisms and procedures which are sufficiently clear, comprehensive and accessible to allow the process of technological change to take place continuously and beneficially. Given the complexity and diversity of our industrial and representative structure, it would be impossible and indeed undesirable to attempt to draw up a single model for universal applicability. The TUC has formulated its 'Checklist of Points for Negotiators on New Technology' and suggested that unions can use this as a basis for the pursuit of 'new technology agreements'. The CBI has also published its views on how its members should approach the handling of technological change in 'Jobs — Facing the Future'.

Neverthesless, the TUC and the CBI — recognizing the need for rapid technological change, accepting that this is most likely to be achieved on the basis of a joint approach, and recognizing the responsibilities which consequently face them — agree to set out the key elements of practices most conducive to the successful pursuit of major technological adaptation.

DECISION-MAKING ABOUT TECHNOLOGICAL CHANGE

We believe that decision-making will benefit from the input of all parties involved. Therefore the decision to introduce major new technology should involve communication and consultation between management, employees and their representatives with the shared objective of making advances on the basis of mutual understanding and common consent. It is in the interests of all concerned with the enterprise that different options are explored and that none are foreclosed without an evaluation of the relevant aspects of the process of change. Moreover, the establishment of such processes can generate the confidence, expertise and understanding which will allow for constant and flexible adaptation to technological advances in the future.

Provision of Information
Access to information from the earliest possible stages of the decision-making process is vital to a successful approach to technological change. The principles governing best practice for the provision of information are that the information should be relevant, regular, understandable and as full as possible, allowing for discussion before decisions are taken and for the needs of commercial secrecy.

Prior Consultation
Decisions on technological change will require full consultation before the decision to change production systems is taken. Regular consultation between management, employees and recognized trade unions should therefore be a feature of decision-making, and the objectives which new technology is designed to achieve — whether in terms of output, productivity, employment or working conditions — should be clearly specified.

Joint Machinery for Consideration of Technological Change
We believe that improvements in information provision and consultation are most likely to succeed if supported by the creation or improvement,

of joint machinery between management, their employees and their trade unions. The precise form which such machinery takes will clearly be determined by the structure, traditions and practices of individual plants, enterprises and industries. Both management and unions will face responsibilities in this respect since technological developments which initially affect only one part of the workforce or one section of the enterprise may eventually have implications for all. For unions, the challenge will be to give careful attention to means of developing or improving machinery that embraces the largest possible proportion of the workforce — and their unions — so as to provide a coherent and effective input to joint management/union structures. For employers, the challenge will be to adopt an open style of management and to make the process of joint consultation an integral part of the management of the enterprise.

Once decisions have been made, employers and employee representatives involved should fully inform all employees of actions that are to be taken, the reasons behind the choices made and their likely implications for working conditions and job content.

With a view to enhancing employee understanding and input their representatives should receive appropriate training. They will therefore require adequate opportunities to acquire the necessary expertise, including time off with pay to attend agreed courses and conferences.

IMPLEMENTING TECHNOLOGICAL CHANGE

Implementing the decisions taken will involve planning, consultation and negotiation on a wide range of issues. Employers should make every effort to provide security of employment for their employees with adequate opportunities to acquire skills appropriate to the new technologies. For their part, the workforce should be willing to accept suitable opportunities for retraining and redeployment that are offered.

Security of Employment
Technological advance and increased productivity can contribute significantly to more secure and ultimately higher levels of employment in the economy as a whole. At the enterprise level we recognize the importance attached to security of employment. This does not mean that immobility in the present structure of jobs is either sought or desirable. Security of employment can be compatible with large-scale changes in the job structure of the enterprise, skill categories and location. Consequently, we believe that forced redundancies should be avoided wherever possible.

Where application of new technologies necessitates changes in manning levels, every effort should be made to plan the redeployment or relocation of those employees wishing to remain with the firm.

215

Channels should be established to find out employee preferences about their future and efforts made to base plans on them with appropriate relocation allowances. Where, despite these joint efforts, technological change leads inevitably to redundancies, notification should be given sufficiently far in advance to allow for adequate consultation with the Manpower Services Commission on alternative employment and training opportunities. Wherever possible, company efforts should also be made to assist employees in finding employment outside the company.

Manpower Planning
Successful adaptation to new technologies will require systematic manpower planning to meet changes in job content, work organization and manning arrangements. The results should be communicated fully to employees.

Skills, Training and Retraining
As a result of systematic manpower planning, identification of those jobs which will be directly affected by the introduction of new technologies should be possible and measures taken to change the direction of skills and avoid the spread of monotonous and unsatisfying work. Those employees identified should be given the opportunity for training or retraining on the principle of maintained earnings and, if successfully retrained, should be given priority in applying for new jobs wherever possible. Government-sponsored training can make an important contribution to such training and retraining. In our view, such reskilling and the ready acceptance by all concerned of those who have retrained enhance job security and equip the enterprise with the range and flexibility of skills which will be needed in a period of change.

Competitiveness and Growth
We share the view that technological change can improve efficiency, living standards and job opportunities. We see it as a means of producing goods and services at more competitive prices, of higher quality, and in greater volume. This will involve exploring new markets for existing products, alternative product ranges and the scope for import substitution, in other words, using technology to expand and revitalize the enterprise. In this process the views of the workforce and their recognized unions, and the work of the Sector Working Parties and Economic Development Committees of the NEDC should be recognized as having an important contribution to make.

DISTRIBUTING THE BENEFITS

Improvements in productivity and competitiveness resulting from the successful adoption of new technology can benefit companies, their employees and customers, resulting in higher living standards. For companies, new technology offers the prospect of increased profitability and greater output and sales. For employees it can bring improvements in terms and conditions of work and more secure employment. Customers can benefit from lower prices and improvements in the quality of goods and services. A joint understanding on the distribution of the benefits can play an important part in implementing technological change.

Terms and Conditions
The successful adoption of new technology and resulting increases in productivity can benefit individual workers, and provide general and continuing improvements in terms and conditions of work on the basis that companies are able to improve their competitive performance and attract new customers.

Where employees have to develop new skills and undertake greater responsibility as a direct result of the application of new technology, this should be taken into account in establishing terms and conditions of work. Job evaluation systems may need revision to reflect changed skill requirements.

Harmonization of Terms and Conditions
Since the introduction of new technology may transform traditional divisions within the workforce between manual and non-manual employees, it may provide the opportunity for greater harmonization where differences exist among employees with regard to hours, holidays, sick pay, pensions, the working environment and special leave arrangements.

Reorganizing Working Patterns
The advent of new technology offers an opportunity to break away from low productivity, systematic overtime and low pay. The introduction of new technologies can lead to an increase in productivity and efficiency and it may thus be appropriate to discuss the organization of working time. Imaginative agreements to redesign shift systems, to eliminate systematic overtime, and to fit the working time preferences of individuals and groups into a more flexible framework can all increase the efficiency with which work is organized and resources used and result in greater leisure.

HEALTH AND SAFETY

The implications of new technology for health and safety at work must be considered carefully taking account of the statutory duties of employers under the Health and Safety at Work etc, Act 1974.

Although application of new technology may reduce the exposure of employees to hazards it may also create new ones. Employers should always obtain information from manufacturers and health authorities on the health and safety aspects of new equipment. It is important that employers discuss new procedures in advance with employees and their representatives and fully disclose information about hazards, including the conclusions of research undertaken by medical or other experts. All equipment should be subject to a strict maintenance programme. After new equipment has been installed, employee reaction to the environmental aspects of the machinery should be carefully assessed.

REVIEWING PROGRESS

Whatever the extent of co-operation and understanding on the introduction of new technology, there will be areas of uncertainty about the precise way in which new machinery and processes will operate in practice. There will therefore be a need to ensure that procedures exist to monitor developments and to review progress against objectives. Where they do not, an effective response may be joint union/management study teams with the responsibility for monitoring the detailed effects of the implementation of new technology. It is also important to enable any difficulties which arise in the trial or adjustment period to be dealt with rapidly. Attention should therefore be given to the adequacy of established grievance and disputes procedures.

Index

219

223